THE PHARISEES
and the
TEMPLE-STATE *of* JUDEA

THE PHARISEES
and the
TEMPLE-STATE *of* JUDEA

Richard A. Horsley

CASCADE *Books* · Eugene, Oregon

THE PHARISEES AND THE TEMPLE-STATE OF JUDEA

Copyright © 2022 Richard A. Horsley. All rights reserved. Except for brief quotations in critical publications or reviews, no part of this book may be reproduced in any manner without prior written permission from the publisher. Write: Permissions, Wipf and Stock Publishers, 199 W. 8th Ave., Suite 3, Eugene, OR 97401.

Cascade Books
An Imprint of Wipf and Stock Publishers
199 W. 8th Ave., Suite 3
Eugene, OR 97401

www.wipfandstock.com

PAPERBACK ISBN: 978-1-6667-4863-5
HARDCOVER ISBN: 978-1-6667-4864-2
EBOOK ISBN: 978-1-6667-4865-9

Cataloging-in-Publication Data:

Names: Horsley, Richard A., author.

Title: The Pharisees and the temple-state of Judea / Richard A. Horsley.

Description: Eugene, OR: Cascade Books, 2022. | Includes bibliographical references and index.

Identifiers: ISBN: 978-1-6667-4863-5 (PAPERBACK). | ISBN: 978-1-6667-4864-2 (HARDCOVER). | ISBN: 978-1-6667-4865-9 (EBOOK).

Subjects: LCSH: Pharisees—Historiography. | Josephus, Flavius—Views on Pharisees. | Jews—History—To 70 A.D. | Jesus Christ—Conflicts. | Bible—Gospels—Criticism, interpretation, etc.

Classification: BM175.P4 H57 2022 (print). | BM175.P4 (epub).

VERSION NUMBER 090722

Dedicated to the memory of Anthony J. Saldarini,
whose innovative critical scholarship has prepared the way for a
more adequate understanding of the Pharisees and scribes

CONTENTS

Acknowledgments | ix

List of Abbreviations | x

Introduction | 1

1 The Unstable Imperial Situation of the Judean Temple-State | 6

2 Assessing the Sources | 21

3 The Political Position of Scribes in the Judean Temple-State | 45

4 The Pharisees—Sometime Administrators of the Judean Temple-State | 63

5 The Pharisees in the Politics of the Judean Temple-State | 85

6 The Pharisees as Retainers of the Temple-State and Jesus' Woes in Q | 116

7 Pharisees and Scribes in the Gospel Stories | 141

Bibliography | 155

Index | 161

ACKNOWLEDGMENTS

The author and publisher gratefully acknowlege the previous publications of two chapters in this volume:

Chapter 3 originally appeared as "The Political Roots of Early Judean Apocalyptic Texts," in *To Break Every Yoke: Essays in Honor of Marvin L. Chaney*, edited by Robert B. Coote and Norman K. Gottwald, 262–78. Social World of Biblical Antiquity Series 2/3. Sheffield: Sheffield Phoenix, 2007.

Chapter 6 is partially adapted from "The Pharisees and Jesus in Galilee and Q," in When Judaism and Christianity Began: Essays in Memory of Anthony J. Saldarini, edited by Alan J. Avery-Peck, Daniel Harrington, and Jacob Neusner, vol. 1, 117–45. Journal for the Study of Judaism Supplements 85. Leiden: Brill, 2004.

ABBREVIATIONS

Ancient

1QH	Thanksgiving Hymns from Qumran Cave 1
1QpHab	Commentary on Habakkuk from Qumran Cave 1
1QS	Community Rule from Qumran Cave 1
4Q171	Commentary on Psalms from Qumran Cave 4
4QMMT[a]	Miqṣat Ma'aśê ha-Torah[a] from Qumran Cave 4 (4Q394)
4QpNah	Commentary on Nahum from Qumran Cave 4 (4Q169)
Ag. Ap.	Josephus, *Against Apion*
Ant.	Josephus, *Antiquities of the Judeans*
b.	Babylonian Talmud (Babli)
CD	Damascus Document
Legat.	Philo, *Legatio ad Gaium* (Embassy to Gaius)
Life	Josephus, *The Life*
m.	Mishnah
War	Josephus, *The Judean–Roman War*

Modern

LCL	Loeb Classical Library

INTRODUCTION

WHILE WORKING ON MY first attempt at a more appropriate and critical consideration of the historical Jesus in his historical context in the mid-1980s, I realized that most Christian scholars were woefully unprepared to deal adequately with the Pharisees and Jesus' conflict with them. My principal purpose in launching the project on *Jesus and the Spiral of Violence* was to replace the anachronistic construct of "the Zealots" that had served as the foil for an irenic apolitical Jesus with a more critical account of the protests and popular movements that were emerging in the historical context of first-century Roman Palestine. A careful reading of the histories of Josephus led to the realization that available constructions of the Pharisees were applying inappropriate concepts and/or based on an uncritical grasp of the multiple sources. This meant that I too was woefully unprepared to deal with the Pharisees and their conflict with Jesus—and this during a time that biblical scholars were struggling with how to deal with the roots of Christian anti-Judaism in biblical interpretation and biblical scholarship's complicity in the Holocaust. So in the 1987 book I simply left unaddressed the conflict between Jesus and the Pharisees that is so prominent in the Gospel sources, fully intending to devote major attention to a fuller, critical understanding of the Pharisees in the next several years.

In 1991 I began to sketch chapters and in the early 1990s even secured a contract for a project seeking a critical understanding of the Pharisees and their conflict with Jesus in a more comprehensive analysis of the historical context. But other lacunae in the scholarship on the historical context seemed important to address first, such as the difference in regional histories of Galilee and Judea that had simply been ignored or glossed over. And then lines of new research came along that required further rethinking of biblical studies in general. Those other projects indicated that further work remained to be done on the sources and conceptual apparatus for the Pharisees and their conflict with Jesus according to the Gospel stories. Through these other projects, however, it was possible to move toward a more comprehensive treatment of the historical context, a more critical assessment of the sources, and critical construction of the Pharisees in the politics of the Judean temple-state in Roman Palestine. In the 1990s and 2000s I produced several articles and papers that explored the sources for, the social-political position of, and changing historical relations of the Pharisees and scribes, with some attention to their conflict with Jesus. Seven of those are included in this volume.

The essays in this volume bring together several important lines of rethinking what we know and do not know about the Pharisees in their historical context.

Important for our overall historical conceptualization is the recognition that in the ancient world religion was not separate and separable from political economy. In the fields of biblical studies and Jewish history the controlling constructs of Judaism and Christianity often block recognition of the concrete social and institutional forms in which life was lived. At the highest level the context in which both the Pharisees and scribes and Jesus and other Galilean villagers lived was the Roman Empire, which was preceded by the Hellenistic Empires. Those empires ruled indirectly, in Judea and later other areas of Palestine, through the Judean temple-state headed by a high priestly aristocracy. The vast majority of people in Palestine, as in any ancient society, lived in village communities under the rule of the empire and the empire's client rulers, in this case the temple-state in Jerusalem. Far from there having been a stable "Jewish society" in Palestine in late second-temple times, both the overarching imperial rule and that of the temple-state and other local client rulers were changing dramatically, with sharp social and political conflicts.

Second, in our graduate training in the fields of biblical studies and Jewish history—at least until recently—we were taught to focus narrowly on a manageable topic or issue and to gather particular evidence, mainly from passages or text fragments from ancient texts directly pertinent to that topic or issue. More recently some are realizing that short passages and text fragments are components in whole texts, the adequate evaluation of which is more complicated. It is important to consider whole texts, their social location, viewpoint, and interests, and what they are about, in order to use them appropriately as sources for the (re-)construction of particular aspects of particular historical contexts and actors.

Third, for various reasons, including frustration with the theological orientation and the old "historical-critical" approach in biblical studies, many of us coming through graduate training in the 1960s and 1970s began looking to the social sciences for alternative approaches that might bring us closer to more concrete social contexts. In my "extracurricular" reading during the 1960s and 1970s I became critical of what appeared to be uncritical adaptation of the then-dominant structural-functional sociology and anthropology in biblical studies.[1]

Historical sociology, such as that of Gerhard Lenski, appeared to offer more help for "biblical" historians and other interpreters. Rather than borrowing a model based on a variety of cross-cultural studies and setting it down onto biblical and other texts, however, historians and biblical interpreters can use those comparative studies to formulate questions to address to their sources that may produce deeper understanding of texts and their historical context. My good friend and colleague Marvin Chaney had used Lenski to advantage in investigation of eighth-century Judea and Israel under their monarchies and of sharply critical prophecies condemning exploitation of Israelite peasants by the kings and their officials. During the mid-1980s while working on a book on the historical Jesus, I was in frequent conversations with the late Tony Saldarini, who was working on applying Lenski's historical sociology and other social-scientific studies to the Pharisees and scribes.

Those conversations helped me considerably in thinking through ways in which Lenski's historical sociology of "advanced agrarian societies" could help in understanding the historical context in which Jesus lived and worked, and ways in which Lenski's model did not apply. Both Tony and I concluded that Lenski's description of retainers that served rulers of agrarian societies could illuminate the social-political position and role of Pharisees and scribes in the temple-state as portrayed in our sources.[2] Discussion of Lenski's historical sociology continued, and his complete model of multiple "classes" in agrarian societies was touted by New Testament scholars as a model or mirror of Judean society. Partly in response to the suspicion in biblical studies of imposing social-science "models" onto texts, it occurred to me that the political-economic-religious structure and dynamics of life in Hellenistic or Roman Palestine/Judea could be discerned by careful examination of some key sources. In the 1990s, in collaboration with Patrick Tiller, I laid this out in a lengthy article that included explanation of ways in which Lenski's model was or was not applicable to second-temple Judea.[3] That led to an article that summarized how Lenski's historical sociology is

1. Horsley, *Sociology and the Jesus Movement*.

2. This can be seen in the first chapter of *Jesus and the Spiral of Violence*, although perhaps too subtly sketched. Saldarini laid out a fuller and more detailed interpretation of the Pharisees and scribes as retainers of the high priestly rulers in *The Pharisees, Scribes, and Pharisees* the next year.

3. Horsley and Tiller, "Ben Sira and the Sociology of the Second Temple."

helpful in understanding the position and role of scribes such as Ben Sira and the *maskilim*, who produced the historical visions in Dan 7–12, an article that appeared in the Festschrift for Marvin Chaney.[4] That critical discussion illuminating the role of scribes, which also reflects the earlier discussions with Saldarini, is included here as Chapter 3, since it helps us discern the social-political position and role of the Pharisees in the Judean temple-state. The critical discussion of how Lenski, as applied by Saldarini, helps illumine the political role of the Pharisees and of their conflict with Jesus continues in the first part of Chapter 6 below, which is an adaptation of an article in memory of Saldarini, whose highly promising work was cut short by leukemia.[5]

Fourth, far from being a stable situation, the historical context in the late Second Temple Era was full of conflict at the level of the empires and that of the rulers in Palestine. Ordinary people, including both Jerusalemites and villagers, periodically mounted resistance and even revolts against exploitative and/or domineering rulers. Pharisees and scribes, sometimes as retainers of the temple-state but sometimes as dissident retainers, usually attempted to mediate tensions and conflicts but also offered resistance at certain crisis points. With broader critical assessment of the sources and a clearer sense of the changing social-political context, it is possible to construct a (provisional) history of the Pharisees' political position and role in, or in opposition to, the temple-state in Judea under imperial rule. In what is now Chapter 1, I attempted to set this up in a short analysis of the multiple factors in the history of second-temple Judea under a succession of imperial regimes.

Chapter 4, composed in 1991, was my first attempt at this based on a careful reading of Josephus's historical accounts in order to discern the position and function of the Pharisees in the Judean temple-state. Upon discovering that Steve Mason had published a critical book-length survey of Josephus's accounts, I put away my paper. His book *Flavius Josephus on the Pharisees* (1991) included a telling criticism of the Smith-Neusner-Cohen thesis of a pro-Pharisee *Antiquities* that provided part of the basis for Neusner's thesis that the Pharisees had become a mere sect before jumping back into politics after the great revolt. Mason, however, had confined his study to Josephus's perspective (as a necessary step toward using the histories in historical reconstruction) but still focused on the passages without considering the broader historical accounts. And he did not consider what Josephus's histories were about—that is, the history of the temple-state

4. Horsley, "The Political Roots of Early Judean Apocalyptic Texts."
5. Horsley, "The Pharisees and Jesus in Galilee and Q."

amidst the vagaries of imperial politics. My 1991 paper had considered Josephus's broader historical accounts and what they are about for what they indicate about the particular historical contexts in which the Pharisees operated, although it was only a provisional sketch.

Chapter 5, composed in 2004, then more fully considers Josephus's broader historical accounts (along with important clues from certain Dead Sea Scrolls) and what they are about (that is, the unstable history of the temple-state under imperial rule) as the context in which the Pharisees acted in their position as retainers or dissident retainers.

Chapters 6 and 7, finally, consider the portrayal of the Pharisees and the conflict between the Pharisees and Jesus in one of the coherent speeches that comprise the "source" of Jesus' prophetic teaching usually referred to as Q and in the sustained narratives of the Gospel stories. These chapters are attempts to move beyond the scholarly habit of focusing narrowly on individual sayings of Jesus or "pronouncement stories" taken out of narrative context. The analysis in Chapter 6 discerns a difference between, on the one hand, the rhetoric of Jesus' woes that complain about the Pharisees' obsession with purity and tithing, and, on the other hand, the speech's deeper concern about the effects of the scribes' and Pharisees' role (in the temple-state) on the life of the people. This concern is thus yet another text that attests the scribes' and Pharisees' role as the "retainers" of the Judean temple-state, which Saldarini had brought to the fore from Lenski's historical sociology. Chapter 6 was originally published as a tribute to the memory of Saldarini in 2004.

Chapter 7 (another paper from 1991) moves beyond a focus on individual pronouncement stories to consider the portrayal of the scribes and Pharisees in the overall Gospel stories of Mark, Matthew, and Luke. The Markan and the Matthean stories present the Pharisees and scribes as representatives of the Jerusalem temple-state who press their scribally cultivated laws and traditions on the people. Their conflicts with Jesus include purity issues, but the deeper issue is the effect of the traditions on the social-economic life of the people.

Health permitting, I will continue to explore some of the lines of new research that bear directly or indirectly on the Pharisees and their conflict with Jesus and Jesus movements. Meanwhile, I hope that these essays can provide a basis on which others can join in the exploration of more comprehensive critical analysis and reconstruction.

1

THE UNSTABLE IMPERIAL SITUATION OF THE JUDEAN TEMPLE-STATE

THE MORE WE LEARN about the history of Judea and surrounding areas in the second-temple period, the greater becomes the disconnect with the standard constructs in which we have been understanding ancient Judeans—including the Pharisees. The most prominent standard construct in the fields of Jewish history and biblical studies has been Judaism. A somewhat more social construct has been a temple-community in which the high priests, and sometimes also the scribes and Pharisees, were "the leaders." The construct of Judaism is rooted in the emergence of rabbinic Judaism, which of course did not happen until late antiquity, long after the Romans had destroyed Jerusalem and the temple. So to indicate the time when the temple was still operating we speak more precisely of "second-temple Judaism." It is a common generalization that Judaism rested on two pillars: the temple and the Torah. In the second half of the twentieth century second-temple Judaism was understood to include the principal sects of the Pharisees, Sadducees, and Essenes (often thought related to the Qumran community since the discovery of the Dead Sea Scrolls).

However, by temple what are we thinking?

(1) Are we thinking of the relatively small structure in Jerusalem—a city that sill had a small population just before and after the Maccabean Revolt—or are we thinking of the huge "wonder of the (Roman) world" massively reconstructed by Herod in grand Hellenistic style, over the gate of which was a golden Roman eagle, symbolizing its subordination and allegiance to the Roman Empire?

Or (2) are we thinking of the sacred precincts to which villagers brought their animals for sacrifices performed by the priests, who then enjoyed the prime cuts of meat? *Or* perhaps we're thinking of the central holy place of festivals, where, once the priestly "leaders" had successfully insisted that the people come to celebrate the Passover, which had formerly been a local family celebration of the people's deliverance from central control, the people coming to the festival in the first century CE mounted mass protests against the rule of the Romans and their high priestly clients. In their repressive response, the Roman governors posted a cohort of Roman troops atop the porticoes of Herod's temple to attack the people if they protested too vigorously.

Or (3) the holy structure that certain circles of learned scribes thought had been "polluted" from the start, hence would not be rebuilt atop the "house" of the Judean people that would finally be restored in God's new deliverance from domination by the superhuman forces of imperial rule (see 1 Enoch 90; the vision in Dan 10–12 also does not include a restored temple).

And by the *high priests* as the leaders, what are we thinking?

Are we thinking about how the high priest "received the portions from the hands of the priests, as he stood by the hearth of the altar with a garland of brothers (all the sons of Aaron in their splendor) around him," in the paean of praise by Ben Sira (Sir 50:12–13)? Or are we thinking of the high priests appointed by the Roman governors from among the four elite families (and who collected the tribute for Caesar), who not surprisingly sided with the Romans when the people mounted protests, and who became downright predatory on the villagers, according to Josephus and memories in rabbinic texts?[1]

Recently researchers are also raising questions about the other principal pillar of Judaism, the *Torah*, the core of the sacred Scripture that supposedly "all" or "most Jews" would have read, known, and faithfully followed. (1) Only about three percent of the people (mainly learned scribes) could have read the scrolls, which were kept mainly in the temple or in scribal communities (such as Qumran) and hence were not accessible.[2] Also, (2) among the texts found in the Dead Sea Scrolls were other, alternative texts of torah, such as the Temple Scroll and copies of the book of Jubilees, that claimed even higher authority than the pentateuchal books. Moreover (3), the Pharisees were known for giving laws "from the traditions of the ancestors" (that Josephus contrasts with those "written in the laws of Moses").

1. Discussed with references in Horsley, "High Priests and Politics."
2. Harris, *Ancient Literacy*; Hezser, *Jewish Literacy*.

These have standardly been understood as "oral torah." Together these factors suggest that the "books" of the Pentateuch held only relative authority even in scribal and priestly circles such as the Qumran community, leaving it unclear to what extent nonliterate villagers may have known about them. The Pharisees are thought to have been the principal interpreters of the laws. But now we must wonder just what the laws they were supposedly interpreting included besides their "traditions of the ancestors/elders."[3]

And by Pharisees, are we thinking of the Pharisees who refused to submit to the loyalty oath to Herod and Caesar and the scribal and Pharisee leaders of the "Fourth Philosophy" who, says Josephus, agreed in everything with the Pharisees except for their passion for liberty and organized resistance to payment of the tribute to Caesar (son of god) as against the first two commandments of the Mosaic covenant? *Or* are we thinking of "the leading Pharisees" who joined the high priests in forming a provisional government in the summer of 66 CE to attempt to hold a lid on the revolt until they could negotiate with the Romans? Moreover, while the concept of *sect* as a group that separates or withdraws from the dominant society or religion may fit the Qumran community,[4] it hardly applies to the Pharisees, whom Josephus portrays as high-level intellectual-legal advisers of the high priests, who also in certain circumstances mounted resistance against them.

Just these several examples of the conflictual political-religious relations—between the high priests based in the temple and the people, between the Pharisees and Herod or the high priests, and between the high priests and the Romans—indicate political-economic-religious structure and dynamics that the construct of Judaism has been hiding in the second-temple period. The high priests were the heads of a temple-state that was itself subject to an empire, ruling and collecting revenues from the people, with the Pharisees serving as advisers of the high priestly rulers, but in certain circumstances resisting. This has been recognized in the fields of biblical studies and Jewish history, but scholars continue to revert to the deeply rooted constructs that are obscuring these concrete conflictual relations.

There is yet another dimension, however, to what is hidden by our conceptual apparatus in these fields. If I may use my own experience as an illustration, during graduate training in the 1960s I was already arguing with my mentors that we should switch to the more appropriate concept of a temple-state. But I was still thinking of the Judean temple-state in fairly constant terms as having a stable structure in a stable historical situation.

---

3. Also found among the Dead Sea Scrolls were manuscripts of the pentateuchal books. Further deliberations about the Torah and other Judean laws will have to consider the findings of text-critical experts on these manuscripts.

4. Baumgarten, *Flourishing of Jewish Sects*.

Yet the examples cited above give the lie to that also. In order to discern and understand the historical context in which the Pharisees originated, and the social-political position in which they operated, it is necessary to recognize that the temple-state was not stable, and its imperial context was not stable.

CONFLICTING INTERESTS IN THE TEMPLE-STATE UNDER A SUCCESSION OF EMPIRES

During the entire second-temple period Judea and the Judeans were subject to a succession of empires, as the Persians replaced the Babylonians, Alexander the Great conquered the whole area from Egypt to Persia, and his successors, the Ptolemies and then the Seleucids, ruled Judea and were replaced with Rome's conquest of the eastern Mediterranean. During the Persian period a temple-state consolidated control in Judea with Persian permission or perhaps sponsorship. The successor empires then retained the temple-state as the local representative of the imperial regime until the Romans finally destroyed it in 70 CE. The continuing or recurrent conflicts inherent in the relations between the imperial regimes, the temple-state, and the agrarian people they ruled and from whom they extracted produce all contributed to the inherent instability of the imperial dynamics throughout. For light on the position and role of the Pharisees (and related groups) we are particularly interested in where they fit in the network of relational conflicts. The results and implications of the interrelations were cumulative from empire to empire. It is probably best to proceed step by step with each imperial period in order to discern those results and implications.

The Origins of the Temple-State under the Persian Empire

The Babylonian armies not only destroyed Jerusalem and its temple and deported the ruling elite from Jerusalem, but they also devastated the countryside and decimated the populace. Persian imperial policy was almost the opposite, insofar as the regime permitted or encouraged the descendants of the previously deported rulers and their dependents to resume their local rule in areas such as Judea. With Persian permission or sponsorship, the descendants of the former Jerusalem rulers returned to rebuild the temple. Sometime during the Persian period a priestly elite gradually consolidated their control of tiny territory[5] as the local representatives of the Persian

---

5. Archaeological explorations have estimated the population of Judea at the start of this period at hardly more than 30,000 people in villages mainly in the hill country

regime, and collected revenues to support the temple and themselves and to send as tribute to the empire. Such indirect rule had advantages for the imperial regime.[6] The regime compromised the priestly aristocracy by giving them an economic stake in the imperial system. Also, the people subject to the temple-state would focus on rendering tithes and offerings to the house of "the God who is in Jerusalem" (Ezra 1:3), and not on paying tribute to the emperor. Or, depending on the response of the subject people, their resentment would be focused on their own aristocracy while the imperial rulers were unseen and remote. This institution of the temple-state headed by the high priesthood continued under the successive imperial regimes for six centuries, until the Romans destroyed Jerusalem and the temple. This meant that the very mediator of the Judean people and their God was also the local representative of the dominant imperial regime. And this at points became a serious focus of conflict and instability in the system.

During the time that the priestly elite was consolidating affairs in a temple-state, a series of conflicts developed among the wealthy and powerful families and clans in the area. The local wealthy families had been exploiting the peasants economically. In attempts to stabilize the nascent temple-state the Persian regime sent a series of governors and envoys. The best known were Nehemiah and Ezra, both Judeans in Babylon who were high-ranking Persian officials. Nehemiah came with military forces to enforce order between the feuding magnates and regional big men such as the sheik Tobiah, based in the Transjordan area. He also intervened to counter the serious results of exploitation of the subsistence peasants by their wealthy fellow Judeans.

The episode in Neh 5:1–13 is a classic case of how wealthy elites exploit subsistence peasants/villagers, in this case their fellow Judeans, who desperately need survival loans to feed their families in order to pay "the king's tax," that is the imperial tribute. The story has Nehemiah sufficiently familiar with Judean/Israelite customs of aiding families who have fallen into debt that he makes the exploiting elite cancel debts and release their debt-slaves, with the forceful suasion of the back-up forces he commands. But despite his being an imperial official, he does nothing to mitigate "the king's tax." Both of these causes of instability would have recurred through the history of the second-temple period: conflicts between different factions of the wealthy elite, including factions in the priestly aristocracy, and economic exploitation of the subsistence peasants that threatened the economic base

---

around Jerusalem and the temple.

6. This discussion of "indirect rule" is informed by a critical reading of a discussion of modern colonial rule by Peter Worsley, *Third World*, 21–49.

of both the temple-state and the imperial regime. Unusual in this case is that the imperial official took action that indicated that Judean/Israelite customs had some influence in the crisis.

Sources for the Persian period and the early Hellenistic period are fairly rare. In the tiny principality of Yehud, however, in a time when literacy was extremely limited, there was evidently a vigorous scribal culture. Learned scribes, virtually the only people trained in reading and writing, further developed at least the earlier forms of texts such as Deuteronomy, which authorized the consolidation of power in the Jerusalem temple-state, and Leviticus as instruction that authorized priestly rule and regulated the priestly procedures of the temple and temple-state. In Deuteronomy the scribes adapted many laws and customs that had originated in village culture to guide social-economic relations in a way that maintained the viability of component households or families to almost the opposite effect: that is, to serve the centralization of power in the temple-city, "the place that God had chosen for his name to dwell." It would probably be impossible to gauge whether this had much effect on the villagers. But this adaptation of popular tradition justified political-economic centralization. The scribes who produced such texts were serving the emerging priestly rulers of the temple-state.

Other scribal activity during the Persian period must have included the continued cultivation of various kinds of wisdom (for instance, cosmological and meteorological wisdom). Jerusalem's cultural and political elite, deported to Babylon in the early sixth century, would have had contact with such wisdom for which Babylonian scribes serving in the imperial regime were famous. The legends eventually included in Dan 1–6 suggest Judean scribes may well have trained and functioned in the imperial court. Prophets such as Nahum appear to have been agents of the temple, exhorting the people to support the temple, with prophetic rhetoric that seems almost like religious extortion: If you do not bring your crops to the temple storerooms, God will not guarantee the productivity of your land (see Nahum). Latter-day disciples of earlier prophets and/or scribal circles also remembered and collected their prophecies and further developed them with additional prophecies that give assurances of the future imperial glory of the temple-city of Jerusalem itself (e.g., the rather grandiose visionary rhetoric in Isa 60–61).

Crisis for the Judean Temple-State under the Hellenistic and Roman Imperial Regimes

The imperial successors of Alexander the Great—the Ptolemies based in Egypt and the Seleucids based in Syria—imposed Hellenistic political and cultural forms in addition to the usual imperial exaction of tribute. Both regimes sponsored the foundation of Hellenistic *poleis* in Palestine around the perimeter of Judea, in which indigenous elites joined Macedonian military as the citizen bodies that dominated the peasantry in the surrounding *chora*. But they did not force the issue in Jerusalem. Over the course of the third century, however, a growing number of the priestly aristocracy evidently became enamored of the dominant Hellenistic political culture of life in a *polis*.

In the calm before the crisis, after centuries from which we have only limited textual sources, we have the collection (by a grandson) of various kinds of wisdom from the Jerusalem scribe Yeshua ben Sira, who was a prominent supporter of the Oniad high priestly dynasty. The rich array of his instructional speeches in Sirach also offers a firsthand source for the position and role of scribes in the temple-state.[7] One speech in particular, which glorifies the importance of the scribes in service to the high priestly rulers, gives a clear picture of the structure of the Jerusalem/Judean temple-state (Sir 38:24—39:11). Farmers, who raise the food, and artisans such as potters and smiths and others who work with their hands are crucial in maintaining support for the ruling city. But it is only the scribes who have leisure to learn the law of the Most High and various kinds of wisdom and prophecies who are prepared to serve in the councils of the rulers and, understanding court decisions, can in turn expound judgment in courts and achieve renown from such service in the temple-state. It is Ben Sira who provides the lengthy poetic paean to the Oniad "sons of Aaron," who have taken their place in the glorious chain of famous officeholders such as Moses and Aaron and David and Josiah at the head of the Judean people now in the Jerusalem temple (Sir 44–50). It is perhaps ironic that Ben Sira is so enthusiastic about the glorious high priesthood performing pomp and circumstance in the temple that he does not even mention that it was subordinate to a Hellenistic imperial regime.

From the instructional wisdom of Ben Sira it seems clear that the position and role of the learned scribes (sages) who served "among the rulers" was to assist the priestly aristocracy in governing the temple-state,

---

7. Extended analysis and discussion in research carried out in the early 1990s and finally published in Horsley and Tiller, "Ben Sira and the Sociology of the Second Temple," which includes a critical use of the historical sociology of Gerhard Lenski.

particularly in cultivating a Judean scribal repertoire of torah, prophecies, and wisdom of various kinds (39:1–4). Ben Sira's concern that people pay revenues to the priests/temple and his warning to his proteges to mind their tongue when the high priest invites them to banquets suggest that the scribes/sages were at least partially dependent on the high priesthood for economic support.

Not long after Ben Sira's service in the temple-state and the success of the Seleucids in finally taking control of Jerusalem, however, the controlling faction in the priestly aristocracy, enamored of the dominant Hellenistic imperial political culture, carried out a coup. With the cooperation of the Seleucid regime they transformed the temple-state into a Hellenistic *polis*. The political culture and forms of the Hellenistic *polis* replaced the Judean covenantal constitution and the laws of the Jerusalem temple-state. Scribal circles that had been dedicated to cultivating Judean traditions were understandably concerned. The visionary histories of Dan 7–12 and the Animal Vision in 1 Enoch 85–90 indicate that at least some scribal circles mounted resistance to the reform.[8] And when Emperor Antiochus Epiphanes invaded Judea to enforce the Hellenizing reform, the ordinary priestly Hasmonean family led other villagers in the guerrilla warfare of the Maccabean revolt.

We might well conclude that indirect imperial rule through the Judean high priesthood worked to control the Judeans only so long as the client high priests had credibility as representatives of the people and patrons of the scribes. But something more concrete was also at stake. The transformation of the temple-state into a Hellenistic *polis* undermined the traditional way of life and, in effect, terminated the raison d'etre of both the scribes and the ordinary priests, some of whom lived in villages but pursued their duties several weeks a year in the temple, conducting sacrifices and helping preside at festivals.

After four years of guerrilla warfare (168–164 BCE), the Judeans had fought the imperial army to a standoff and (at least supposedly) had captured, cleansed, and rededicated the temple. But a war of attrition continued for more than another decade between the weakened Seleucid forces still trying to enforce the reform and the rebels led by Jonathan, brother of Judas Maccabaeus. By maneuvering between rival claimants to the Seleucid empire, Jonathan gained appointment as the new high priest in 152, mainly because of his military prowess. And he was succeeded as high priest by his brother Simon and then by Simon's son John Hyrcanus and their successors in the new Hasmonean dynasty. The Hasmonean family of ordinary priests, however, was full of illegitimate upstarts who had replaced the long line of

---

8. This was discussed later in Horsley, *Scribes, Visionaries,* chapters 8 and 9.

hereditary Zadokites as high priests. The power of the Hasmoneans lay in their military, initially a popular militia, later replaced by mercenaries.

It is at just this point in Judea's history, after the temple-state had been restored by Jonathan (and Simon), that the wealthy priest and historian Josephus first mentions the three schools of thought—the Pharisees along with the Sadducees and the Essenes—in his *Antiquities* (13.171–173). This historical timing is evidently confirmed by the pesher Habakkuk (1QpHab 8:8–11), according to which the scribes and priests who formed the new covenant community at Qumran had abandoned Jerusalem in protest against the "Wicked Priest," who is thought to have been Jonathan. The timing is further confirmed by the story Josephus repeats in *Ant.* 13.289–296 that has the Pharisees serving as the "friends" of the high priest John Hyrcanus, nephew of Jonathan, early in his reign. In this capacity the Pharisees had been promulgating laws derived from the traditions of the ancestors for public life. It would appear that the Pharisees were now serving in a role similar to that of Ben Sira and other scribes in the temple-state under the high priests before the crisis of the Hellenizing reform and the Maccabean Revolt.

This restoration of the temple-state by the early Hasmoneans, however, proved no more stable than had the temple-state under the Ptolemies and Seleucids, which had led to the Hellenizing reform, scribal resistance, and revolt by ordinary priests and other villagers. In the power vacuum left by the decline of the Seleucids and civil wars between rival claimants to the throne, the Hasmonean high priests, imitating the pattern of their former imperial overlords, proceeded to attack and conquer the neighboring territories and peoples: the Idumeans to the south and the Samaritans to the north, whose temple they destroyed (*Ant.* 13.254–258, 275–279). Eventually they also took over Galilee and required the residents, if they wanted to remain on their land, to live under "the laws of the Judeans" (*Ant.* 13.318–319). Alexander Jannaeus, in the third generation of Hasmonean high priests, conquered several of the Hellenistic cities around the perimeter of the now vastly expanded set of regions ruled by the Jerusalem high priest and temple-state. The Hasmoneans had carved out an empire of their own in Palestine and Jannaeus proclaimed himself king. In the narrative by Josephus in *Antiquities,* starting under Hyrcanus and escalating under his son Alexander Jannaeus the people of Jerusalem and perhaps some villagers (after Hyrcanus's more intensive exploitation) revolted against their high priests (*Ant.* 13.288, 372–383). The Pharisees evidently joined in the revolt, as intimated by Josephus, which escalated into a civil war, after which Jannaeus exacted brutal retaliation against the rebels. Jannaeus's wife and successor as ruler, Salome Alexandra, brought the Pharisees back into the administration of the temple-state and restored their traditions from the ancestors as state law (*Ant.* 13.405–411). Evidently this arrangement temporarily mitigated the civil conflict. But the more ambitious of her sons, who was heading military officers inherited from his father, soon seized power in the temple-state, setting off a prolonged civil war between rival Hasmonean factions (*Ant.* 13.422–432).

Meanwhile, Roman warlords had been expanding their control of the Mediterranean to the East. The rival Hasmonean factions both appealed for Roman support. And the Romans eventually took the opportunity to seize Palestine and take control Jerusalem and the temple-state. But civil war between rival Roman warlords greatly exacerbated the continuing civil war between rival Hasmonean factions. To finally exercise fuller control in Palestine, the Romans installed the ambitious young Idumean military strongman, Herod, as "king of the Judeans" to rule from Jerusalem the territories that had been conquered by the Hasmoneans (except the Hellenistic cities) . Only with the help of Roman troops was he able to conquer his subjects after a three-year campaign, and then he instituted a repressive rule. By intensely exploiting the peasantry that constituted his economic base, Herod gained the revenue for massive building projects in honor of Caesar: he erected temples dedicated to the emperor, built whole new cities named for Caesar Augustus, and established Roman institutions in Jerusalem itself. He became most famous from his massive rebuilding of the temple in grand Hellenistic form, which became one of the wonders of the Roman imperial world. This was the architectural foundation of his expansion of the high-priesthood with his own appointees, including high priestly families from Egypt and Babylonia. He thus turned the temple-state into an instrument for his own rule.

The Pharisees and any other scribes who had been serving in the temple-state thus experienced a demotion in relative position and influence. But judging from Josephus's reports, they did not withdraw from political activity in Jerusalem. One has the impression from Josephus's account of the widespread opposition to Herod's rule and of initiatives that were contrary to revered Judean tradition that the Pharisees and other scribes continued in a role that was a combination of mediation of Roman, Herodian, and high priestly rule over the people of Judea and other areas, and resistance against actions and policies that seemed to them egregious violations of Judean customs and traditions.

MEDIATION AND RESISTANCE BY RETAINERS

Subjected people do not always acquiesce and cooperate with the imperial or local rulers' designs. In situations where their traditional way of life is crumbling or their traditional culture threatened or under attack, subject peoples often generate movements that attempt to reassert or to adjust their traditional way of life or even move toward new forms of social-economic relations. In modern colonial situations where the standard traditional forms have disintegrated beyond the possibility of renewal, subjected people have developed new forms for their survival.[9]

From the structure and dynamics of imperial or colonial situations, some groups were more likely or able to mount resistance. Especially in situations of indirect rule, the local aristocracy had a serious stake in maintaining the established imperial order. If the conditions of the peasants degenerated into and brought about the disintegration of village communities as villagers became debt-slaves dependent on their wealthy and powerful creditors (often also officers of the state), they no longer had a collective basis of mutual support to mount a revolt. Although peasant revolts are rare historically, villagers are more likely and able to revolt when they see their traditional social forms disintegrating. This was likely the situation after decades of intense economic extraction by the Ptolemies. And then the Hellenizing reform and the Seleucid invasion and enforcement directly threatened their whole traditional way of life.

Intellectual-legal retainers are caught in the middle. They must struggle between their dependency on their patrons (the wealthy rulers) on the one hand, and their commitment to the traditional laws and relational forms, on the other. The retainers who enjoy positions immediately subordinate to the local or regional rulers also may have a realistic sense of the concrete imperial power relationship, which would incline them to a more conservative political stance. But at least some scribal circles, such as the maskilim and the Enoch scribes, found that the impending reform and its implementation eliminated their position and whole raison d'etre.

The imperial situation of Roman, Herodian, and high priestly rule in Judea and the rest of Palestine was, in effect, a prolonged crisis of instability. This may be most dramatically illustrated by the several widespread popular revolts that framed the period of late-second temple history from Herod to the Roman destruction of the temple and beyond. The Judeans and especially the Galileans who were to become Herod's subjects fought persistently for three years against his campaigns to subject them. After his death, widespread revolt erupted in all the principal districts of his realm;

---

9. Again this discussion is informed by Worsley, *Third World*, 21–49.

some locations achieved a degree of independence for as much as three years. Preceded by numerous movements of renewal, resistance, and protest, the great revolt took hold in Galilee and throughout Judea, from 66 to 70. Seventy years later, the second major revolt against Roman rule erupted in Judea, from 132 to 135.

In the imperial situation of early Roman Palestine renewal and resistance movements took forms informed by stories of movements of deliverance under legendary leaders of the people.[10] Judging from the accounts of the wealthy Judean priest Josephus, the widespread popular revolts against Roman and Herodian rule after the death of Herod in 4 BCE were patterned after the stories of the young David having been "messiahed" by (the elders of) the Israelites to lead them against Philistine incursions. In the great revolt of 66–70, one of the principal popular fighting forces took the same form, with peasants from the countryside acclaiming Simon bar Giora as their king. In the revival of time-honored Israelite laws, customs, and mechanisms, he declared the liberation of debt-slaves in the areas of the countryside he and his movement controlled. As the political-economic-religious order in Judea disintegrated further in the mid-first century, a series of popular movements emerged under the leadership of popular prophets, such as Theudas and the Judean prophet "from Egypt," in anticipation of a new act of deliverance from their (Roman and high priestly) rulers patterned after the foundational movements of hoary antiquity led by Moses and Joshua. The movements of resistance and the popular revolts were thus deeply rooted in Israelite/Judean popular tradition.

The Judean (and broader range of Israelite) peasants, however, did not have a monopoly on renewal and resistance movements. Even though they were conservative and obedient by training and political-social position, including because of economic dependency on the priestly aristocracy, circles of learned scribes or sages also engaged in resistance and even revolt. From their devoted professional cultivation of Judean traditions of "the teaching/law of the Most High" and prophecies, as well as forms of wisdom, learned scribes developed a sense of their own authority that transcended the authorization they had from the high priests. Particularly when their high priestly patrons abandoned the traditional covenantal relationship between God and the priestly rulers and the Judean people, embodied in the institutions of the temple-state headed by the high-priesthood, scribes must have

---

10. Discussed, with new translations by Hanson, in Horsley with Hanson, *Bandits, Prophets, and Messiahs*; based on a series of articles with documentation and discussion, including Horsley, "Popular Messianic Movements," and "Popular Prophetic Movements." See the collection of these articles in Horsley, *Politics, Conflicts, and Movements* (forthcoming).

struggled over competing loyalties: to the traditional God-given covenantal relations in the temple-state or to their high-priestly patrons.

We can detect this struggle coming to a head earlier in the "Enoch" scribal circle that produced the texts eventually collected in 1 Enoch and in the circle of *maskilim* who produced the visionary histories in Daniel 7–12. When the dominant priestly aristocracy abandoned the Judean covenant that held together the temple-state and carried out their reform to transform Jerusalem into a Hellenistic *polis*, these circles of now-dissident retainers mounted resistance. In their visionary histories, moreover, they projected a restoration of the Judean people that did not include a temple(-state) (Dan 11–12; 1 Enoch 90).

Fast-forward two centuries to the imperial situation under direct Roman rule, to what Josephus calls the "Fourth Philosophy," led by a Pharisee and another scribal teacher (*sophistes*) who agreed with everything the Pharisees advocated, including refusing to pay the tribute to Caesar (a violation of the first two covenantal commandments), in defiance of the high priests who were charged with its collection (*Ant.* 18.3–9, 23–25). And more radical yet were the *Sicarioi* ("dagger-men"), who, in their utter frustration over their high priests' collaboration in Roman rule, began to assassinate leading high priestly figures during the crowded conditions of festivals in the Jerusalem temple (*War* 2.254–256).[11]

In passing or limited references, however, Josephus gives the impression that under Herod the Pharisees, individually or collectively, were "political realists" who continued their service in the temple-state that Herod had retained but subordinated to his rule, presumably partly to mitigate or mediate his rule in Judea. Practically this meant that the Pharisees were trying to mediate but in certain circumstances resisted or checked his rule. According to Josephus, Herod honored—or perhaps tolerated—the Pharisees because, in their realistic estimate of how he would be backed by overwhelming Roman power, Samaias or Pollion and Samaias had warned the Jerusalemites to submit to Herod's rule lest they simply be destroyed (*Ant.* 14.172–174; 15.3–4). And indeed, Herod regularly eliminated those who resisted or opposed him or were "in the way." The Pharisees, evidently collectively, refused to submit to a loyalty oath (perhaps once, perhaps twice), an oath to support Caesar as well as Herod himself. Whether it was to mediate or to resist, a circle of Pharisees managed to find a place in Herod's court and to cultivate some Herodian family members, including the wife of his brother Pheroras (*Ant.* 17.41–45). She paid the "fine" Herod had slapped

---

11. These two movements are discussed in Horsley with Hanson, *Bandits, Prophets, Messiahs*, 190–210.

on them for refusing the oath. Josephus, likely depending on an account by Herod's court historian Nicolaus of Damascus, says that they delivered a prophecy that Pheroras would replace Herod as king. Herod retaliated against these conspirators. But Herod evidently did not simply get rid of them all, as he did others who resisted him.

That Pharisees were able to continue some functions in the temple-state or otherwise in Jerusalem is indicated, perhaps, by the example of two highly regarded sages and teachers, accounts of whom Josephus includes toward the close of his narratives about Herod (*War* 1.648–653; *Ant.* 17.149–154). Hearing that Herod lay dying, these two sages, revered by the populace as teachers of the youth, instructed (or was it inspired?) their proteges to cut down the golden Roman eagle from atop the gate of the temple. This symbol of loyalty to Rome and Caesar, of course, was in direct violation of the first two commandments of the Mosaic covenant: commandments not to have any other gods (Caesar was honored throughout the empire as a "son of god") in exclusive loyalty to the God of Israel, and not to bow down and serve (symbols of) other gods with their resources (as in the tribute to Caesar). After the sages had carried out this brazen demonstration, Herod had them burned alive. But this is an example of sages and scribal teachers continuing to operate and teach openly in the temple city and just waiting until they could get rid of Herod's "innovations" that were utterly counter to sacred Judean traditions and laws.

It may be more difficult to understand the action of "leading Pharisees" in the circumstances of the beginning of the great revolt. This may be largely because standard interpretation of the revolt appears to have been influenced by Flavian imperial propaganda that glorified the great victory of the Roman imperators Vespasian and Titus over the Judean people in general, who had so audaciously revolted against the Pax Romana. This was impressively embodied in the massive monument of the Arch of Titus erected in the Roman forum. Even though interpreters of Josephus's *War* have bought into this interpretation, Josephus does not provide solid support for it. In the *War* he portrays the high priests and leading Pharisees as at first taking refuge from the insurgents in a fortified place in the summer of 66. Then they timidly venture out and semi-agree to pursue the revolt with the rebels. In his later *Life* (17–29), a self-defense against the charge that he was helping lead the revolt, which seems more credible, Josephus states more clearly that he along with the high priests and leading Pharisees, who formed a sort of provisional government amid the chaos of the revolt, were trying to contain it until they could negotiate with the Romans. They knew that if they could not manage to control the people that the Romans had charged them to govern, the Romans would have no more use for them. But the revolt had expanded beyond the point that they could restrain it. And the scorched-earth way the Roman troops pursued their reconquest, destroying villages and driving people into the hills, simply created an expanding revolt. The Pharisees' realism may have been right: that the revolt was madness in the face of Roman power. It provoked the Roman destruction of the temple and temple-state in which the Pharisees had functioned for several generations as intellectual-legal retainers.

2

ASSESSING THE SOURCES

How we understand the Pharisees and their role and relations with others in late second-temple Judea depends heavily on how we assess and use the sources. Approaches to and analysis of the sources became steadily more critical in the last three decades of the twentieth century. Studies of the Pharisees in the fields of biblical studies and Jewish history, however, still look somewhat narrowly to text fragments and passages taken out of their literary context as the sources. Considering the fragments and passages in their literary and historical contexts, however, may lead to an understanding of the Pharisees more in accord with the changing historical contexts in which they lived and operated.

Constructions of the Pharisees in the last century drew on three principal sets of sources: the accounts of the Judean historian Josephus, the polemical stories in the Christian Gospels, and rabbinic traditions of their views and opinions on particular issues. Since the discovery of the Dead Sea Scrolls, brief polemical attacks in some previously unknown texts on the "seekers of smooth things," a derogatory epithet for the Pharisees, may provide a fourth source.

It was simply assumed in biblical studies and to a degree in the field of Jewish history that the way to proceed was to focus on text fragments such as particular passages and even on particular sayings or rulings taken out of broader context in texts and without much consideration of historical context. Different constructions of the Pharisees have depended heavily on how the sources were read and on the scholarly conceptual apparatus employed. Most earlier interpreters simply took their text fragment sources at face value. It was standard to form a composite picture by combining impressions from the different sources. In New Testament studies composite pictures were framed and informed by a basic Christian theological scheme of Judaism as a legalistic religion from which Jesus and Paul broke away toward a more universal religion centered on a direct spiritual relationship with God. Jewish constructions understandably sought ways of countering that standard scheme. In both fields the Pharisees were understood as the principal representatives of Judaism.

Leading scholars took steps toward a more critical assessment and reading of the accepted sets of text fragments during the last fifty years. In groundbreaking analysis of rabbinic sources, Jacob Neusner demonstrated how rabbinic text fragments could be critically analyzed for (ostensibly) appropriately dated information on figures reputed to have been Pharisees (or on the disputes between Pharisees and Sadducees or between Hillelites and Shammaites).[1] He further insisted that the pertinent text fragments in each of Josephus's works be considered separately, although he continued to lump the Gospel traditions about the Pharisees together (to then be treated according to topic). In the (1973) textbook *From Politics to Piety* that became highly influential in New Testament studies, Neusner delineated the different portrayals of the Pharisees in the different sets of text fragments: passages from the works of Flavius Josephus, purposely isolated sayings from the Gospel stories, and carefully evaluated traditions of the Pharisees from rabbinic texts. He then explained the difference in portrayals by positing a change in the Pharisees' social position and relations. From the accounts taken from Josephus he concluded that the Pharisees started as political "administrators" of the Judean state under the Hasmonean high priests. The rabbinic traditions he found reliable focused on issues of purity and food, issues that were also attested in text fragments from the New Testament. He took these to indicate that the Pharisees retreated under Herodian repression to become a pious eating club focused on purity. He read Josephus's later accounts in the *Antiquities*, however, as indicating that after the great revolt and the Roman destruction of Jerusalem and the temple, Josephus was backing the Pharisees' aim of returning to political life if only the Romans would entrust the leadership of the Judeans in Palestine to them.

Neusner eventually insisted on the importance of reading whole treatises to discern their focal subject matter and presentation. But in critically ferreting out the rabbinic traditions of the Pharisees, he did not begin with the overall rabbinic enterprise evident in the tractates of the Mishnah and Tosefta so that it informed his investigation of the relation between those treatises and the views and rulings of earlier sages and Pharisees.

---

1. Neusner, *Rabbinic Traditions about the Pharisees*.

As for the passages from Josephus's works, Steve Mason insisted that it was important to evaluate Josephus's perspective and view of the Pharisees before moving toward use of the passages for historical reconstruction.[2] He called attention to how the political-intellectual ethos of Flavian Rome, where Josephus was living and composing, affected his views. And Mason's selective word-studies contributed toward more appropriate translation and understanding of some of Josephus's statements. He followed the standard procedure of focusing mainly on the passages directly pertinent to the Pharisees without considering the broader literary context and thus missed how Josephus's narratives indicate their social-political position and role in the (shifting) institutional structure of Judea.

Treatment of the Pharisees in New Testament studies lags behind in considering the text fragments concerning the Pharisees in broader literary and then social context, to which the literary context may be the best guide. Accordingly discussion of the disputes between Jesus and the Pharisees proceeded by focusing on individual fragments such that they are pulled back up into the standard scheme of early Christianity making its break from the Pharisees as spokespersons for early Judaism.

A MULTIFACTOR APPROACH TO THE SETS OF SOURCES

With ever-expanding studies of texts and historical contexts, it should be possible to explore a more comprehensive multifactor approach to what constitute our sources and to how we assess and how we use those sources for the Pharisees and other scribes/sages in late second temple Judea.

Most investigations and constructions of the Pharisees have taken the text fragments that (may) pertain to them out of literary and historical contexts, as if the fragments were the sources. There is increasing awareness, however, that the broader literary contexts of the pertinent fragments contain key clues to how those fragments can be assessed. It is important to evaluate the text fragments' portrayal of the Pharisees in the broader texts of which they are components, that is, the broader contents, focus, and purpose of each text and set of texts. These—and not separate fragments and passages—are the sources.

Moreover, there is increasing awareness that texts are situated in particular historical contexts but portray other, often earlier historical contexts. This increasing awareness of the social situation of texts lends importance to the consideration of the perspective of the texts. The social location of (the producers of) the sets of texts are fundamental in determining the

---

2. Mason, *Flavius Josephus on the Pharisees*.

perspectives of the four principal sets of sources about the Pharisees. The works of Josephus, which supply accounts of the Pharisees' position and activities over several generations, provide a view from above, that is the viewpoint of a precocious, wealthy priest who claimed to be a descendant of the Hasmonean high priests. One does not have to read very far into his historical narratives to realize that he not only despises the peasants who live in villages of the *chora*, but also despises the ordinary people of Jerusalem. He is also evidently jealous of the Pharisees, who have moved into what he sees as the prerogatives of the priestly aristocracy to know and expound the laws.

The Gospels are unusual not just as texts from the ancient Mediterranean but in the world more generally as foundational stories of Jesus movements among ordinary people. They thus have a view from below that is often polemical against the rulers in Jerusalem and the Pharisees.

The other two sets of sources are from groups that parallel the social position of the Pharisees—from associations of educated people devoted to cultivating the Judean scribal reservoir of torah and other traditions. First, the Dead Sea Scrolls, discovered in the mid-twentieth century, come from a dissident priestly and scribal group that withdrew in protest from the Jerusalem temple to form a tight-knit covenantal community in the wilderness. These texts view the incumbent high priest as illegitimate and articulate sharp polemics against "the seekers of smooth things." Second, the circles of the rabbis whose rulings and observations are extant in the tractates of the Mishnah and Tosefta and related texts appear to occupy a social position somewhat similar to that of the Pharisees, but now in the absence of the temple that the Romans had destroyed.

Consideration of the broader literary context of text fragments and limited passages opens toward recognition of the historical context that the texts portray. This should serve as a check on assimilating text fragments into the inherited conceptual apparatus of the academic fields of biblical studies and Jewish history that may not be attested in the sources. It should also lead toward recognition of the complexities of the historical context and social conflict that are attested.

THE WORKS OF JOSEPHUS

In social location and perspective, Josephus saw himself as a member of and operated among the wealthy, ruling priestly aristocracy that headed the Judean temple-state under the overarching rule of Rome. Central to Judean elite tradition, God, through Moses, had placed the priestly aristocracy in charge of Judeans (Israelites) in the central institutions of temple and priesthood and given them the charge and responsibility and privilege of knowing and administering the torah/laws. In the course of second-temple history, the scribes/sages had gradually taken responsibility for knowing and applying the torah/law, which would have led to some tension between priests and sages/scribes. Moreover, during the Judean revolt against Roman rule, Josephus came into serious conflict with leading Pharisees in a delegation sent by the provisional priestly government attempting to control the revolt to relieve him of his prized command in Galilee. So when he came to composing his historical accounts, he had reason to downplay and denigrate the Pharisees and their role in the temple-state.

A hundred years ago, Josephus was viewed not only as a traitor to the Jewish people but as a mindless copyist unable to smooth out the contradictions between the various sources he used in constructing his histories. The hypothesis that Josephus did not assimilate the sources he copied proved particularly useful with regard to the clearly negative portrayal of the Pharisees in both the *War* and the *Antiquities*. The only way scholars could explain such negative representations of the Pharisees from a writer they all believed was himself a Pharisee (on the basis of *Life* 12) was that he had mindlessly copied from Nicolas of Damascus, Herod's house historian. In the last eighty years or so, interpreters have come rather to recognize that Josephus was well aware of standard historiographical conventions and wrote his histories with distinctive concerns and an agenda of his own.[3]

In using Josephus's works as sources for Judean history, I have been consistently attempting to follow three procedural steps (albeit without walking through each step explicitly here): (a) consider critically his *social location* and the perspective from which he composed his works; (b) in what has been called *composition criticism*, examine each work as a text with its own integrity, attempting to ascertain its distinctive purpose, interests, and agenda, and what the work is about,[4] in the circumstances of its composition; and (c) examine how each source represents the Pharisees (in relation with others). With both the overall agenda of each work and its portrayal of the Pharisees in particular in mind, I will in subsequent chapters reason critically from the source's representations to historical judgments and constructions of the social location and role of the Pharisees. Josephus's portrayals themselves and in some instances portrayals in the Gospel stories

---

3. Mason, *Flavius Josephus on the Pharisees*, chapters 2, 3, 7; in particular see his comments on the influence of Laqueur (*Der Jüdische Historiker Flavius Josephus*, 1920) through Thackeray (*Josephus: The Man and the Historian*, 1929).

4. Although Mason considers Josephus's perspective and interests, he does not consider what his works are about.

and Qumran texts may provide clues to or illumination of the accounts' value as historical evidence.[5]

Three of Josephus's works offer portrayals of and/or passing references to (the) Pharisees. While it is the last of the three to be written, his *Life* contains what has been read as a claim that he himself was a Pharisee. Since this passage has been the key to modern scholarly reading of Josephus's references to the Pharisees, we will begin with examination of the *Life*.

The Life and Its Representation of Pharisees

Josephus himself indicates that his *Life* was written as an appendix to the *Antiquities* (*Ant.* 20.266; *Life* 430; and all but one of the manuscripts combine them), although it may have been written a bit later than 93/94.[6] The principal purpose and agenda of this "autobiography," the bulk of which (*Life* 28–406) concentrates on the five months of Josephus's actions in Galilee during the great revolt (67 CE), is to defend himself against the embarrassing charge leveled by the rival historian Justus of Tiberias of having fomented the revolt in Tiberias. Still debated is whether the whole document, including the introduction (1–27) and conclusion (414–430) and the accounts of all the incidents, or only the bulk of them, are part of the defense against Justus's charges. The introduction, an account of Josephus's priestly lineage and education that includes all three of the principal "philosophies," certainly a bridge to the self-defense in the bulk of the *Life*, could more easily be read as documentation of his own claim to "accuracy" (*akribeia*) in the conclusion to the *Antiquities* (20.266).[7] This link with the ending of the *Antiquities* is significant for how Josephus's representations of the Pharisees in *Life* are understood.

Pharisees figure at only two points in the *Life*. The first has been the key to most modern interpretation of Josephus on the Pharisees, because nearly all scholars have taken Josephus to be representing himself as a Pharisee. Most scholars have then also assumed Josephus's (supposed)

---

5. Thus, in contrast to some earlier studies, particularly of the Gospels as evidence for the historical Jesus, I am not trying to identify and then peel away the views or "biases" of Josephus, supposedly leaving a deposit of historical data. I am attempting rather both to take Josephus's views into account as we reason from his accounts to the historical situation and relationships he represents and to consider ways in which Josephus's own concerns may illuminate history, whether his own situation or the situation he represents in his historical accounts.

6. On dating of Josephus's works, see especially Cohen, *Josephus in Jerusalem and Rome*.

7. Mason, *Flavius Josephus on the Pharisees*, 324.

self-identification as a Pharisee in their interpretation of his histories, while a few have recently taken it as a new assertion by Josephus to ingratiate himself with the Pharisees and/or to help persuade the Romans to place the Pharisees in charge of Judea. A close examination of this key passage is therefore in order. The key sentence comes in *Life* 12b, and as always it must be understood in context.[8]

After elaborating his illustrious priestly pedigree, including descent from the Hasmoneans, he discusses his education. This focuses particularly on his "very precise/accurate" (*akribesteron*) knowledge of the ancestral laws of his people, in which he was precocious for a lad of fourteen. In Judean society, of course, the priests were traditionally responsible for cultivation of the laws. At sixteen he determined to gain direct experience of the three main schools of thought, of the Pharisees, the Sadducees, and the Essenes, anticipating that after investigating all he could choose the best. Having passed through the three courses, however, he was still not content, and then became the devoted disciple of the ascetic hermit Bannus in the wilderness. "With him I spent three years" (thus he obviously could not have spent long with each of the three schools of thought) "and, having (finally) satisfied my longing, returned to the city" at age nineteen (*Life* 11–12a). Then comes the key sentence, *Life* 12b—after which comes narrative of his early career in Judean political life, including participation in a delegation to Rome and his long account of his attempting to take control of affairs in Galilee during the great revolt.

In the almost unanimous conventional English-language understanding and translation, the key sentence in *Life* 12b is taken to say that Josephus became a Pharisee, that he "attached himself to," "chose to follow," "joined," "began to follow," "chose," or "began to adhere to" the Pharisees. Thackeray's translation (in the LCL: "I began to govern my life by the rules of the Pharisees") and those influenced by it are clearly projecting modern Western individualism back into the Greek text. And those who take the statement as indicating a kind of conversion to or choice for a particular religion or religious sect are projecting the modern separation of religion from political life into Josephus's account. Mason's thorough critical analysis now offers a persuasive and, it seems, definitive translation that differs dramatically from the standard understanding. The key statement in Josephus's Greek text has two clauses: a main clause, *erxamen politeuesthai*, and a subordinate clause, *te Pharisaion heiresei katakolouthon*. The sense (and adequate translation) of the statement hinges on three things: the meaning of *politeuethai*, the

---

8. The following analysis depends on Mason, "Was Josephus a Pharisee?"; and Mason, *Flavius Josephus on the Pharisees*, chap. 15.

relation between the clauses, and how the statement fits the flow of the narrative context.

In Greek literature and philosophy, the term *politeuomai* usually had a clearly political meaning, associated with life in the fundamental political form, the *polis*: "live as a citizen, take part in political life/government, hold public office, etc." Liddell and Scott also list a special meaning of "behave" or "deal with (in private affairs)" that is (supposedly) attested only in Jewish and Christian texts. That reading of the term in those texts, however, is apparently a projection of modern religious individualism onto ancient Jewish and Christian texts in which the meaning is still, in effect, "to conduct one's political-economic-religious life in the community," as can be seen in the texts scholars list: 2 Macc 11:25; Acts 23:1; and Phil 1:27. German interpreters and translators of Josephus have consistently recognized this.[9] Except for a few occurrences in *Antiquities* 17, with its recognized stylistic peculiarities, Josephus almost always uses the term in the political or public-life sense: "to govern, hold office, enact policy, act as a leader, participate in politics" (e.g., *Ant.* 4.13; 13.432; 14.91; 20.251; *Life* 258, 262). This is clearly the meaning in *Life* 12b as well: After his three years with Bannus, having satisfied his yearning, at age nineteen Josephus returned to the *polis* (Jerusalem) and "began to participate in political life." After his preparation in the wilderness—a common preparation for political life, as in the cases of Moses, Elijah, and Jesus—he was now ready to enter, as had his father and other ancestors before him, upon the public career expected of one from a prominent priestly family (*Life* 1–7). And sure enough, by age twenty-six he was sent as part of a delegation to Rome and at age thirty sent to take control of Galilee.

The verb of the dependent clause, *katakolouthon*, ordinarily means "to follow, obey, emulate, imitate," and Josephus uses it often in connection with the laws or God's will. In this case its meaning is determined by its subordination to the main verb, "to participate in politics/public life." That is, in his participation in Jerusalem politics, Josephus was "following" the Pharisees' school of thought. But that does not mean that he was a Pharisee or had joined the Pharisees' school. He has already mentioned that "whenever [Sadducees] come into public office, they defer, albeit unwillingly and by necessity, to what the Pharisee says, because otherwise they would become intolerable to the common people" (*Ant.* 18.17). When he "followed the Pharisees' school" in his participation in political life, Josephus did not become a Pharisee any more than those officeholding Sadducees did. The concluding comparison of the Pharisees' school with that of the Stoics fits

---

9. See the list in Mason, "Was Josephus a Pharisee?," 38.

the same context of public/political life. Since Stoicism had become the dominant philosophy in Hellenistic cities, its influence on political life was considerable, as can be seen in other philosophies of the time and in Stoic commonplaces that found their way into public discourse. Just as non-Stoics in the Greek cities had to follow Stoic political philosophy in their conduct of public life, so in Jerusalem Josephus followed the Pharisaic school of thought in political life. But in *Life* 12b he does not say that he joined the Pharisees. It seems that, contrary to previous scholarly consensus, Josephus did not claim to be a Pharisee.

The other reference to Pharisees in the *Life* comes toward the middle of Josephus's narrative of events in Galilee. John of Gischala, Josephus's rival for control of affairs in Galilee, appeals to Simon son of Gamaliel to persuade the provisional government in Jerusalem to relieve Josephus of his command in Galilee. Simon is identified as a Jerusalemite from an illustrious family and as belonging to the school of the Pharisees, "who have the reputation of being unrivalled in accuracy concerning the ancestral laws/customs/rulings" (*nomima*, 190-192). When he cannot persuade the high priests Ananus and Jesus, who head the Jerusalem *koinon*, he arranges for Ananus to be bribed into sending a delegation to relieve Josephus without the knowledge of others in the city. Three of the four members of the delegation are Pharisees, including Jonathan, who appears later as the leader. In the ensuing narrative Jonathan and the others of the heavily Pharisaic delegation are represented as being devious, dishonest, duplicitous (*Life* 216-245, 274-275, 281-283, 290-303). They may have had a reputation for expertise in the laws, but they are hardly admirable characters in the narrative. This portrayal, of course, should not be surprising, since these Pharisees are Josephus's opponents. This passage is important, however, because it is one of the few in Josephus to indicate that the Pharisees were still active in prominent positions in the high priestly government in Jerusalem. It is also the only passage in Josephus's histories to place the Pharisees in Galilee, however briefly.

The Judean–Roman War

Josephus's *Judean–Roman War* has for some time been taken as pro-Roman propaganda, written at the behest of Josephus's patron, the emperor Vespasian, as a vehicle of imperial policy in the East. After all, this Jewish traitor who deserted to the Romans and then helped them conquer Jerusalem and destroy the temple was living in the emperor's villa when he wrote the work. Its earlier version in Aramaic was supposedly written to dissuade eastern barbarians from joining the Parthians in a war against Roman forces in Syria. That view is no longer convincing. Even if his lavish praise of Vespasian and his son and successor Titus reflect his gratitude for their patronage, his appreciation of Roman "power," his claim that "Fortune" (even God's providence) had passed to the Romans, and his conviction that the Judean and Galilean people must inevitably submit to Roman imperial rule can be easily explained by his own aristocratic station in life. The Roman imperial order, after all, was based on the alliance and collaboration between the imperial power and wealthy and powerful provincial elites. And Josephus had been born and socialized into just such a political-economic position and shared the interests and views of what has been called "the ruling class of Judea."[10]

Recent critical studies of Josephus and other ancient Greek and Roman writers have recognized that the prologue to a work of ancient historiography provides the key to its concerns and agenda and the way the whole writing should be read.[11] In the prologue to the *War* Josephus states clearly that his principal concern, following the paradigmatic Greek historian Thucydides, is to present his account with "accuracy" and "truth" (the Greek terms *akribeia* and *aletheia* occur repeatedly throughout the prologue). But he claims his own account is important because he was himself a direct participant in the events, in contrast both to those who had distorted the truth about the Judean-Roman War, and to Greek historians of the time, who wrote simply about events of the distant past.[12] He also deliberately takes liberties with standard canons of historiography to include both laments over the sufferings of his people and assignment of blame for the destruction of the Judean people to the Judean "tyrants" who spearheaded the revolt, while also taking care not to blame the Romans.

While sharing the view of Judean and other provincial elites like himself, he writes as a Judean who intends to set the record straight, who argues that the Jerusalem *demos* (especially respectable people like himself) were not to blame, while castigating the bands of "bandits" from the countryside of Galilee and Judea and the Jerusalem riffraff who foolishly began and continued the revolt that inevitably brought destruction on the suffering Judean land and people.[13] In the middle of the work, he even portrays himself as

10. Goodman, *Ruling Class of Judea*; Rajak, *Josephus*, 185; Mason, *Flavius Josephus on the Pharisees*, 59-60.

11. Attridge, *Interpretation*, 44-45; and Mason, *Flavius Josephus on the Pharisees*, 62-81, have given telling attention to precisely this.

12. Mason, *Flavius Josephus on the Pharisees*, 64-74.

13. It is worth noting that he could later refer to the work as his "Book of Judaica" or "the Judaica" in *Ant.* 13.173, 298.

the great Judean general who constituted a worthy opponent for the Roman generals who became the emperors, Vespasian and Titus.

Josephus's Attitude toward the Pharisees in the War

In the *War* Josephus first mentions the Pharisees in the middle of his account of the Hasmonean rulers. He views the early Hasmoneans positively, starting with Mattathias and his sons, who led the resistance to the brutal Antiochus Epiphanes. He characterizes Simon's rule as "excellent" (*War* 1.50). And he praises John Hyrcanus as the high point of the dynasty, having received all three of the coveted gifts of divinely blessed rulership: "the rule of the people and the high priesthood and prophecy" (*War* 1.68). His sons Aristobulus and Alexander Jannaeus, however, turned out to be, respectively, a "catastrophe" and an oppressive tyrant who touched off civil war (*War* 1.69, 85–104). Things looked more promising at the accession of Alexander's queen, Salome Alexandra, because of her great piety (i.e., adherence to the ancestral traditions or laws). But the Pharisees, "with a reputation for great piety and accuracy on the laws," exploited her piety and gradually took over as the real wielders of royal power. With such power they began to attack "the most eminent men," conveniently not mentioning that these had been the highest-ranking officers and closest advisers of the tyrant Alexander Jannaeus, who had brutally killed thousands of his people and even crucified hundreds who had rebelled against him.

Josephus's sharply negative portrayal of the Pharisees here led earlier scholars to attribute the account of the Pharisees in *War* 1.110–112 to Nicolaus of Damascus, Herod's court historian, who would presumably have been negative toward them. This judgment, however, was rooted in the assumptions that we now recognize as questionable, particularly that the Pharisees were tantamount to Judaism, and that Josephus himself was a Pharisee, hence would not write such a negative account.[14] While his principal source for Hasmonean history after the end of 1 Maccabees may well have been Nicolaus of Damascus, Josephus has overwritten his source in this case. The terms Josephus uses in his characterization of the Pharisees, as "having a reputation" for extraordinary "piety" and "accuracy in keeping the laws," are his own standard vocabulary, which he uses in two other contexts to similarly characterize the Pharisees (*War* 2.162; *Life* 191), passages that are almost certainly his own formulations.[15]

---

14. E.g., Moore, *Judaism*, vol. 1, 62 n4, 65 n3.
15. Mason, *Flavius Josephus on the Pharisees*, 85–96, 113.

Josephus mentions the Pharisees a second time in the *War* in his account of Herod. In the *War* Josephus presents Herod in a highly favorable light, as pious, humane, and brave, while blaming all his problems on the women of the court.[16] His brother Pheroras's wife is said to be particularly subversive and is accused, among other things, of "supplying a reward/money to the Pharisees" to oppose the king (1.567–571). Accusation of "the love of money" was a standard slander of one's opponents in antiquity, one that Josephus brings against the Pharisees elsewhere as well (*Ant.* 17.42–43; *Life* 195–196; cf. Luke 16:14; 1 Tim 6:10; 2 Tim 3:2; Titus 1:11).[17]

Josephus finally presents his principal account of the Pharisees, the Essenes, and the Sadducees as he moves from the Roman deposition of Herod's son Archelaus to the turmoil in Judea under the Roman governors. After noting, in connection with the incitement by Judas of Galilee (elsewhere Judas of Gamla/Gaulanitis) of resistance to the Roman tribute, that he introduced a party/school (*hairesis*) that had nothing in common with the others, he devotes a lengthy sequence of very positive paragraphs to the Essenes (*War* 2.119–161), followed by three short paragraphs on the Pharisees and the Sadducees (*War* 2.162–166). His presentation of the Pharisees seems positive enough until we compare it with his highly appreciative treatment of the Essenes. The Pharisees have a reputation for accuracy in the laws (*War* 2.162), but the Essenes "are most accurate" in their court cases and Sabbath observances (*War* 2.145, 147). The Pharisees are devoted to each other (*War* 1.166), but the Essenes are "more devoted to one another than the other schools/parties" (*War* 1.119). Josephus mentions in a passing phrase that the Pharisees cultivate "concord/harmonious relations" with the community, but devotes two paragraphs to the Essenes' unusual concord (*homonoia*, 1.122–127). And these characterizations and comparisons are Josephus's own judgments, since the key vocabulary throughout is typical of his style.[18]

The *Judean Antiquities*

Josephus's apologetic aim in the *Antiquities* to present the history and philosophy of the Judeans as ancient and admirable has been consistently recognized by modern scholars. They have thus spent far less energy searching for its supposedly ulterior motive, and attend to Josephus's own stated

---

16. Mason, *Flavius Josephus on the Pharisees*, 116–17.

17. Mason, *Flavius Josephus on the Pharisees*, 117–18; Karris, "The Background and Significance of the Polemic of the Pastoral Epistles."

18. Mason, *Flavius Josephus on the Pharisees*, 173–77.

purpose in the prologue. The main teaching of the *Antiquities*, says its author, is that God rewards those who pursue virtue by obeying the laws with "happiness" (*eudaimonia*, *Ant.* 1.14, 20). "Happiness," of course, was the goal of Greek philosophy, the principal goal (*telos*) of humans (Aristotle, *Nic. Eth.* 10.6.1–3). Josephus is thus presenting the history and "constitution" of the Judeans (*politeia*, which he pairs and identifies with the Mosaic laws, *Ant.* 3.332; 4.198, 310) as a philosophy, which means not simply a system of thought, but a way of life, in this case one of hoary antiquity, which would make it all the more appealing to his non-Judean Greek-speaking audience.

The earlier view that the *Judean War* was written as pro-Roman propaganda has led to the frequent assumption of a dramatic difference between the *War* and the *Antiquities*. Josephus, no longer living under imperial patronage, has supposedly rethought his position twenty years after the *War* and come around to the apologetic agenda laid out in the *Antiquities*. If we take the prologues and the overall presentation in both works seriously, however, there is not much difference between them. In both works Josephus is concerned to present history with "accuracy" and, against others' misrepresentations, to set the record straight on Judeans, their history, and heritage. In the still later work, *Against Apion*, Josephus claims that in aiming at the "truth," he has "fully accomplished this in both works" (*Ag. Ap.* 1.53–56). The main difference lies in their respective genres and materials, the *War* being an account of recent historical events in which the author participated, and the *Antiquities* being *archaiologia*. In addition, of course, he has revised his views and evaluations of particular events and main figures, the most obvious being Herod the Great, whom he criticizes sharply in the *Antiquities*.

Josephus's Attitude toward the Pharisees in the Antiquities

Until the last generation, scholars saw no difference between the *War* and the *Antiquities* on their treatment of the Pharisees. A number of factors seem to have converged in stimulating a new theory of Josephus's accounts of the Pharisees. In the aftermath of the Holocaust, both Jewish and Christian interpreters were questioning the synthetic and overly simple standard construct of ancient Judaism. Due partly to the discovery of the Dead Sea Scrolls, modern interpreters were forced to come to grips with the diversity of prerabbinic Judaism. Perhaps there was no normative Judaism, and the Pharisees were not as central and important as previously thought. In response to long-overdue criticism, interpreters began to realize that it was not appropriate to project later rabbinic views back into late second-temple times. In reaction to the quest for sources behind ancient documents, scholars were gaining an appreciation of the creativity, purpose, and particular agendas of ancient intellectuals. Faith in the continuity between the Pharisees and the rabbis, however, remained relatively firm.

Morton Smith pioneered, and then Jacob Neusner gave decisive formulation, to a new view of both Josephus's accounts of the Pharisees and of the history of the Pharisees.[19] In this view, Josephus's portrayal of the Pharisees in the *War* is negative (as noted above). But suddenly in the *Antiquities* twenty years later, he presents them as indispensable to the rule of Judea and even claims to be a Pharisee himself in the *Life*. The explanation must be that, faced with a new situation in Roman-dominated Judea, Josephus had himself come to a new view and strategy. While other groups were eliminated in the Roman devastation of the countryside and destruction of Jerusalem and its temple, the Pharisees had regrouped at Yavneh on the coastal plain. Josephus now, perhaps partly to ingratiate himself with the Pharisees, reconfigured history, particularly the role of the Pharisees, in order to commend the Pharisees to Rome as the only viable option to place in charge of Judea. Particularly his portrayal of the Hasmonean Alexander Jannaeus stating that Judea cannot be ruled without their support because of their influence with the people in *Ant.* 13.400–404 (far more pointed than the corresponding passages in the *War*) would supposedly have convinced the Romans to back the Pharisees.

Neusner's special contribution to the new hypothesis, as noted above, was that while starting out as a politically active group, the Pharisees had withdrawn "from politics to piety" once Herod took over and became politically active again only during the revolt in 66–70.[20]

With hindsight, we can see a number of problems with this view, which became very influential particularly among New Testament scholars. In the years since its formulation, scholars have raised questions about the assumptions on which it is based. The evidence for who was involved and just what (supposedly) happened at Yavneh in the aftermath of Roman defeat is not all that clear. It is questionable, moreover, whether the Romans were even interested in placing some Judean group in charge of Judea in the late first century CE. The Roman policy in the East was either to support provincial rulers, such as Herodian kings and Judean high priestly families, where they could (as in the case of Agrippa II in eastern Galilee and the Golan), and otherwise to deploy Roman governors and/or to urbanize

---

19. Smith, "Palestinian Judaism in the First Century."
20. Neusner, *From Politics to Piety*, 45–56.

Roman rule, with cities in control of the surrounding countryside (as with Sepphoris in western Galilee after the death of Agrippa I).

It is also questionable whether Josephus's portrayal of the Pharisees in the *Antiquities* can be made to support the new hypothesis about the history of the Pharisees.[21] The latter depends primarily on the portrayal of the Pharisees in *Ant.* 13.288-298 and especially 13.400-411. The claim that the Pharisees' "influence with the common people was so great that even when they spoke against a king or a high priest, they would immediately gain credence" (13.288), however, was hardly likely to have carried much weight with the Romans, who were extremely suspicious of urban mobs. And the statements that the Pharisees had so much influence with the multitude that "they could injure those whom they hated," that they virtually usurped Salome Alexandra's royal power, and proceeded to attack the military aristocracy (13.401-411) would have positively frightened the Romans, who depended on their own and the provincial aristocracy to control the empire. Josephus changed his representation of Queen Salome Alexandra from *War* to *Antiquities*; she is no longer deeply pious. But he does not suddenly present the Pharisees positively. If anything they appear more ominously scheming in the *Antiquities* than in the *War*.

In fact, a closer examination of Josephus's portrayal of the Pharisees in the *Antiquities* indicates that it differs little from the negative evaluation in the *War*. When he introduces them as the first (or leading) of three schools of thought among the Judeans in *Ant.* 13.171-173, he defers to his account in *War* 2.119-166, which highlights the Essenes as "more accurate."[22] When Josephus recounts their activities under the Hasmoneans, he presents them first as having been dismissed by Hyrcanus (*Ant.* 13.288-298), the ideal ruler who was blessed with the gift of prophecy and the high priestly office as well. His framing of the story of that break claims that the Pharisees' influence with the populace (of Jerusalem) leads to trouble for the ruling high priest or king. When the Pharisees are brought back into the Hasmonean administration by Salome Alexandra at her dying husband Alexander Jannaeus's suggestion, Josephus portrays them as retaliating against Alexander's high military officers who had carried out his brutal crucifixion of his opponents (who, Josephus fails to mention, probably included Pharisees; *Ant.* 13.401-411).[23] In *Ant.* 17.41-46, the Pharisees are presented as refus-

21. Mason, *Flavius Josephus on the Pharisees*, presents a complete critical survey

22. Mason, *Flavius Josephus on the Pharisees*, chap. 8, explains carefully how *Ant.* 13.171-173 "serves the apologetic-didactic interests of *Antiquities*," including its minor differences with *War* 2.119-166.

23. Mason's presentation of Josephus's accounts of the Pharisees under Hyrcanus and Salome Alexandra is an exaggeration. He largely ignores or downplays Josephus's

ing to take an oath of loyalty to Caesar and their own client king Herod, prophesying against him, whereupon Herod executes some of them. The Romans and loyal provincial elites would have found this subversive.[24] One of the few individual figures that Josephus names as a Pharisee, Saddok, is the other principal leader, along with Judas of Gaulanitis, in organizing the resistance to the Roman tribute, the "insurrection" on which Josephus places greatest culpability for the eventual outbreak of the disastrous Judean revolt (*Ant.* 18.4–10). In the immediately ensuing account of the three main philosophies among the Judeans, however, Josephus's portrayal of the Pharisees is relatively neutral. And he adds there that they "happen to be persuasive in these matters to the townspeople," who perform prayers and sacred rites according to their interpretation (*Ant.* 18.12–15). His rhetorical purpose in this account, however, is to contrast the "intrusive Fourth Philosophy" with the other three, which he portrays as politically innocuous by contrast, as well as similar to the standard Greek philosophies familiar to his readers. When he returns to the "Fourth Philosophy," moreover, he points out that except for its intense passion for liberty, the new school "agrees in all other respects with the opinions of the Pharisees" (*Ant.* 18.23), hardly a comment that would commend them.

Josephus's overall presentation of the Pharisees in the *Antiquities* can thus hardly be taken as positive. It differs little in tone and substance from his earlier treatment in the *War*. In an extensive presentation of the laws/constitution of the Judeans as a philosophy (way of life) comparable to those

---

broader narrative of historical events before, between, and following the accounts of the Pharisees: the popular resistance to Hyrcanus, the widespread popular revolt against Alexander Jannaeus, and Jannaeus's grossly brutal killing of thousands of those opponents, including his crucifixion of eight hundred, and the subsequent seizure of power by the warlike older son of Jannaeus and his military officers. Focusing mainly on the passages that focus on the Pharisees, Mason can thus attribute blame for the demise of the Hasmoneans primarily on them. Read in broader narrative context, far from upsetting "the delicate balance of the kingdom by taking revenge on their enemies among Alexander's high officers," the Pharisees Salome Alexandra brought into the administration help her restore public order and, at least for a decade, set up a delicate balance between their operation of domestic affairs and the military officers led by Aristobulus who were allowed to take over the fortresses around the country. As Josephus explains in the subsequent narrative, the military officers and Aristobulus then seized power and set off a prolonged civil war between rival Hasmonean factions. Josephus's historical narrative of the Hasmonean rulers includes multiple factors that are interwoven or treated sequentially.

24. Again Mason exaggerates Josephus's presentation, claiming that he portrays the Pharisees in a far more negative light than Herod. But again Mason does not consider Josephus's broader narrative of events that is bluntly critical of Herod's rule as increasingly repressive, and presents the Pharisees court conspiracy as one among many actions of resistance by Herod's subjects.

already familiar to his readers, it is not surprising to find Josephus representing the Pharisees as one of three principal schools of that philosophy. But, of course, he had done the same in the *War*, more extensively. And there he made it clear that he most admired the Essenes. His portrayal in the *Antiquities* of the Pharisees' conflicts with the Hasmoneans and Herod would have been particularly troubling to readers with a stake in the Roman imperial order.

THE GOSPEL STORIES

The greatest source of distortion of the Pharisees as historical figures and defamation of their character has been the Christian reading of the Gospels. The Christian construction of the Pharisees as "leaders" of "Judaism" as a religion obsessed with the law and conspirators against Jesus, who offers direct access to God and love of enemies, is deeply inscribed in academic handbooks and commentaries as well as in sermons and Sunday school lessons. Even scholarly interpreters who have devoted major studies in attempts to oppose the worst of the Christian stereotype of the Pharisees as law-obsessed still read the texts according to the standard old paradigm: Judaism as a religion, the Pharisees as leaders of that religion, whose main focus is still the law. It is important, therefore, to cut through centuries of caricature of the Pharisees as obsessed with law-keeping and adamant enforcers of purity codes. For Christian theologians the law and the Pharisees as its interpreters may still be the central issue in the conflict between Jesus and the Pharisees as portrayed in the Christian Gospels. But that is not necessarily the issue in the Gospels themselves and for use of the Gospels as sources for the Pharisees and scribes or for the conflict between Jesus and the Pharisees and scribes.

The obvious first step is simply to abandon the old paradigm and the standard controlling concepts in the fields of Jewish history and New Testament studies that have been blocking recognition of historical contexts and historical relations and conflicts.

A second obvious step would be to stop focusing on text fragments such as controversy stories taken out of the context of the Gospels and their historical settings. The Gospels were and are not mere collections of "pericopes" such as "controversy stories" in which Jesus comes into conflict with the scribes and/or Pharisees. In the 1970s and 1980s Gospel scholars (re)discovered that the Gospels are sustained narratives, whole stories with speeches that had plots, settings, and characters, often in conflict. It soon became evident, moreover, that the Gospel stories-with-speeches fit into what appear to have been their historical context as known from other sources (especially the histories of Josephus).[25]

The basic overall story of the Gospels (each of which has its own distinctive features) is of Jesus' prophetic mission of renewal of the people of Israel in villages of Galilee and nearby areas over against the rulers of the people, both the Roman conquerors and their client rulers in charge of the temple in Jerusalem (and Herodian figures in Galilee). In the main plot of the Markan story and of the Matthean story, the scribes and Pharisees, evidently representatives of the Jerusalem temple-state (that no longer had jurisdiction over the territory of Galilee), having come "down from Jerusalem," appear to be keeping surveillance on the actions of Jesus and his disciples. Jesus responds to their challenges with mockery and condemnation. In the climax of the all the Gospel stories, Jesus goes up to Jerusalem where he confronts the high priestly rulers. Scribes and Pharisees appear, speaking and working in tandem with the high priests in the confrontation. The high priests finally arrest Jesus and hand him over to the Roman governor, who orders him crucified.

This opens up the possibility of investigating how each Gospel portrays the Pharisees in a distinctive way. Comparison between the Gospels then enables interpreters to weigh the different portrayals for differences grounded in and expressive of particular distinctive emphases, interests, and historical circumstances. More detailed recent research on the potential historical contexts of particular Gospels then enables interpreters to contextualize the portrayals more precisely.

The recent research into several interrelated aspects of the historical contexts of the Gospels requires far more complex considerations than before. The Gospel stories derive apparently from movements among ordinary people, while the Pharisees were evidently associated with the high priestly and Herodian rulers. This division between the rulers and the people living in hundreds of villages has been investigated, largely separately, in its political-economic aspects and in its cultural aspects.

No less than Josephus's histories, the Gospels and gospel materials reflect and portray the sharp political-economic division and continuing conflict between the rulers and their representatives, on the one hand, and the peasantry who formed the vast majority of Galileans and Judeans, on the other. The earliest Gospel materials apparently derive from Galilee, which came under Jerusalem's rule only about a hundred years before the lifetime of Jesus, and had then been subjected to the rule of Herod Antipas during

---

25. See Horsley, *Hearing the Whole Story*; Horsley with Draper, *Whoever Hears You Hears Me*.

Jesus' lifetime. Now that we are more acutely aware of how widely Galilean history diverged from that of Jerusalem and Judea prior to the Hasmonean takeover of Galilee in 104 BCE, the regional differences must be taken into account when reading the Gospels.

The cultural differences that correspond to the political-economic division have become evident as a result of several largely separate lines of research into ancient communications media. Only recently have we begun to recognize that literacy was extremely limited in the Roman empire generally and even more severely in Judea and Galilee in particular. Given the predominantly oral communication environment, the Gospel stories would have been developed in and by communities or movements of Jesus-loyalists and then regularly performed in those communities, with varied further developments. The Gospels can thus no longer be read simply like archival written sources.[26]

Bringing the implications of these aspects together, the Gospel stories and speeches were clearly the products of communities of ordinary people. Since Jesus' mission and the communities that responded were based initially in Galilee, the Gospel stories-with-speeches were rooted in Galilean village communities and articulate the perspective and interests of villagers subjected by the Romans and ruled by their client rulers. Thus it should not be surprising that they articulate hostilities and criticisms typical of or similar to those found in studies of other agrarian societies/peasantries under rulers and their representatives.

For a final significant illustration of the implications of the new recent research, evidence of the scrolls of the Pentateuch and prophetic books found among the scrolls at Qumran reveal that instead of a standard text, there were multiple versions of scriptural books all still undergoing development. If there was no standardized scriptural text among temple and scribal circles who had access to the cumbersome and expensive scrolls, however, it is highly unlikely that there was a standardized Israelite tradition among village communities that lacked both scrolls and the ability to read them. We must reckon with the likelihood that at least the earliest (oral) Gospel sources derived from people embedded in a popular version of Israelite tradition and only indirectly aware of the official and partially written version of Israelite tradition that originated in and was still undergoing development in Jerusalem priestly-scribal circles. To put it bluntly, we must (re-)learn how to hear (as well as read) the Gospels and gospel materials as oral-derived texts and then figure out how to use these oral-derived texts as

---

26. Again, see Horsley, *Hearing the Whole Story*.

historical sources and to interpret them in their historical context for which we now have far more precise knowledge than previously.

Considering the episodes focused on the scribes and/or Pharisees in the overall Gospel stories-with-speeches, they focus on the impact of their role in the temple-state on the villagers lives. Standard scholarly reading of these episodes has been rather flat, superficial, and unimaginative. Peasants are every bit as capable as well-educated literate elites of rhetorical flourishes such as hyperbole, caricature, mockery, and sarcasm. Galilean and Judean peasants would have been fully aware that although the scribes and Pharisees did not despise them (as did Josephus), they looked down their noses at them as boors (even the serving-woman in the high priest's mansion viewed Peter as an *idiotes*). A more sensitive, subtle reading might consider whether Jesus may be mainly mocking Pharisees' obsession with rules of purity and the fine points of tithing. That would mean that much of the previous Christian interpretation has been mistaking Jesus' mocking of the Pharisees for his real concern: the effects of the Pharisees' role in the temple-state on villagers.

RABBINIC TEXTS

In the early twentieth century, Jewish scholars, followed by Christian scholars, believed that the rabbis were the direct successors of the Pharisees. Hence rabbinic texts were thought to be relatively solid and immediate sources for the Pharisees' knowledge and interpretation of the Torah. This continued, on a much-reduced scale and with far greater selectivity in the pathbreaking scholarship of Jacob Neusner, who set scholarly treatment of rabbinic texts onto a whole new critical basis. Neusner eventually insisted on the importance of reading whole treatises in order to discern their focal subject matter and presentation. But in critically ferreting out the rabbinic traditions of the Pharisees, he did not begin with the overall rabbinic enterprise evident in the tractates of the Mishnah and Tosefta so that it informed his investigation of the relation between those treatises and the views and rulings of earlier sages and Pharisees.

Since Neusner's pathbreaking work there has been growing skepticism, including his own, about how much information can be gleaned about the Pharisees from rabbinic texts. Neusner claimed to have identified as many as fifty Pharisees by name, most of them active in the first century CE. A more recent survey of the pertinent sources, however, identified only a dozen Pharisees, some of them still questionable.[27] In another measure,

27. Sievers, "Who Were the Pharisees?"

the plural term *perushim* ("Pharisees") occurs seldom in the Mishnah, while *hakamim* ("sages") occurs with considerable frequency, suggesting that the rabbis remembered the sages, not the Pharisees, as their principal predecessors. In any case, the limited number of traditions of the Pharisees in rabbinic texts are mainly about their opinions or rulings on only a few particular issues. These are hardly a solid basis from which to form judgments about their social roles and functions and relations in the temple-state or in Judean life more generally.

Any approach, old or new, critical or not, is closely connected with and dependent on its interpretive categories. The effect of Neusner's revolutionary new form-critical approach was to break through and abandon the Christian paradigm and the problematic Christian theological categories. Yet some of the most basic old assumptions and categories remained. Judaism was still understood as a religion. As traditions of the Pharisees were transferred from their containers in rabbinic tractates to scholarly reconstruction according to the controlling scholarly constructs and concepts, those traditions were assumed to give evidence for a Jewish sect. Presumably, if we were to follow Neusner's own method to its logical conclusion, we would also need to find dateable evidence, in order to claim that the Pharisees constituted a sect. "Sect," however, is as much a modern scholarly construct as are many (other) key Christian theological categories.

With regard to how we use rabbinic traditions of the Pharisees as sources for the Pharisees, the relatively recent critical way of reading rabbinic literature has resulted in some serious questioning of old assumptions based on a more confident reception of these sources. When Neusner did his early work on the rabbinic traditions of the Pharisees, it was still generally assumed that Johannan ben Zakkai founded a rabbinic academy at Jamnia/Yavneh that became the effective local governing authority for Palestinian Jews, and that Gamaliel II achieved official recognition by the Romans for his own "Patriarchate" and the (proto)rabbis as the self-government of the Jews. Critical examinations of the rabbinic texts on which assumptions such as the re-formative academy at Yavneh were based, however, have concluded that they are late foundational legends that may not provide solid historical evidence.[28] The eventual emergence of a "Patriarchate" under Judah the Prince may have more to do with his wealth and network of influence than with any official Roman approval. Studies of a wider range of rabbinic texts have found that the rabbis themselves said repeatedly that they did not enjoy much authority among the populace, who ran their own village affairs quite

---

28. Saldarini, "Johanan ben Zakkai's Escape"; Schäfer, "Die Flucht Rabban Johanan ben Zakkai"; Levine, "Jewish Patriarch."

independently of rabbinic rulings. It has been estimated that the rabbis did not take over leadership of the synagogues until the seventh century.[29] Such new, more critical readings of rabbinic literature in general and revision of previously accepted notions of rabbinic history and authority may seriously alter our assumptions about what rabbinic literature represents and its role and authority in Jewish society of its own time—and hence the way we use the rabbinic traditions of the Pharisees as historical sources.

The continuing projection of the construct of Judaism onto ancient texts and history tended to block recognition of the respective roles of the rabbis and the Pharisees in their respective historical contexts. While the contexts were dramatically different, considering the destruction of the temple and high priesthood and the emigration of rabbinic circles from a devastated Judea to Galilee, there was evidently some continuity. Like their Pharisaic predecessors, the rabbinic sages were also focused on the preservation and further development of the elite Judean scribal culture that had previously been cultivated in service of the temple-state. In quite different circumstances, directly under Roman rule and no longer under and in service of the temple-state (which was in turn subject to Roman rule), the rabbis occupied a position somewhat analogous to the position the scribes/sages, including Pharisees, had held under the high priestly heads of the temple-state.

As Tannaitic texts attest, rabbis and their proteges were engaged in remembering and advancing traditional rulings about a very broad range of issues in Jewish life in Palestine under Roman rule during late antiquity. Because such rulings were traditional, the precedents of what earlier sages and others had said were the essential basis for subsequent rulings. At some points, fairly rare in the broad set of tractates, the memory of what earlier figures, who may have been Pharisees, had said or ruled or of what earlier circles of sages/scribes had debated were important to evaluate and assimilate and develop. The result is a small pool of Pharisaic opinions/rulings on only a few issues that were remembered. Since Pharisaic opinions or rulings on other issues were evidently not remembered, we simply do not know whether or not one or more (supposed) Pharisees may have addressed them. The result of this assessment is that rabbinic texts provide only a smattering of evidence about the Pharisees' view on a few particular issues. It seems quite unwarranted to imagine, for example, that because they were concerned about eating food in purity (as priests were required to do), they therefore formed an eating club or a sect concerned about erecting distinguishing and group-defining barriers around themselves. That the rabbis

---

29. Cohen, *From the Maccabees to the Mishnah*, 221.

remembered and further developed some of the Pharisees' rulings along with many more rulings of "the sages," however, evidently indicates that they also were engaged in scribe-like cultivation of some of the reservoir of torah, teaching, or law in the temple-state of late second-temple times.

THE DEAD SEA SCROLLS AND THE QUMRAN COMMUNITY

The discovery of the Dead Sea Scrolls seventy-some years ago provided yet another set of sources for the Pharisees. The texts from the Qumran community are the earliest identifiable sources for the Pharisees, even contemporary with the group. The community that produced and cultivated the texts, moreover, occupied a similar social position to the Pharisees. The community that kept and hid the scrolls discovered in the wilderness of Judea in 1947 was evidently a group of dissident scribes and priests who rejected the upstart Hasmonean high priesthood and in protest withdrew from Jerusalem in a new exodus and formed a renewed covenant community at Qumran. The Qumran scrolls are no less hostile to the "interpreters of smooth things" than the Gospels are to "the scribes and Pharisees." But whereas the Gospels derive from popular attitudes toward the Pharisees, the Qumran texts represent a rival scribal group. The community was heavily engaged in cultivating Judean scribal tradition, but in sharp animosity to those their texts refer to as "seekers after smooth things," which was evidently their code name for the Pharisees who were serving or in authority in the temple-state. Some of the texts inscribed on the scrolls provide a source for three things in particular: (1) references (in code) to figures and their actions that evidently parallel references in Josephus's accounts that are relevant to the Pharisees—hence the Qumran references confirm the reliability of his accounts; (2) sharp criticisms of the policy and actions of the "seekers of smooth things"; and (3) an idea of what Pharisees may have been doing in a parallel cultivation of Judean scribal tradition, focused on keeping the torah/laws.

(1) Josephus narrated at some length Alexander Jannaeus's brutal crucifixion of those who had opposed him in an account that some interpreted as a reference to the Pharisees. The *pesher* (interpretation) of Nahum (2:12) from Qumran includes references to "the furious young Lion" who strikes by means of his great men" against those who seek smooth things and hangs men alive" in one of many passages in which "those who seek smooth things" is thought to be a code word for the Pharisees (4QpNah 1:4–7, applying Nah 2:12).

(2) In application of "the mistress of seduction" in Nah 3:4, the *pesher* (interpretation/application) condemns "Ephraim," thought to be another code word for the Pharisees, who lead astray "kings, princes, priests, and people" through their false teaching and their lying tongue (4QpNah 2:7–10). That is, the Pharisees as the teachers in Judea, lead rulers, priests, and people all astray.

(3) Some scroll scholars have found correlation between purity practices in 4QMMT[a] and rabbinic traditions that stem from or are similar to those of the Pharisees. On the hypothesis that the rabbis are indeed successors of the Pharisees (the Pharisees the predecessors of the rabbis), it then seems likely that the Qumranites must have been attacking the Pharisees' views in these polemical passages. Greater caution may be necessary in these comparisons, however. The concepts in which these comparisons are made may themselves have been developing from the time the Qumran texts were composed to the time the rabbinic literature was redacted centuries later. It may not be warranted to assume either that the Qumranites engaged in formulating *halakhah* on the basis of study or exegesis of scriptural texts, or that *halakhah* remained more or less the same from the first century BCE to the third century CE and after.[30]

The importance of the Scrolls as sources, albeit indirect sources, may be that they attest how a contemporary scribal community cultivated the laws, customs, and other traditions in the Judean scribal repertoire. This possibility is still largely unexplored. Such exploration, however, will require fuller acquaintance with texts and practices of the Qumran community and fuller acquaintance with lines of recent research into ancient communications media.

In the essays below I have attempted to consider the multiple factors delineated at the outset above in order to work toward a critical approach more adequate to the sources for the Pharisees in their changing historical context.

---

30. Contra Schiffmann, *The Halakhah at Qumran.*

3

THE POLITICAL POSITION OF SCRIBES
IN THE JUDEAN TEMPLE-STATE

THE HISTORICAL SOCIOLOGY OF Gerhard Lenski has exerted a formative influence on the sociology of biblical history and literature that blossomed in the last few decades.[1] His historical sociology of agrarian societies can be critically adapted in analysis of second-temple Judean society, particularly to understand the position and role of learned scribes in the temple-state.

Recent studies focused on particular sociological issues have not yet been combined into a critically formulated overall picture of the structure and dynamics of Judean society under the Persian or the Hellenistic empires. The result is that during the last few decades scholars have continued to project onto ancient Judea assumptions and constructs that are rooted in their own societies or their knowledge of early modern European history.

The most influential interpretation of this last generation, that of Martin Hengel,[2] further developing the view of Victor Tcherikover, for example, portrayed second-temple Judea as suddenly teeming with commercial activity in the Hellenistic period.

> Ben Sira frequently mentions merchants and their pursuit of profits, and these passages again reflect the new period which began in Judaea under Greek rule, when the money economy, the opportunity to invest one's means in profitable enterprises,

---

1. Lenski, *Power and Privilege*; adapted, for example, by Chaney, "Bitter Bounty"; and Saldarini, *Pharisees*.

2. Hengel, *Judaism and Hellenism*.

and lively and absorbing commercial traffic had begun to develop.[3]

By synthesizing fragments of archaeological and textual evidence, Hengel claimed that Greek agents and merchants penetrated even into village life, increasing circulation of coins and monetarizing the economy, and that foreign trade increased as Judea became more prosperous. He explained the Maccabean revolt as well as Ben Sira's harangues (supposedly) against merchants as the conservative reactions of a particularist traditional "Judaism" against the entrepreneurial individualism and cosmopolitan spirit of "Hellenism."

It simply did not occur to Hengel, and others who share the standard orientation of biblical studies, to ask questions of social location rooted in a sense of the broader social structure of the historical situation. What he saw as merchants and traders were mainly agents of the Ptolemaic imperial regime. The vast majority of coins were found at Samaria, Shechem, and Scythopolis, outside of Judea, or at Beth Zur, site of a military garrison, hence hardly evidence for the monetization of the economy in general. The wine jars from Rhodes in the Aegean Sea were found on the Phoenician coastal plain, outside Judea, and inside Judea only at military garrisons, again hardly evidence of a commercialization of Judean society in general. It is not difficult to recognize that Hengel was projecting onto the Hellenistic period the sort of social-economic relations that he was familiar with from early modern Western society, with its rising "middle class" and commercialized economy. Indeed, much of the standard picture of ancient Judea as of the Hellenistic social and economic world in general was based on the monumental research and reconstruction by the great scholar Michael Rostovtzeff, who projected into ancient times the evolving capitalism of his native Russia in the early twentieth century.[4] Lacking in studies of second-temple Judean history and literature has been any clear sense of the overall concrete historical political-economic-religious structure and how it might have been different from that of modern Europe.

While Lenski's study of advanced agrarian society may not prove as applicable to second-temple Judea as it did to monarchic Judah and Israel, it may well be helpful in significant ways. In contrast to other structural-functional sociology, which has been developed on the basis of complex modern societies but then applied to New Testament materials,[5] Lenski has care-

---

3. Tcherikover, *Hellenistic Civilization and the Jews*, 149.

4. Rostovtzeff, *Social and Economic History of the Hellenistic World*.

5. Theissen, *Sociology of Early Palestinian Christianity*. See the criticism by Elliott, "Social Scientific Criticism of the New Testament"; and Horsley, *Sociology and the Jesus*

fully articulated a genuinely historical sociology. Recognizing that societies have undergone great changes over long period of time, he has constructed models of different types of social structure. Most significantly for biblical studies, he fully recognizes that agrarian societies of the past involved a pre-market economy. In significant respects, however, Lenski's complex model of agrarian society is not applicable to second-temple Judea. His construction of an elaborate system of social stratification in twelve "classes" tends to obscure the fundamental social conflicts attested in Judean literature. It seems fairly clear from the outset that a separation of a "priestly class" from "the ruler" and "governing class" and "retainer class" does not fit a temple-state such as Judea.

It is not a question of whether we utilize a particular model of society. In recent years even biblical scholars have recognized that, consciously or not, when we (re)construct history we make use of particular models of social structure and social relations. The key is whether we do so with some critical awareness and some basis of comparison with studies of similar societies. I am convinced that literary and historical analysis remain primary in our attempt to understand ancient literature and history, with sociological and anthropological analysis playing an ancillary role. Rather than start from a model, therefore, I would like to begin with information in Judean sources.

ROLES AND RELATIONSHIPS IN JUDEA AS REPRESENTED BY BEN SIRA

It so happens that a principal text from the Hellenistic period, the book of Sirach, contains a great deal of information about social structure and social relations in Judea. Patrick Tiller and I have presented a fuller sketch of the religious political-economic structure of Judean society based mainly on analysis of information provided by the scribe/sage Jesus ben Sira and comparative materials used by Lenski.[6] Here we can focus mainly on the most informative passage regarding the key political-economic roles in Judean social structure.

> How can *one who handles the plow* become wise, ...
>   *who drives oxen* ... and whose talk is about bulls?
> He sets his heart on plowing furrows,
>   and he is careful about fodder for the heifers.

Movement.

6. The following is heavily dependent on the research and analysis done with Patrick Tiller, published in "Ben Sira and the Sociology of the Second Temple."

So too is every *artisan and master artisan*.
> those who cut the signets of seals . . .

So too is *the smith*, sitting by the anvil, . . .
> he struggles with the heat of the furnace . . .

So too is *the potter* . . . turning the wheel with his feet . . .
He molds the clay with his arm, . . .
> and he takes care in firing the kiln.

All these rely on their hands, . . .
Without them no city can be inhabited,
> and wherever they live they will not go hungry.

Yet they are not sought out for *the council* of the people,
> nor do any of them attain eminence in the public assembly.

They do not sit on the seat of a court,
> nor do they understand the decisions of courts;

They cannot expound discipline or judgment,
> and they are not found among *the rulers*.[7]

But they maintain the fabric of the world,
> and their concern is for the exercise of their trade.

How different the one who devotes himself
> to the study of the law (torah) of the Most High!

He seeks out the wisdom of all the ancients . . .
He serves among *the great ones* (*megistanon*)
and appears before *the rulers* (*hegoumenon*);
> he travels in foreign lands

and learns what is good and evil in the human heart.
> (Sir 38:25–35; 39:1, 4 abridged, italics added)

In Ben Sira's glorification of the importance of the scribes and sages, the principal social roles in the political-economy of Judea appear simple and uncomplicated. The city is habitable because agricultural laborers provide the food, and manual laborers such as artisans and smiths supply the necessities and amenities of civilized living. The scribes are devoted to the intellectual labor of perpetuating the culture and maintaining the knowledge necessary for the social and political life of the city. And "the great ones" and "rulers" at the top evidently sit in command on the whole. By supplementing this skeleton of information from Ben Sira's praise of the high priest(hood), we can flesh out this picture a bit more.

Ben Sira's praise of High Priest Simon II (Sir 50) portrays temple, state, and society (undifferentiated) all headed by the high priest surrounded by

---

7. Although this verse is not extant in Hebrew, the original must have read *bemoshlim* [*bmwshlym*], which was misread by the Greek translator as *bemashalim* [*bmshlym*] = *parabolai*, as Patrick Skehan has shown in Skehan and DiLella, *The Wisdom of Ben Sira*, 448.

the inner concentric circle of "his brothers," the aristocracy among "the sons of Aaron." The priesthood is, in turn, surrounded and supported by the outer concentric circle of the people, "the whole assembly of Israel" (esp. 50:1, 12). From the praise of Aaron in the preceding "Praise of the Ancestors" (officeholders: 45:6-22) and from Ben Sira's exhortations to dutifully bring produce to the priests (45:14, 16, 20-21; 7:29-31), it is clear that the priestly aristocracy is economically supported by the tithes and offerings of "the whole assembly of Israel" (45:14, 16, 20-21; 50:12-15). The offerings to the Most High that supported the priesthood constituted a tax on Judean agricultural producers.

Information gleaned from Ben Sira's instructional speeches fills out an overlapping picture. A collective aristocracy with wealth and power stands at the head of society, somewhat in tension with the scribes who serve them in governing, and in sharper conflict with the people in general. Ben Sira refers to them with a variety of interchangeable traditional terms, such as "the great," "rulers," "nobles," "elders," etc. with "priests" notable by its absence. The artisans, smiths, potters, and others mentioned as foils to the scribes, who cultivate wisdom, were the other residents of the capital city built around the temple, who provided supporting services for the ruling aristocracy (38:24-34). The merchants whose buying and selling Ben Sira abhors as sinful (26:29—27:2) were not the same as the wealthy he refers to in other speeches, and in fact must also have serviced the lifestyle of the wealthy and powerful "great ones" in Jerusalem. What makes all this possible economically appears to have been the portions, the first fruits, the offerings, and so forth that were to be given to the priests as an expression of devotion to God (7:29-31; 35:6-12). Although Ben Sira does not refer explicitly to the Judean peasantry as the agricultural producers who would have been the only source of such revenues, he does mention "the poor," who are often in desperate straits economically and vulnerable to exploitation by the wealthy and powerful.

This picture of Judea gleaned from Ben Sira's instructional speeches thus resembles the picture in the praise of High Priest Simon II in the fundamental political-economic-religious structure of a ruling aristocracy supported by tithes, offerings, and sacrifices from the agricultural produce of ordinary Judeans. But the picture is complicated by the addition of scribes who assist the rulers, artisans who supply basic services in Jerusalem itself, and merchants who supply luxury goods from the outside, which fits well with the picture in Sir 38:24—39:4. Read with a critical eye, Ben Sira's speeches on topics such as the relations of the rich and the poor and the obligation to pay tithes and offerings point fairly clearly to the fundamental division and conflict in second-temple Judea, which corresponds with that in similar "tributary" societies. Ben Sira also offers fairly clear hints of the power relations and potential conflict between aristocracy and the scribes.

Ben Sira, however, totally ignores what may have been the determinative factor in the dynamics of relations between scribes such as himself and the Judean priestly aristocracy whose rule he and his fellow scribes served and on whom they were economically dependent. The temple-state in Jerusalem had been instituted as an instrument of Persian imperial rule, as the books of Ezra and Nehemiah make clear. The Ptolemaic imperial regime that took over Judea after Alexander the Great's conquest of the Near East continued this imperial arrangement for the control and economic exploitation of Judea. The decree that the Seleucid emperor Antiochus III issued shortly after wresting control of Judea in 200 BCE indicates that the Jerusalem aristocracy that ruled Judea was subject to, dependent on, and representative of their imperial rulers (in Josephus, *Ant.* 12.138–144). The subordination of the Judean aristocracy to the often shifting and conflictual contingencies of imperial regimes is a major factor that, because it is ignored in an influential source such as Sirach, has usually not been taken into account in biblical scholarship.

COMPARATIVE SOCIOLOGY OF AGRARIAN SOCIETIES

While Lenski's model of agrarian society does not fit Ben Sira's representation of social relations and roles in second-temple Judea in fundamental respects—his elaborate scheme of stratification into multiple classes tends to obscure power relations and structural conflict—it is very useful for two important reasons. It is relatively familiar to biblical scholars, having been used to advantage on the monarchic period. And since Lenski's discussion draws on such a wealth of studies of comparative materials, it provides a well-grounded basis on which we can discern the dynamics of political-economic structure and conflict in Judea under the Hellenistic monarchies.

In a moment of self-criticism that is refreshing among scholars, Lenski mentions in a footnote that Robert Bellah, in response to his discussion of agrarian societies, had argued for division of agrarian societies into three subtypes: city-states, bureaucratic empires, and feudal regimes.[8] In fact the differences between precisely those three kinds of societies keep cropping up when Lenski discusses variations within his broad model. In European feudal societies, for example, the "state" is strikingly diffuse when compared with the far more centralized "state" of ancient Near Eastern, Indian, Aztec, Inca, and African societies. Or, in feudal Europe a good deal of mercantile

---

8. See Lenski, *Power and Privilege*, 191 n5a.

or artisan specialization developed independently of feudal lords, whereas trade and artisans do not appear to have been independent of the 'state' in the ancient Near East and in other bureaucratic empires. Again in feudal European societies higher lords granted 'fiefs' to lower lords, which included both relatively independent political jurisdiction together with a hereditary claim to the produce of the peasantry and even to the land. By contrast, in the ancient Near East rulers granted their high officials incomes from large landed estates without hereditary rights and without independent political jurisdiction.

Focusing, with Lenski, on the different social strata leads to a vertical categorization of a populace into many classes. If we focus instead on the basic political-economic-religious relations between those social strata, e.g., on the relations between the ruler and governing class on the one hand and the peasant producers on the other, then we can better appreciate the dynamics as well as the structure of agrarian societies. The differences between the three subtypes of feudal societies, city-states, and bureaucratic empires constitute a decisive, systemic variation in those fundamental political-economic relations between ruler, governing class, and peasantry. In some of the societies among Lenski's comparative materials, the ruler was the sole political authority figure who then economically supported the governing class with goods appropriated by the state from the peasants. On the basis of the materials available to him from British colonial records, Marx thought such societies were characterized by an "Asiatic" mode of production. A more appropriately descriptive term used by recent critical analysis is a "tributary" political economy. In others among his agrarian societies members of the governing class enjoyed a combination of political authority over the peasantry and hereditary rights to the land or the produce of the land. Most of Lenski's materials illustrate the former system. For study of second-temple Judaea and other ancient Near Eastern societies and ancient empires, which display such decisive differences from both feudal Europe and ancient city-states of antiquity, a far more precise comparative model of agrarian societies could be constructed by focusing on the majority of Lenski's materials. The excluded feudal European materials and city-states of Greco-Roman antiquity could then be used as illustrating different systems for comparison and contrast.

Some of the remaining problems with Lenski's model are rooted in the basic systemic difference just outlined. A key example for dealing with second-temple Judea is his delineation of the "priestly class" as separate and different from "the ruler," the "governing class" and the "retainer class." The Western differentiation between church and state, spiritual power and temporal power (religious and political institutions and roles), would appear to have become normative for his model. In much if not most of his materials, however, these dimensions of life have not been differentiated, or have been unevenly differentiated at different levels. The very use of terms such as "king" or "priest" or "manager" may be a projection based on a more differentiated social system. Since in fact the category of "the priestly class" is not central or determinative in the majority of Lenski's materials, making a distinction between priestly and other aristocrats or rulers does not seem appropriate. Such a distinction is certainly inapplicable to second-temple Judea.

To better appreciate the dynamics as well as the basic structure of tributary societies, therefore, it makes sense to focus on the fundamental political-economic-religious relations, using the wealth of comparative materials that Lenski has pulled together (but not an elaborate scheme of social stratification, a predilection of much American sociology). By thus refocusing our inquiry, it becomes clear that the fundamental and controlling relationship lies between the rulers and the agricultural producers, the peasantry who compose the vast majority (90 percent) of the people of such a tributary society. By virtue of their power, military and other, the rulers are able to demand rent, tithes, or tribute from the peasant producers whom they rule (but who are otherwise virtually self-sufficient in the village communities of many agrarian societies). Then, as Lenski himself explains variously, the rulers (official ruler and governing class) use part of what they appropriate from the peasantry (a) to support a staff of military and legal-clerical "retainers" through whom the society is "governed," (b) to support traders who obtain the luxury and other goods the rulers desire,[9] (c) to pay artisans who make the various products needed by the rulers and their retainers and supporters in the cities.[10] That is, the retainers, merchants,

---

9. Lenski's discussion of the merchant class draws mainly on medieval European, even nascent capitalist evidence, and on agrarian societies which had been affected by early modern mercantile or modern capitalist systems. Perhaps it was true in late medieval Europe that "from a very early date merchants managed to free themselves from the direct and immediate authority of the ruler and governing class" (*Power and Privilege*, 250). But that should not be projected onto ancient Judea. In the Ptolemaic empire which dominated Palestine just before the time of Ben Sira, trade was a virtual monopoly of the imperial regime. It seems highly unlikely that things were any different in a far smaller entity such as the Judean temple-state.

10. Some of Lenski's principal points about the "artisan class" also appear to be based on evidence from medieval European towns, and may not apply to most traditional agrarian societies. There is certainly little evidence from the ancient Near East generally that would indicate either that artisans were "originally recruited from the ranks of the dispossessed peasantry" or that "the majority of artisans were probably employees of the merchant class" (*Power and Privilege*, 278–79). Nor is there evidence of artisans rebelling against those in authority over them. In the case of a temple-city such

and even the artisans are all dependent upon, as well as subordinate to, the ruling class. That is a much simpler model than Lenski's, but it enables us better to appreciate the fundamental divide in tributary societies as well as the dynamics between rulers and their retainers as well as between rulers and peasants.

Lenski is sensitive to the fact that modern Western assumptions about private property tend to obscure our understanding of political-economic-religious relations in traditional agrarian societies (which is not generally noticed by biblical scholars who use his model). This is of greatest importance in understanding how the ruler or state can lay claim to such a huge share of a society's productivity. As Lenski noted, a king or emperor was at the head of every advanced agrarian state. If we approach tributary societies with the modern capitalist concept of private property in mind, it must appear that the monarch is the owner of the land. But then how do we explain that the peasants in such societies are by and large not slaves but free (to a degree), and that they also have certain claim to the land and its produce? The concept of private property or ownership may simply be inapplicable. More appropriate to tributary societies would be to reconceptualize property *in terms of rights not things*, with the possibility of overlapping rights to the land, or, perhaps better, to the produce of the land and the labor of the peasants.

Accordingly, Lenski suggests "a proprietary theory of the state," as a way of understanding what "property" or "ownership" might mean in the concrete relational terms in which such societies apparently operated. The common or corporate "ownership" can be understood as vested in the head of state. "*All agrarian rulers enjoyed significant proprietary rights in virtually all of the land in their domains.*"[11] It may thus be possible to understand how rulers appear to be owners or rather part-owners' not only of their own royal estates but of all other lands that they grant as prebends to their officials, or from which they extract taxes or tribute.

The "proprietary theory of the state," however, does not yet help us understand the Judean temple-state. It is curious that in this connection Lenski does not discuss the mechanism by which such "proprietary rights in virtually all of the land in their domains" is legitimated for the monarchs of traditional agrarian societies. Ironically, Lenski focuses almost exclusively on the material level, while the *dialectical materialist* Karl Marx provides

---

as Jerusalem (or for that matter in any capital or royal city), the artisans would have been economically dependent on the (priestly) rulers in command of the temple, city, and society. In the case of a temple-community, one wonders the extent to which the ordinary priests and/or Levites may have performed some of the supportive services.

11. Lenski, *Power and Privilege*, 215–16 (italics original).

a less reductionist approach—one that takes the religious dimension more fully into account. Lenski does mention in passing, with regard to the advanced horticultural system of Dahomey (in west Africa), that the rulers were regarded as divine or semidivine and thus the owner of all property in the land.[12] And he notes the ancient Mesopotamian conception of the land as the estate of the society's god(s), the temple(s) as the house of the god(s), and the king or high priest as the chief servant of the god(s). But it is Marx who recognizes more generally that in such societies it is by virtue of being the symbol of the society as a whole, the head of the whole body, that the god or the god's regent is the controller (and beneficiary) of the tribute taken from the members of the social body. Biblical scholars can surely appreciate that the working of such a societal system is dependent on just such an ideology or mythology of god(s) and king and/or high priest as the representative(s) and symbol(s) of the whole.

Lenski's model of agrarian society, moreover, perhaps because of its part in his overall evolutionary scheme, does not take into account the fact that most concrete examples of agrarian societies are parts of larger agrarian empires. This is a serious omission, as the previous two chapters above should make clear. As John Kautsky explains,[13] the aristocratic rulers of a large agrarian empire usually compose a different society from the peoples they rule, and the subordinate states often rule over different societies or peoples. Since many large aristocratic empires ruled their subject peoples indirectly through the native aristocracies or monarchies, the overall political-economic-religious system was usually more complex than Lenski's model allows. This subordination of one society to another and one ruling class to another should then be juxtaposed with the previous point about how the social system was held together by an ideology of a god and/or king or high priest at its center as a symbol of the whole. This juxtaposition enables us to discern the interrelated issues of (a) the "legitimacy" of the ruler(s), local and/or imperial, and (b) the potential conflict between the levels of rulers with different legitimating ideologies.

THE DYNAMICS OF RULER-RETAINER RELATIONS IN HELLENISTIC JUDEA

The central figure and institution in the Judean temple-state, as well as symbolic head of the society as a whole, was the high priest(hood) and the center of a priestly aristocracy. Although Ben Sira does not mention them,

---

12. Lenski, *Power and Privilege*, 154–55.
13. Kautsky, *Politics of Aristocratic Empires*.

and Lenski's discussion of the governing class gives them scant attention, factions were a recurrent feature in the ruling aristocracy in Judea. One of Nehemiah's principal tasks as Persian governor was to check the squabbles that were disrupting the operations of the temple-state. Under the Ptolemies, leading figures in the Tobiad family who had intermarried with the high priestly family for several generations managed to gain considerable power within Judea by shrewd maneuvering at the imperial court.[14] Ben Sira's celebration of the ceremonial solidarity of "the sons of Aaron" hides the factions that were already apparently prominent in the Jerusalem aristocracy of his day.

In order to understand the workings of the tributary political economy in general as well as ruler-retainer relations in particular, we must devote attention to the religious dimension focused on the high priesthood (again as represented by Ben Sira), a dimension neglected in Lenski's model. The people were to fear and to serve "the Most High," who is explicitly understood as "the king of all." Correspondingly, the whole temple-state apparatus was structured ostensibly toward the service of God. The priesthood headed by the high priest(hood) was the people's representative to God as well as God's representative to the people, established by everlasting covenant and given "authority and statutes and judgments" over the people. Therefore the people were to honor the priest with their tithes and offerings as the way of "fear[ing] the Lord" (see esp. Sir 45:15–21; 7:29–31).

Ben Sira thus presents a "proprietary theory of the state," but in a combination of theocratic and hierocratic terms (not taken into account by Lenski). God, as the ostensible head of state, was the proprietor of the land, with the (high) priest(hood) as regent and actual head of (temple-)state-and-economy. In that position Aaron was granted a "heritage" but no "inheritance" among the people or in the land (Sir 45:20–21). The modern Western concept of private property gets in the way at this point. The priesthood had no land of its own because as the head of the whole it received a (special) heritage of "first fruits and sacrifices." Ideologically at least, the high priest(hood) and priests had no individual or personal wealth and power separate from their wealth and power as public figures representative of the whole. The high priest and other members of the priestly aristocracy may well have used their public wealth and power as a means of generating what would appear as private wealth or property (e.g., by charging interest on loans made from the stores or wealth they controlled as representatives

---

14. See what is called the "Tobiad Romance" retold by Josephus in *Antiquities* 12.160–224; and the discussion of factions in Horsley, *Scribes, Visionaries*, chap. 2.

of the whole). But the basis of their wealth, power, and privilege was their position as the representative head of Judean society.

This particular hierocratic understanding of the Judean state is the key to understanding the internal relations of the temple-state, both between the rulers and ruled and between the rulers and retainers. Insofar as the (high) priesthood was the representative of and had authority over the whole, then it would both have claimed support from the agricultural producers and have commanded whatever governing apparatus was developed in addition to the priesthood itself.

Judea, however, was not an independent society. The priestly aristocracy with the high priesthood at its center served two masters, the imperial regime as well as its own divine King. In connection with the temple-state as an instrument of imperial rule, the priestly aristocrats interacted with the dominant imperial culture as well as officials of the imperial regime. To the extent that (a leading faction of) the ruling aristocracy in Judea appeared to compromise with or sell out to the ideological or institutional forms of imperial rule, it would presumably have lost legitimacy with Judean priests and scribes. This would have happened especially among those who strongly believed in and had a stake in the theocratic, hierocratic ideology.

The learned scribes or sages that Ben Sira speaks about clearly fit into the group that Lenski called "retainers," who assisted the rulers in "governing" a tributary society in various legal, educational, and cultural-religions respects. They even played a role in councils of state and judicial courts, as the ones who could "understand the decisions of courts" and "expound discipline and judgment" (Sir 38:33-34).[15] The sages and scribes appear not only to have served the priestly aristocracy but to have been dependent economically on the rulers as well. Ben Sira repeatedly cautions his scribal students about the deference incumbent on them in their close contact with their powerful patrons. The sage must bow low to the ruler (Sir 4:7). When invited to dinner by rulers, they must know how to handle themselves prudently, so as not to give offense (Sir 13:8-11; 31:12-24). Their exhortations about the importance of tithes and offerings thus involved a certain self-interest.

---

15. The role of scribes must have overlapped with those of ordinary priests and Levites, who would seem to have functioned somewhat as did the retainers Lenski describes in other agrarian societies, i.e., mediating between the high priestly rulers and the common people, including "effecting the transfer of the economic surplus from the producers to the political and religious elite" (*Power and Privilege*, 246). Lenski's "priestly class" does not apply to ancient Judea, since the priestly aristocracy were the rulers, ordinary priests had more "retainer"-like functions, and scribes performed functions that Lenski ascribes to "the clergy" in societies of limited literacy.

Despite their economic dependence on the aristocracy, the scribes and sages also had a certain authority of their own, independent of the authority derived from their service of the priestly aristocracy. In their own mind, at least, their authority stemmed from their knowledge of wisdom and their faithful cultivation of and adherence to the torah and commandments of the Most High. Just as the high priesthood had its power, privilege, and authority from God through an eternal covenant, so also the sages had their authority as the custodians of divine revelation in the torah of God and in prophecies. They themselves were the heirs of earlier generations of sages.

Viewed in the broader political-cultural context of the Hellenistic imperial situation in which they were operating, this dedication to the cultivation of Judean cultural traditions and sense of independent higher authority should alert us to the potential for social-political conflict. Insofar as the sages' professional role was the cultivation and administration of the traditional Judaean covenantal torah as (at least in effect) the official state law, their dedication to covenantal torah would have been far more than a matter of individual morality. The sages had a clear sense of their own, independent of their patrons, of how the temple-state should operate, i.e., in accordance with (their understanding of) the covenantal laws. Scribes, or some scribes at least, may have been concerned about high priestly interactions with the imperial regime or imperial culture that seemed to compromise the ancestral covenantal laws and service to the God whose torah they cultivated professionally.

Presumably the high priestly rulers accepted this semi-independent role of the sages because it was part of the foundation of their claim to divine authority, and this made the sages able to provide the ideological basis for the priests' rule. Ben Sira's praise of the ancestors provides a prime example of how a staunchly partisan sage could play this role faithfully. It served the interests of the wealthy indirectly as well, insofar as the scribal circles that defended the interests of the poor may have provided a legitimate (but nonthreatening) outlet for frustration that may have developed among the impoverished peasantry.

POLITICAL-CULTURAL CRISIS IN THE TEMPLE-STATE AND SCRIBAL RESISTANCE

The potential for conflict in the political-economic-religious relations between the priestly aristocratic rulers of the Judean temple-state and their scribal retainers came to a head in the late third and early second centuries BCE. The key factors were two: (1) the potential conflict between the legitimating religious ideology of the temple-state and the dominant imperial culture into which the priestly aristocracy was drawn by their role as agents of the imperial regime; and (2) the conflict between scribes loyal to the ancestral traditions of the Judean temple-state and a high priestly faction prepared to compromise those traditions in their assimilation to the ways of the dominant imperial culture and politics.

Under the Persian Empire, the Jerusalem temple, dedicated to "the god that was in Jerusalem" (Ezra 1:3), was set up purposely to provide a basis for the temple-state in traditional local Judean culture. The high priests stood at the head of Judean society as the mediators with the God of the Judeans, even as they also delivered tribute to the Persian court and shaped the temple-state according to the commands of the Persian governors. In their service among the high priests, "the scribes of the temple" took responsibility for the shaping and cultivation of Judean culture focused on the legitimation of the temple and priesthood. As noted above, however, Judean scribes had developed a sense of their own authority as devoted to the keeping of the commandments and cultivation of other traditional culture, an authority semi-independent of their (economic) dependency on aristocratic patrons.

The Ptolemaic and Seleucid imperial regimes left the Jerusalem temple-state intact with its traditional Judean cultural forms of temple and priesthood and authorizing history and law codes. In the surrounding territories, however, they fostered the formation of cities (*poleis*) on the pattern of Greek polity and culture. Inconsistent policy and rival factions within and between the Ptolemaic and Seleucid imperial regimes, moreover, created opportunities that encouraged power struggles within the Jerusalem aristocracy. And some aristocratic families were attracted by the dominant Hellenistic imperial culture as well as Hellenistic political-economic prominence.

To the degree that leading members of the priestly aristocracy appeared to be compromising the commandments of God and the temple's and priesthood's devotion to the God of the Judeans, however, scribes strongly devoted to the traditional culture would have been increasingly torn between obedience to the commandments and loyalty to their aristocratic superiors. Scribal circles apparently split into different factions, probably in correlation with factions among the aristocracy.

The crisis in Jerusalem came to a head in 175 BCE when the faction that had become dominant in the priestly aristocracy spearheaded a Hellenizing reform with the permission of the new emperor, Antiochus Epiphanes. They transformed Jerusalem into the city of Antioch with a Greek constitution and bought the high priestly office from the emperor for Jason, ousting his more traditional brother, Onias III. After several years of continuing fighting among aristocratic factions, Antiochus's plunder of the temple treasury and the beginnings of organized resistance to the reform and to Antiochus's invasion, Antiochus attacked Jerusalem, replaced the temple ceremonies that served the Judean God with alien rites, and forbade the observance of the covenant law (c. 167 BCE). At that point more widespread popular resistance coalesced around the Maccabees, who led guerrilla warfare against the imperial armies.

This escalating crisis was the context in which circles of Jerusalem scribes produced the first texts that have been called *apocalyptic*—sections later included in 1 Enoch, such as the Animal Vision (1 Enoch 85–90), and the visions-and-interpretations in Daniel.[16] Although biblical scholars often think mainly of wisdom books as having been written by scribes or sages, the books of both Enoch and Daniel represent themselves as wisdom revealed to scribes or sages. Enoch is the prototypical sage: he is trained to write petitions and deliver them orally before a royal court (God's); he is addressed as "righteous scribe" and as the recipient of heavenly wisdom, which he wrote down for his children. Such characterizations resemble Ben Sira's self-portrayal. Daniel is portrayed in the tales that precede the visions as a professional scribe in the royal court, a retainer like Ben Sira (in Lenski's terms). The principal difference between Daniel and Ben Sira is that while Ben Sira is suspicious of dreams and dream-interpretation, Daniel is highly skilled in this standard branch of the scribal-sapiential repertoire. Both Enoch and Daniel, of course, are figures that different circles of scribes and sages identify with as the source of the revelation that they have received about the escalating political-religious crisis in which they are living.

The Animal Vision in 1 Enoch 85–90 and the parallel symbolic visions in Dan 7–12, which originated as responses to the crisis of reform, repression, and resistance in early second-century Judea, are the earliest texts that scholars have called "historical apocalypses." They are revelations received in visions, narrated either by the scribe/sage to his "children" (1 En) or by a heavenly messenger to Daniel (Dan 7; 8; 10–12), and written as a "book" to be delivered to a later generation (in the time of crisis on which they focus). In their overall and component forms, and in many of their motifs and allusions alike, these revelatory visions of the future are developments of prominent features of the prophetic tradition of which scribal circles had long become the cultivators (see the scribal curriculum or repertoire

---

16. Fuller discussion in Horsley, *Scribes, Visionaries*, chaps. 8 and 9; for fundamental research and interpretation on the Animal Vision in 1 Enoch and the book of Daniel, I am heavily dependent, respectively, on Tiller, *A Commentary on the Animal Apocalypse of 1 Enoch*; and Collins, *Daniel*.

in Sir 39:1–4).[17] They are grand surveys of Israel's history of domination by foreign rulers, from the beginning of creation in the Animal Vision, during the Second Temple Period in the Daniel visions. Insofar as the recipients of the revelation stand at the beginning of the history recounted, the narrative consists of what has been called *ex eventu* prophecy. The history of successive rulers becomes increasingly violent and destructive under the succession of imperial regimes in second-temple times, in effect beyond the ability of the Judean scribes to understand in normal historical terms. The extreme violence of imperial rule in Judea can be understood in the Animal Vision only as a result of God having given over domination of the Judeans to heavenly powers that do not obey the divinely imposed limits on their oppression and exploitation. The visions of Daniel represent the succession of empires as a sequence of predatory beasts, with the fourth, symbolizing the Hellenistic empire(s), becoming so severely violent that even challenges the divine sovereignty over history (and over Judea).

The portrayal of this escalation of violence against "the sheep" (Israel/Judeans) and "(the people of) the holy ones of the Most High" (Judeans/Jerusalem/the temple/the covenant) clearly corresponds to the crisis in Jerusalem that reaches its climax in 175 BCE and the ensuing years. In the Animal Vision and the narrative of Dan 10–12 it is possible to discern references to fairly specific events such as the deal made by the reformers who "rejected the covenant" with Antiochus Epiphanes, the beginnings of resistance by certain scribes or sages (the ones who produced the Animal Vision [1 Enoch 90:6–19]), imperial violence against Jerusalem and the temple, and the martyrdom of some of the scribes/sages (the *maskilim* who produced Daniel; Dan 11:31–35). Clearly these visions-and-interpretations of second-temple history were produced by the very scribal circles who were caught up in the crisis on which they focus, as is commonly observed by scholarly interpreters.

What is not often observed by those interpreters, however, is the difficult position in which the crisis placed the scribal circles who produced these visions. Their adherence to the cultural traditions of which they were the professional guardians and cultivators led them into active opposition to their own priestly aristocracy as well as to oppressive imperial rule. As sketched above, scribes and sages, as the intellectual retainers of the temple-state were engaged in service of Judea's high priestly rulers, and were politically and economically dependent on them. Yet they had their own sense of authority directly under God, independent of their high priestly patrons.

---

17. Collins, *Daniel*, 52, 55, etc.; Carr, *Writing on the Tablet of the Heart*, esp. 143–51; and Horsley, *Scribes, Visionaries*, chap. 6.

The conflictual function of the priestly aristocracy, however, as local agents of imperial control and taxation set up a serious potential conflict. The attractions of the "western" imperial culture and political forms of the Hellenistic empires and the opportunities to enhance their position and power locally proved more than many of the priestly aristocracy could resist. And as the dominant reforming faction in the Jerusalem aristocracy moved to transform the temple-state legitimated traditionally by Israelite-Judean covenantal and prophetic culture and temple rituals, certain scribal circles must have begun to dissent.

Probably in response to the reform in 175, they began to mount more serious and organized resistance. And as imperial repression reinforced the reform, they persisted in their resistance even if it meant martyrdom. Their dissent, resistance, and martyrdom were informed by the visionary revelation that they produced in the Animal Vision and the visions-and-interpretations of history in Dan 7–12. What scholarly interpreters often miss, largely because they separate the religious dimension from the political-economic, is just how strong is the negative evaluation of imperial rule. In fact, it stands under divine condemnation and will be destroyed in the divine judgment. But the scribal circles who produced this literature had moved even further from the tenuous position they occupied in the temple-state hierocracy. The Daniel visions are horror-struck at the arrogant emperor's attacks on the Jerusalem temple and its rituals in service of God. Perhaps it is thus understandable that in the scenarios of restoration of "the people of the saints of the Most High" (7:27; 12:1), they give no hint of any interest in the restoration of the temple with a now faithful high priesthood. The Animal Vision and other texts in the circle of "Enoch" scribes does indicate its views of the temple and high priesthood, however, and it is sharply negative, a clear rejection. Since the beginning, the second temple has been illegitimate, and in the restoration of the people ("new house") there will be no new temple ("tower"; 1 Enoch 89:73; 90:28–29).

In sum, the earliest "apocalyptic" texts, at least the earliest "historical apocalypses," were produced by scribal circles "caught in the middle." Their traditional institutional function was to serve (among) the high priestly rulers of the Judean temple-state. But when the "westernizing" faction that had become dominant in the Jerusalem aristocracy moved to transform the traditional institutions of the temple-state and their legitimating religious ideology into Hellenistic political-cultural forms, they opted for loyalty to the traditional culture of which they were the professional guardians. Thrown back on those traditional cultural resources, they adapted forms and motifs from the prophetic segment of the Judean cultural repertoire into revelatory visions. Those visions helped explain that their God was ultimately still in control of a history that seemed to be spinning out of control, and that their own role was to resist their erstwhile patrons who had abandoned the covenant with God.

As will become clear from critical examination of the histories of Josephus and the narrative of 1 Maccabees, the restoration of the temple-state as the controlling political-economic-religious institution in Judea followed the by then traditional pattern evident in the instructional speeches of Ben Sira. Josephus's portrayal of the Pharisees as the "friends" of the high priest John Hyrcanus and of their prominent role in the temple-state under Salome Alexandra indicate that they became the successors of the earlier scribes/sages, such as Ben Sira. These Hasmonean rulers sanctioned the laws derived from "the tradition of the ancestors" as the laws of the temple-state. The historical sociology of Lenski, as critiqued in this chapter above, will again prove helpful in discerning the structure and dynamics of the temple-state and the potential for conflict between the rulers and the retainers. When Alexander Jannaeus, son of Hyrcanus, proceeded to flout the laws and traditions of the Judeans, the Pharisees were faced with a situation similar to that faced by the earlier scribes who produced the Animal Apocalypse and the historical visions in Dan 7–12. The Pharisees who had been the retainers serving in the temple-state became part of the resistance to the unacceptable imperial practices of the incumbent high priest. This will be a significant step in the reconstruction of the history of the Pharisees to be sketched in the following chapters.

4

THE PHARISEES
—SOMETIME ADMINISTRATORS
OF THE JUDEAN TEMPLE-STATE

Discerning the position and role of the Pharisees is of considerable importance for understanding the origins of both Judaism and Christianity and the relations between them. Until the mid-twentieth century the general assumption, shared even by those who caution about its evidentiary basis, was that the Pharisees were the predecessors of the rabbis who shaped normative Judaism. Thus, while we are now aware of how little evidence we have for the Pharisees themselves, particularly for their views on particular issues, it was still legitimate, in study of "early (formative) Judaism" and "early Christianity" to believe that they were similar to the rabbis known through the Mishnah and other early rabbinic literatures. This seems to have been the basis for continuing to use the concept of Judaism with reference to anything prior to the compilation of the Mishnah, around 200 CE. On the assumption that their views were similar to those whose views were found in the Mishnah, scholars proceeded on the further assumption that the Pharisees provided a sort of baseline or norm for what was constructed as normative Judaism or sectarian Judaism in late second-temple Palestine. The Mishnah ostensibly provided continuity with the twin "redemptive media" of "early Judaism" insofar as its *halakhah* supposedly continued interpretation of the Torah and many of its tractates and individual rulings pertained to the temple and priestly matters.

As more critical study of the textual sources has developed in recent decades, students of Jewish history and religion were concerned to defend maximum continuity between the Pharisees and the rabbis consistent with the canons of critical scholarship. The massive project of critical analysis of the forms, transmission, and function of the voluminous rabbinic literature of late antiquity by Jacob Neusner and others has made unavoidably clear just how little reliable information about the Pharisees is actually available from rabbinic texts, even from the Mishnah, compiled around 200 CE. Yet even that minimal information was used as the decisive basis for reconstruction of the Pharisees in the crucial transition period of the first century CE. Neusner's own careful and sophisticated analysis of "rabbinic traditions about the Pharisees," including the more popularized presentation, *From Politics to Piety*, concluded that Josephus's accounts of the Pharisees as heavily involved in politics under the Hasmonean regime must yield to the limited and reworked yet (supposedly) more reliable representation of the Pharisees in rabbinic literature even though it dated from much later. Since those reliable rabbinic traditions of the Pharisees pertain primarily to agricultural tithes and offerings and ritual purity—"that is, sectarian interests"—the Pharisees must have been basically a Jewish sect devoted to table fellowship and the keeping of ritual purity outside the temple. Then, after 70 CE, "this small group of learned men eventually [became] the leaders of the whole nation," starting from their base in the academy at Yavneh, with Gamaliel II achieving "Roman recognition as head of the Jewish community" already by around 80 CE.[1]

This picture of the Pharisees, still based on rabbinic representations, however limited and reworked the evidence, proved attractive and influential in the historical study of ancient Jewish religion and New Testament studies. That the Pharisees had moved "from politics to piety" suited the professional agenda of religious studies and theology, with their frequent assumption that religion is a dimension of life that can be studied apart from political-economic life, even in ancient societies which preceded the historical Western structural differentiation of religious, political, and religious institutions. Equally determinative for historical reconstruction of "early Christianity," moreover, was the (continuing) assumption that the rabbis moved quickly into prominence if not control of the Jewish community in Palestine following the Roman destruction of Jerusalem and the temple.

Studies of the Gospels, Jesus, and the development of the synoptic tradition have been taking into consideration how little we actually know about the Pharisees, including how polemical and self-justifying the Gospel

---

1. Neusner, *From Politics to Piety*, 99.

portrayals are. Simplistic older assumptions about direct conflicts between Jesus and the Pharisees over the law have yielded to more nuanced discussions of Synoptic Gospel representations of the Pharisees as involving competing Jewish groups and particular concerns for purity and boundary definitions. Because of the skepticism about the historical veracity of Gospel portrayals of the conflict between Jesus and the Pharisees, however, the assumption about the continuity between the Pharisees and the rabbis has become determinative for the reconstruction of Christian origins in important ways. Two recent treatments of key facets of Christian origins by scholars to whom I have looked as mentors provide illustrations.

According to Burton Mack's stunning construction of Christian origins, the Pharisees whom the Jesus people encounter in the Galilean synagogues play the crucial role of competing authority figures for what he calls the "synagogue reform movement" out of which the Markan pronouncement stories and eventually the Gospel of Mark itself developed.[2] It seems unlikely that Jesus ever encountered the Pharisees in Galilee in the early 30s CE insofar as the Gospel of Mark is the only source that represents the Pharisees as active in Galilee (it is commonly assumed that Matthew and Luke were following Mark). On the assumptions of continuity between Pharisees and rabbis and that the Pharisees-become-rabbis were recognized by the Romans as the Jewish authorities in Palestine shortly after the destruction of the temple in 70 CE, however, it seems credible that a Jesus movement encountered the Pharisees as leaders of the synagogues thirty-some years later as they were gearing up to assume political authority throughout Palestine.

Howard Kee's "deconstruction" of the unwarranted assumption that "synagogues" in the first century CE were buildings still assumes that these "assemblies" were basically religious.[3] The assumption of direct continuity of the Pharisees and the rabbis, including their dominance in post-70 Judaism, then determines the focus of his argument. Even in the Gospel of Mark, the synagogues were "the assemblies of the Pharisees."[4] Matthew 23, moreover, "is filled with detailed references to what by the end of the first century CE were in the process of becoming normative practices in the emergent institutional synagogue."[5] One can thus find parallels in leadership roles between Matthew's community and "emergent Pharisaic-rabbinic Judaism." The "Jewish leaders" in this emergent movement were, it seems obvious, the Pharisees. While he has them more directly involved in the synagogues, Kee

2. Mack, *Myth of Innocence*.
3. Kee, "Transformation."
4. Kee, "Transformation," 14.
5. Kee, "Transformation," 15.

like Mack has the Pharisees gaining in authority and clarity of profile as they move toward "post-70 Judaism."

But—if I read them right—a number of critical studies have recently demonstrated in various ways how uncertain is the continuity between the Pharisees and the rabbis, given the extremely disruptive historical events of the late first and early second centuries CE, and how long it was before the rabbis had much authority and influence in the society at large.

The standard assumption has been not only that the Pharisees-becoming-rabbis formed an academy and a council (sanhedrin) at Yavneh after the destruction of Jerusalem and the temple in 70 CE, but that this academy/council (or its head, the rabbinic patriarch) was given authority over affairs in Palestine by the Roman government. It now turns out that such a construction rests on thin threads of evidence. Anthony Saldarini and Peter Schäfer explain that the four rabbinic accounts of Yohanan ben Zakkai's escape from besieged Jerusalem, of his encounter with Vespasian, and of his request to start a school at Yavneh, while all perhaps stemming from an original story, are different versions of a rabbinic "foundational legend."[6] The several similarities the rabbinic accounts display to Josephus's story of his own escape from the siege of Jotapata and encounter with Vespasian confirm their legendary character. We need not doubt the existence of an academy, but the foundational legend makes no mention of such. More importantly perhaps is the lack of solid evidence that the Romans recognized the (political-religious) authority of the "rabbis" at Yavneh. The principal proof text is m. Eduyot 7:7, which represents Gamaliel (II) going to the Roman governor in Syria to obtain "authority" (*reshut*), apparently to teach. The text does not suggest a more political dimension such as receiving authority over affairs in Jewish Palestine.[7]

The first substantial evidence of "the patriarchate" wielding some political power, possibly with Roman approval, pertains to Judah the Prince, around 200 CE. Although there is little doubt about the full Roman recognition of the political authority of the patriarchate by the middle or end of the fourth century, there are serious problems with the continuity of the evidence for the patriarchate before that.[8] Nevertheless a variety of sources indicates that Judah the Prince must have risen rapidly to power by the

---

6. Saldarini, "Johanan ben Zakkai's Escape"; and Schäfer, "Flucht Rabban Johanan ben Zakkai," 98.

7. Review of the evidence in Levine, "Jewish Patriarch"; Levine, *The Rabbinic Class of Roman Palestine*, chap. 4.

8. See the review of the kinds of evidence and the attendant problems by Levine, "Jewish Patriarch," esp. 649–54. The following is dependent on Levine's critical reconstruction of Judah's emergence and powers, 654–74.

beginning of the third century. Taking advantage of a certain rapprochement between certain prominent Jews in Palestine and the Roman imperial regime just prior to 200, Judah apparently cultivated a close relationship with the emperor Antoninus, one which became legendary in rabbinic literature. Thus enabled to obtain certain favors from the emperor, such as land grants, and to cultivate social ties with wealthy and powerful families in and around Galilee, Judah emerged with unprecedented power in the affairs of the society. For example, he could make judicial and communal appointments, alter the level of tithing and sabbatical year obligations, and even collect certain taxes. But this sudden rise of Judah the Prince to prominence and power around 200 CE makes all the more striking how different the situation must have been with his predecessors. There is simply little or no evidence that either Simeon ben Gamaliel or his father and predecessor Gamaliel II were recognized by the Romans or otherwise held much social-political authority in Palestine.[9] Nor would that be surprising, given the disastrously disruptive events of revolt and reconquest in both 66–70 and 132–135 and the resultant relocation of the rabbinic academy to Galilee in the mid-second century.

Moreover, in the Mishnah and the Tosefta the rabbis repeatedly witness to their own lack of authority with the people (now in Galilee) during the second century.[10] The principal areas in which they made rulings were limited primarily to concerns such as purity and tithes. But matters such as the disposal of bodies and Sabbath observances, like the affairs of the synagogues and civil and criminal court cases, were left to local communities, their customs and authorities. In the areas where they did attempt to assert some authority—that is on purity, tithes, sabbatical year observances, or laws of mixed kinds (of crops)—the people often disregarded their rulings. Again this may not be surprising given the serious disruptions in Palestine and the rabbinic move to Galilee in mid-second century.

Finally, the rabbis apparently had little interest in, let alone authority over, the local synagogues in the first century or so after the destruction of the temple. As just noted, the Mishnah had almost nothing to say about the synagogues and very little even on prayer. As will be explored further below, synagogues were local community institutions with their own heritage of customs and traditional leadership roles. In sum, it appears that the rabbis

---

9. Levine, "Jewish Patriarch," 654–55. For the following sketch, see especially 93–111, and his notes with numerous references to evidence from Mishnah and Tosefta.

10. This is the principal thesis of Goodman, *State and Society*. For the following sketch, see especially 93–111, and the notes with numerous references to evidence from the Mishnah and Tosefta.

had very little influence on Jewish life in Palestine for several generations after the destruction of the temple. As Cohen observes candidly,

> the rabbis were opposed by various segments among the wealthy and the priesthood, and by the bulk of the masses in both Palestine and the diaspora ... The rabbis triumphed over their opponents among the aristocracy and priesthood by absorbing them into their midst ... The rabbis triumphed over the indifference of the masses by gradually gaining control of the schools and the synagogues. The exact date ... was not earlier than the seventh century.[11]

Clearly we can no longer assume direct and substantial continuity between the Pharisees and the rabbis. These critical studies which demonstrate how slowly the rabbis were in gaining authority in Jewish society have pulled the props out from under the recent tendency to believe that the evidence for the Pharisees, particularly for their activity in Galilee, is better the further we move toward 70 and after. But the Pharisees are centrally important to reconstruction of early Jewish history and the origins of Christianity, virtually the hinge on which most issues turn, either directly or indirectly. Hence we cannot go much further in the field without simply generating more confusion, without reexamining the evidence for the Pharisees and securing a more reliable sense of their place and function in late second-temple Palestine.

In the course of pointing out how different the pictures of the Pharisees are in our three principal sources, i.e., Josephus, the Gospels, and rabbinic traditions, Neusner commented that "for all we know, all reports are correct."[12] Perhaps it is time to explore that possibility. We might do well to abandon essentialist assumptions that our different sources are each representing "the nature of" the Pharisees so that either one or more must be dismissed as wrong or propaganda or polemic, or the Pharisees must have changed from the politicians of Josephus to the religious sect of the rabbinic traditions. It is more likely that our different sources not only have their own particular point of view but are each representing only certain aspects of the Pharisees. To appreciate the different facets of the Pharisees that the sources may characterize we will need an approach that takes into account their historical context, particularly the historical social relations in which they may have been involved. Thus, while taking critically into account the particular point of view and interests of the respective sources—Josephus, the Christian Gospels, and rabbinic traditions—we can investigate how our

---

11. Cohen, *From the Maccabees to the Mishnah*, 221.
12. Neusner, *Rabbinic Traditions about the Pharisees*, vol. 3, 244.

different sources may shed light on the social position, roles, and relationships of the Pharisees in late second-temple Palestine.

CLAIMS OF JOSEPHUS'S PRO-PHARISAIC PROPAGANDA IN *ANTIQUITIES*

The claim that the Pharisees retreated from active political involvement to conventicles of piety at the beginning of Herodian rule is based on allowing only Josephus's *War* as evidence, to the exclusion of the *Antiquities*, and on a reading of the rabbinic and Gospel evidence according to certain presuppositions. Josephus's treatment of the Pharisees in *Antiquities* is excluded on the claim that it is tendentious propaganda on their behalf as they are about to be entrusted by the Romans with authority over Jewish Palestine, supposedly in the 90s CE.

It is argued that the *Antiquities* is blatantly pro-Pharisee, in contrast to the *War* in which "we find no claim that the Pharisees are the most popular sect and have a massive public following, or that no one can effectively govern Palestine without their support."[13] This argument, however, can now be seen as flawed in several respects.

(a) The claim that the Pharisees-turned-rabbis at Yavneh were negotiating with the Romans for recognition of their authority in Palestine is without good evidence: Not only can the story of Yohanan ben Zakkai's escape from Jerusalem and audience with Vespasian now be seen as a later foundational legend,[14] but the authority that Gamaliel II obtained from the Roman governor in Syria appears to pertain only to teaching (*m. Eduyot* 7:7). Josephus gives no indication that he even knew about Yavneh.

(b) The argument apparently assumes that the Romans, whose consistent policy was to govern subject peoples through urban and native aristocracies, would have been interested in a sect with a popular following in the exceptional case of the Judeans.

(c) The argument is based on selective criticism of Josephus's accounts of the Pharisees, taking virtually at face value his portrayals of them as a philosophy, without examining Josephus's manner of presentation to a Hellenistic-Roman readership. The argument also does not consider the possibility that Josephus may be dependent on Nicolaus (Herod's house historian), while focusing exclusively on the issue of the Pharisees' influence with the people: the political motif that he wants to explain away.

---

13. Neusner, *From Politics to Piety*, 53, 64–65, citing at length from Smith, "Palestinian Judaism in the First Century," 75–76.

14. Again see the articles by Saldarini and Schaefer cited in n. 6 above.

(d) The argument overplays the difference between Josephus's two portrayals of the Pharisees: For example, he writes in both histories that the Pharisees were "the principal," "the first," or "the leading" party (*ten proten hairesin*, *War* 2.162; *Ant.* 13.171). In the *War* Josephus also has "the most notable Pharisees" working with the nobles and the chief priests to control the insurrectionary populace in the summer of 66 CE (2.411)—that is, in Josephus the Pharisees are still politically active, just as he has the leading Pharisees "consulting with the high priests" on how to deal with the insurrection in his *Life* (21–22), written at about the same time as the *Antiquities*.

(e) The portrayals of the Pharisees in *Antiquities* as moved by envy to subvert or combat rulers, particularly Rome's own client Herod, and as refusing an oath of loyalty to Caesar (*Ant.* 13.288; 17.41–45) would hardly have commended them to the Romans. Thus even if Josephus happened to be quoting a source such as Nicolaus of Damascus in these cases, he would have edited more carefully if he had been advocating the Pharisees' case.

The last point would appear to be decisive in favor of taking the accounts of the Pharisees in *Antiquities* seriously as representative of the Pharisees' political engagement, since Josephus's portrayal of their disrupting activities do not serve his own political or apologetic purposes.[15] If we now consider the accounts in both *War* and *Antiquities* along with those in *Life*, the Pharisees appear to have been continuously involved in political affairs, from Hasmonean through Herodian times and into the great revolt of 66–70.

THE PHARISEES' CONTINUOUS INVOLVEMENT IN POLITICS

The Pharisees' integral involvement in political affairs under the Hasmoneans is not in dispute. They enjoyed considerable influence with John Hyrcanus until he broke with them and worked with the Sadducees. They were apparently involved in bitter conflict with Alexander Jannaeus, only to become "the virtual administrators of the (temple-)state under his wife and successor, Salome Alexandra. But did the Pharisaic party then face "the choice of remaining in politics and suffering annihilation, or giving up politics and surviving in a very different form"?[16] Even the *War* has Herod

---

15. Schwartz, "Josephus and Nicolas on the Pharisees," 159, 161, 169, even suggests that, far from Josephus purposely emphasizing reports of the Pharisees' political activities in *Antiquities*, he suppressed such reports in the accounts of Nicolaus which he was following in *Jewish War*.

16. Neusner, *From Politics to Piety*, 146, cf. 66.

accusing the wife of his brother Pheroras of "subsidizing the Pharisees to oppose him" (*War* 1.571). Clearly they had not all been killed by Aristobulus and Herod. What had they been doing? Judging from Josephus's accounts, certain Pharisees were prominent in the Sanhedrin and influential in Jerusalem. When the Council, convened to try the young Herod for the murder of the brigand-chief Ezekias and his men in Galilee, was intimidated by his brazen appearance before them replete with troops, Samaias, disciple of the Pharisee Pollion, warned them (predicting) that the one they were about to acquit would one day have power over them. A few years later, when Herod was besieging Jerusalem in the course of conquering the kingdom over which Rome had just appointed him king, these two political realists advised the Jerusalemites to submit to Herod's rule (*Ant.* 14.172–176; 15.3–4). Herod thereafter held them in honor. These stories, repeated by Josephus and confirmed by his accounts of the conflicts and intrigue between Herod and the Pharisees that ensued later in the tyrant's reign, indicate clearly that the Pharisees were still heavily involved in political affairs under Herod.

In fact, the Pharisees evidently had sufficient standing in Jerusalem to be able to resist Herod's worst repressive measures while still apparently carrying out some function in the government of the country. Josephus presents two different accounts of a loyalty oath that the Pharisees refused (*Ant.* 14.370; 17.41–42). While it may be impossible to determine whether these represent two different events, they are clearly two different accounts, the second possibly taken from Nicolaus of Damascus, judging from its pro-Herod stance and language, unusual for Josephus (*morion ti Ioudaikon*). In any case, for the information we can glean about the political position of the Pharisees and the dynamics of their relationship with Herod, both are as interesting as accounts as they are for the events that may lie behind them.

The first account of the refusal of the loyalty oath comes at the end of a long section detailing the steps Herod took in imposing a virtual police state, toward the middle of his reign (*Ant.* 15.365–370). Among other repressive measures, the whole populace was required to take the loyalty oath, and those who resisted were simply eliminated, by whatever means. "He also tried to persuade Pollion the Pharisee and Samaias and most of their disciples to take the oath, but they would not agree to this, and yet they were not punished . . . , for they were shown consideration on Pollion's account (370). Such restraint was highly unusual in Herod's otherwise unmitigated tyranny. Those Pharisees must have had some independent base of power, must have played some important function for Herod's government, or both.

The second account is placed amid Herod's increasing paranoia, confusion, and escalating repressive measures toward the end of his reign.

> There was also a group of Judeans priding itself on its adherence to ancestral customs and claiming to observe the laws of which the deity approves, and by these men, called Pharisees, the women (of the court) were ruled. These men were able to help the king greatly because of their foresight, and yet they were obviously intent upon combating and injuring him. At least when the whole people affirmed by an oath that it would be loyal to Caesar and to the king's government, these men, over six thousand in number, refused to take this oath, and when the king punished them with a fine, Pheroras's wife paid the fine for them. In return they foretold ... that by God's decree Herod's throne would be taken from him ... and the royal power would fall to her and Pheroras ... And the king put to death those of the Pharisees who were most to blame and the eunuch Bagoas and a certain Karos ... who was loved by the king ... and also those of his household who approved of what the Pharisees said ... (*Ant.* 17.41–45)

The possibility that this account stems from Nicolaus, Herod's own court historian, and has the Pharisees involved in his court where they could engage in court intrigue makes it all the more credible.

It is clear that Herod had instituted his own royal administration, in effect, above that carried over from the Hasmonean temple-state, in which the Pharisees had been playing an important role. Thus we would assume that the Pharisees generally had suffered a demotion in status and responsibilities. Yet here is a story portraying a number of Pharisees as actively involved directly in the affairs of Herod's court. The colleagues and successors of the political realists Pollion and Samaias have become political opportunists, as was only fitting under Herod's rule, cultivating the women and court figures close to the king. It is difficult to determine from this account the extent to which the Pharisees were conspiring against Herod; perhaps it was only this one incident. The opposition to Herod was evidently wider among Judean sages. Josephus narrates at length how other prominent *sophistai*, Judas and Matthias, "the most learned of the Judeans and unrivalled expounders of the ancestral laws," boldly enough exhorted their disciples to cut down the golden Roman eagle Herod had installed over the great gate of the temple (*War* 1.648–650; *Ant.* 17.149–154).

Completely aside from the presence of some Pharisees in Herod's court and their engagement in court intrigue, however, this second account of the loyalty oath carries two other telling bits of information. The oath that the Pharisees refused was also an affirmation of loyalty to Caesar. One immediately thinks of what Josephus says about the "Fourth Philosophy," whose leaders in 6 CE were Saddok the Pharisee and the sage/teacher (*sophistes*) Judas of Gamala. In all respects, says Josephus, "they agree with the views of the Pharisees, except that they have an intense passion for freedom, on the conviction that God alone is their ruler and master" (*Ant.* 18.4, 9, 23). Resistance to Rome as well as to Herodian rule must not have been completely dormant in Pharisaic and other intellectual circles under Herod's repressive measures. Moreover, while Josephus must be engaging in his typical exaggeration with the figure of six thousand Pharisees, this "group of Judeans" known as the Pharisees was clearly several thousand strong. It is highly unlikely that so many Pharisees were utilized in Herod's court and administration or engaged in instructing proteges the ancestral traditions, like Judas and Matthias. They must have still been performing needed functions and services for the apparatus of the temple-state that Herod left intact underneath or beside his own administration.

Except for Saddok, co-leader of the "Fourth Philosophy" that organized resistance to the Roman tribute in 6 CE, Pharisees disappear from Josephus's narratives from the death of Herod until the beginning of the great revolt in 66 CE. Judging from what Josephus writes about key events in the early stages of the revolt, however, they clearly did not disappear from political affairs in Jerusalem and the areas over which the Jerusalem temple-state claimed jurisdiction. As the insurrection was gathering momentum in the summer of 66, "the *dynatoi* (powerful ones)," called "elders" in the Gospels, assembled with the high priests and "the most notable Pharisees" (*hoi ton Pharisaion gnorimoi*) to deliberate on how they might control the situation (*War* 2.411). Having taken refuge in the upper city and inner court of the temple from the escalating revolt, "the high priests and leading Pharisees" (*hoi protoi ton Pharisaion*) finally emerged again to deliberate on how to moderate the revolt (*Life* 21–22). "The leading Pharisees" at least evidently belonged to the inner circle of those who headed the temple-state in Jerusalem who were dependent on the Romans to maintain their power and privilege. They were hoping the Roman general Cestius Gallus would soon come with his troops and restore their control of the city. The phrases "the most notable men among" and "the principal men of" indicate that the Pharisees were a much larger group than the few in prominent positions, presumably also playing some role in the operation of the temple-state. When the rebels had driven Cestius Gallus and the Roman troops out of Jerusalem and some of the most prominent high priestly figures had fled the city, other prominent high priests and leading Pharisees formed a "council," a provisional government and attempted to control the revolt

(*War* 2.566–568; *Life* 21–22, 28–29).[17] Fairly quickly prominent Pharisees, including Simon son of Gamaliel, appear in the inner circle of that provisional government, and other Pharisees are involved in the implementation of its decisions—as Josephus knows only too well from their having been instrumental in attempting to displace him as the governor/general assigned to control affairs in Galilee (*Life* 190–198).

These Pharisees cannot be dismissed as simply individuals who happen to be Pharisees or as members of a "revolutionary" government. It is clear from Josephus's accounts that these Pharisees worked with the high priests on a regular basis and that there was continuity between the high priests and leading Pharisees who were trying to contain the revolt and the high priests and most prominent of the Pharisees who were controlling affairs in (and from) Jerusalem in late 66 and early 67. It is apparent that the Pharisees had been involved in the government of Jerusalem right along, and that the leading Pharisees had been prominent figures in Jerusalem during the decades prior to the revolt. The representation of Gamaliel in Acts 5:33-39 as "a Pharisee in the council," "a teacher of the law, respected by all the people" and a decisively influential voice in the council's deliberations has considerable historical verisimilitude. His son evidently picked up where he left off: "this Simon was a native of Jerusalem, of a very illustrious family, and of the party of Pharisees, who are recognized as accurate (experts) in the country's laws . . . he could by sheer genius retrieve an unfortunate situation in affairs of state" (*Life* 191–192). If we take Josephus's accounts seriously and read them critically in historical context, it is clear that the Pharisees had remained in politics and not suffered annihilation, and that in the first century CE they were in charge of considerably more than pious eating clubs scrupulous about purity codes and tithing.

---

17. Pace Shaye Cohen, *Josephus in Jerusalem and Rome*, no great difference is discernible between the narrative in the *War* and that in the later *Life* with regard to their respective "apologies" and to the formation and overall strategy of the provisional government formed in Jerusalem after the defeat of Cestius Gallus. All one has to do is "read between the lines" of the passage in *War* 2.562-568 to discern that the principal leaders of the revolt to that point are either not appointed "generals" at all or are assigned to outlying districts (e.g., Eleazar the temple captain to Idumea under the watchful eye of a high priest named Jesus son of Sapphas), and that the "junta" was dominated by prominent high priests, particularly Ananus and Jesus son of Gamalas, who managed to hold the insurrection in check in Jerusalem until the Zealots (proper) finally took effective control of the city in the summer of 68.

THE POLITICAL-RELIGIOUS POSITION AND FUNCTION OF THE PHARISEES

Only recently have we resumed asking questions of social structure and social role in studies of ancient Jewish history. Baron, Finkelstein, and others constructed some suggestive pictures of ancient Jewish social history. Urbach laid out a provocative analysis of "class and class-status" among the sages.[18] More recently, however, we have works of comparative historical sociology based on numerous cross-cultural studies from a variety of comparable "pre-industrial," "agrarian" societies or "aristocratic empires."[19] And we can utilize the more critical historiographical analyses of our literary sources.[20]

The use of models developed by historical sociology may help to locate the Pharisees on a map of social stratification. In a broadly cross-cultural and evolutionary study, Gerhard Lenski developed a model of agrarian societies based on many studies of societies that seem comparable to ancient Palestine, but for which we have more sources, studies, or both.[21] The Pharisees in Josephus's accounts appear to have been analogous to certain kinds of "retainers" in other traditional agrarian societies.[22] "Retainers" in Lenski's scheme were the military, some religious specialists, lawyers, teachers, and other functionaries who served and aided the "ruler" and the "governing class" in controlling the rest of the society, which consisted primarily of peasants and urban artisans. The retainers were generally dependent on the rulers and/or governing class for their position and income. Although offices and prerogatives often became virtually hereditary, retainers could fall out of favor. A change in rulers might entail replacement of retainers, but often did not. Given the dynamics of history, there was no firm boundary between the retainers and the governing class. When the traditional ruling class became weak, the retainers could move into positions of considerable power.

That the Pharisees came to occupy just such a position and function in the political-economic-religious structure of Judea under early Hasmonean

18. Urbach, *Class-Status and Leadership*.
19. Esp. Lenski, *Power and Privilege*.
20. Attridge, *Interpretation of Biblical History*.
21. Lenski, *Power and Privilege*, esp. 214–84.
22. As I outlined briefly in *Jesus and the Spiral of Violence*, chaps. 1 and 5, and as Anthony Saldarini argued at some length in *Pharisees, Scribes, and Sadducees*, esp. 35–45, 86–87, 93–94, 119–20. I continued to work with Lenski's concept of "retainers" in *Sociology and the Jesus Movement*, but was critical of structural-functional sociology that downplays political-economic conflict, chapters 4–5.

rule is evident from Josephus's accounts of their shifting status from Hyrcanus to Alexander Jannaeus to Salome Alexandra. They had been close associates and advisers of John Hyrcanus, who was their "disciple."[23] Their function under Hyrcanus was to cultivate regulations derived from the traditions of the ancestors for the people, regulations that Hyrcanus evidently enforced as laws of the temple-state. Hyrcanus, however, broke with them and looked to the aristocratic party of the Sadducees for advice. Then after apparently being in the bitter conflict with Alexander Jannaeus, the Pharisees became "the real administrators of the state," handling "all matters of royal power" under Salome Alexandra, who reauthorized their regulations as state law (*War* 1.111; *Ant.* 13.405).

The use of Lenski's model of social stratification has certain limitations, two of which should be mentioned. First, to focus heavily on the particular status of the Pharisees as "retainers" in Lenki's scheme of multiple (eight or nine) "classes" may limit our perception of the overall power or class-relations in the traditional agrarian society of Judea (and where the Pharisees may have fit). In terms of fundamental political-economic-religious relations, a traditional agrarian society such as ancient Judea had only two classes, the rulers and the ruled.[24] Retainers are usually dependent on rulers and serve their interests. On the other hand, certain conflicts can develop between the rulers and their retainers, as must be explored below. Josephus's assertions that the Pharisees (sometimes) had influence with the people should be examined critically in this connection.

Second, placing the Pharisees in a model of social stratification does not necessarily indicate the particular social functions or roles they served and the particular social relations in which they operated. Viewing Josephus's accounts through the lenses of Lenski's scheme, Saldarini is skeptical about just how much clarity can be gained about "what functions the Pharisees fulfilled in society" and concludes that as just one among many groups striving for influence with the rulers, they "were a minor factor."[25] On the other hand, a closer look at Josephus's accounts with a focus on the Pharisees' social role and function rather than on classification by social stratum may generate more information.

Broadly speaking, the Pharisees evidently served political-religious functions in the Judean temple-state. We can become more precise initially

---

23. A story similar to the one about Hyrcanus and the Pharisees that Josephus repeats in *Ant.* 13.288–296 appears in a much later rabbinic text as about Jannaeus, in b. Qiddushin 66a.

24. Saldarini, *Pharisees*, 36–37, includes this important point in discussion of comparative social structure, but does not develop it in connection with the literary sources.

25. Saldarini, *Pharisees*, 120, 132.

on the basis of what functions they apparently did not serve, according to the silence of our sources. They had nothing to do with the military. Even under Salome Alexandra, when their power probably reached its height, it was she who, like her predecessors, saw to the hiring of mercenaries (*War* 1.112; *Ant.* 13.409). Also, there is no indication at any point that they were involved in the collection of taxes or tithes. But what Josephus mentions again and again, in the context of historical accounts of a people whose whole life arises out of and is committed to the observance of "the laws" or "ancestral traditions" or "customs," is that the Pharisees are the principal experts in or the unrivaled or most accurate expounders of the laws (*War* 1.110; 2.162; *Life* 191; "interpreters" is not a good translation of these Greek texts). Clearly the Pharisees' cultivation of the laws merits closer attention, but in the context of the governing of the temple-state, as in our sources, and not only in the sense of personal devotion or sectarian piety (as in so much of the modern discussion).

In several large agrarian societies, certain officials who could be understood as intellectual-legal retainers served as guardians and transmitters of the cultural traditions, oral and/or written, according to which social and political affairs were conducted. In this connection such officials might help determine and/or implement the rulers' governing policies. We may think of the ulama in Islamic societies or the mandarins in China. The learned scribes earlier in the history of the Judean temple-state, as described by Ben Sira in Sir 38–39. Josephus mentions a number of things that are suggestive about the Pharisees having served similar functions.

Josephus characterizes the Hasmonean high priest, John Hyrcanus, as a "disciple" (*mathetes*) of the Pharisees (*Ant.* 13.289), a term often used for a student who learns the cultural traditions under the tutelage of a sage or teacher. When he then deserts the Pharisees for the Sadducees, Josephus writes:

> he abrogated the regulations which they had established for the people (*ta hup' auton katastathenta nomima to demo*), and punished those who observed them . . . For the Pharisees had passed on to the people certain regulations handed down from a succession of ancestors [by former generations] and not written [recorded] in the laws of Moses (*nomima tina paredosan to demo . . . ek pateron diadoches, haper ouk anagegraptai en tois Mouseos nomois*). And on account of this, the party (*genos*) of the Sadducees reject these (regulations), holding that only those regulations which are written (*nomima ta gegrammena*) must be observed, while it is not necessary to keep those from the

> tradition of the ancestors (*ta ek paradoseos ton pateron*). (*Ant.* 13.296–297)

Then a generation later when Salome Alexandra restored the Pharisees to power, Josephus writes,

> Whatever regulations (*ta nomima*), introduced by the Pharisees in accordance with the ancestral tradition (*kata ten patroan paradosin*), had been abolished by her father-in-law Hyrcanus, these she again restored. (*Ant.* 13.408)

It is important to draw out several aspects of these key statements by Josephus, not necessarily as accurate historical accounts, but as representative of the functions of the Pharisees under the Hasmonean rulers. First, these *nomima* given by the Pharisees were different from "the laws of Moses," here specified as the regulations written on scrolls. Second, for some time prior to the story, on a regular basis, as part of their political responsibilities, the Pharisees had been promulgating these regulations. Third, the regulations were established for the people, evidently for the regulation of public life. They were not just for the Pharisees themselves and did not rest simply on the Pharisees own authority. Fourth, the rulings were sanctioned (or rescinded) by the ruler, Hyrcanus or Salome Alexandra, as official state law, the policy of the high priestly head of state. Josephus says explicitly that there were sanctions (punishments?) for those who failed to observe the regulations when they were official state law, just as there were for those who continued to observe them when they had been rescinded.

Finally, fifth, these regulations are represented as derived from or being ancestral laws, stemming from the ancestors of old. This basic concept as well as the particular terms Josephus uses are highly suggestive in connection with statements about the Pharisees or the sages elsewhere, particularly in Mark 7 (*paradosis*) and in the rabbinic texts on "the chain of tradition." A standard interpretation is to classify all these in the terms of a later rabbinic concept of *the* "oral law" as a supplement and parallel to the written law. But is that classification warranted? This fifth aspect requires fuller exploration.

A starting point may be to compare this account with other passages in Josephus's works, specifically with three passages in his apologetic treatise *Against Apion*. The most striking comparison is with *Ag. Ap.* 1.39, where Josephus is boasting about the twenty-two "books" of the Judeans. The five books of Moses, he declares, contain "the laws and the tradition" (*paradosis*) from the birth of mankind to his (i.e., Moses's) death. The key term *paradosis* here refers to the "historical" parts of the books as distinguished from the laws/ordinances/customs, both contained in the written torah scrolls. At the beginning of his lengthy discussion of the highly desirable antiquity of the records or history of certain peoples, such as the Egyptians, Babylonians, and Phoenicians, Josephus explains that these peoples have a very ancient and permanent tradition of their memorable past/history (*tes mnemes ten paradosin*; 1.8–9). It was the Phoenicians who made the greatest use of writing "both for the ordinary affairs of life and for the tradition of public events (*pros ten ton koinon ergon paradosin*; *Ag. Ap.* 1.28–29). In this discussion Josephus is emphasizing the recording of peoples' *tradition* in writing so that they are preserved with scrupulous accuracy. A people's *paradosis* is its history, the more ancient the better. But it does not necessarily include the laws/ordinances (1.28–29, 39). The "tradition from the succession of ancestors" in *Ant.* 13.296–297 differs from what Josephus touts in his great apology in two significant respects that are striking: it clearly refers to laws, regulations, rulings, and these are contrasted with the laws of Moses that are written on scrolls.[26]

Josephus's discussion of the importance of the written records of tradition, however, is suggestive for why the Pharisees may have understood their regulations as derived from the succession of ancestors. All scribal cultivation of laws and legends and prophecies in a traditional agrarian society was understood as learned and remembered from the ancestral predecessors, among whom scribal teachers played a prominent role. Under the Hasmoneans the Pharisees had taken up the traditional role of the learned scribes of the temple-state after a hiatus in the high priesthood and operation of the temple-state because of the Hellenizing reform and the Maccabean Revolt. This was exemplified by the highly regarded Yeshua ben Sira only two generations before them. He boasts how the learned scribe or sage learned the laws of the Most High and prophecies, as well as various kinds of wisdom from earlier generations as preparation for serving in the councils of the temple-state rulers (Sir 39:1–4). It is significant that Ben Sira touts the ancestors of hoary antiquity to establish the authority of the high priests and the ancestral traditions of laws and prophecies and officeholders of the people (Sir 44–50). In terms of Judean tradition, the Hasmonean patrons of the Pharisees, who were from an ordinary and not a high priestly lineage, were illegitimate. As their legal-intellectual retainers, it would have been important for the Pharisees to emphasize that the laws and rulings they promulgated for the operations of the temple-state were derived from ancestral tradition. This would have enhanced their own authority and would presumably have helped legitimize the upstart high priesthood. As

---

26. Cf. the claim that the Pharisees' *paradosis* in *Ant.* 13.297, 408 is "consistent with these usages" in Josephus's *Against Apion* by Baumgarten, "Pharisaic *Paradosis*," 64–65.

Hyrcanus consolidated his control of Judea and even launched wars of expansion with newly hired mercenary troops, and expanded his wealth by intensified exploitation of the countryside (*chora; Ant.* 13.249–258, 273) he understandably found the more conservative, wealthy, aristocratic Sadducees more compatible. Their view that the only laws that required observance were the written laws of Moses, left Hyrcanus much more freedom of action, unconstrained by the regulations of the Pharisees promulgated for the current operations of the Hasmonean temple-state.

That the Pharisees were promulgating ordinances derived from the ancestral traditions for the operations of the temple-state that functioned as state law under Hyrcanus and again under Salome Alexandra fairly clearly indicates their position as legal retainers of the temple-state. Contrary to much recent discussion, they were not one religious sect competing with other sects for members from Judean society at large or from a narrower circle of potential clientele.[27] Hyrcanus's replacement of the Pharisees with the Sadducees as his close "friends" (advisers) was also a change in temple-state policy and practice. Under Salome Alexandra the policy and practice changed back. Thereafter the Pharisees appear not to have been one minor group among others vying for influence but were the predominant party in the operation of public affairs in Jerusalem.

That the Pharisees became the advisers of the high priest at some point early in the Hasmonean period is confirmed by references to the "seekers of smooth things" in the *pesherim* (interpretations/applications) and other texts in the Dead Sea Scrolls. The Qumranites who produced these texts evidently originated as dissident scribal and priestly elements who had abandoned what they considered an illegitimate and hopelessly compromised Hasmonean regime ("the Wicked Priest")—and who may have been awaiting their opportunity to return to power themselves. Judging by the complaints against them, it is by the "smooth things" they speak to the Hasmonean regime and the people that cities and families will be brought to ruin (1QH 4:7-14; 4QpNah 2). The context, in the latter text, appears to be the power struggle of "the seekers of smooth things" against Alexander Jannaeus, who crucified several hundred of his opponents (4QpNah 1-3; *Ant.* 13.376–383). Whether in its own condemnation of "the seekers of smooth things" or in its portrayal of "the furious young lion" hanging them alive, the

---

27. The concept of "sectarian Judaism, that is of Pharisees, Sadducees, Qumranites, and early Christians as religious "sects" lends itself to a religious reductionism that loses sight of how, with the exception of the Qumranites who had withdrawn from Jerusalem in protest, Judeans were rooted in traditional corporate social forms and structures. See Baumgarten, "The Pharisaic Paradosis," 76–77.

community at Qumran is referring to political power struggles for control of the society, with the application of the laws as the focus of those struggles.[28]

Key aspects of several of Josephus's accounts of Pharisees' activities in subsequent regimes fit well into this picture of their principal political function (the cultivation of the laws and promulgation of related regulations for public affairs). Herod, like the Romans whose client he was, ruled through the native aristocracy of Judea. Although he set his own creatures, some from diaspora communities, into the office of high priest, that was precisely in the context of leaving intact the apparatus of the temple-state. If the Pharisees had established themselves as being (most) accurate in the laws and traditions according to which the society was still governed, then it is understandable that Josephus mentions that several thousand were still active, some even in Herod's court. The presence of Sammaias in the Sanhedrin (probably irregularly assembled) was surely not unique, whether before, during, or after Herod's reign. And being experts in the laws and knowledgeable in the ancestral customs ranked in importance with being a native of Jerusalem or belonging to a priestly family, at least in the mind of the consummate politician, Josephus (*Life* 191).

THE INFLUENCE OF THE PHARISEES AMONG THE PEOPLE

The claim that the Pharisees had a following among or influence with the masses also can become intelligible in this connection. One might well be skeptical of a wealthy aristocratic historian's claim that anyone in a position of authority had influence or popularity with the ordinary people. It is clearly from the rulers' point of view that the claim is asserted. One might also question just what is meant by "the multitude/populace" (*to plethos*) in such accounts, and in what respect the Pharisees "have influence."

A close examination of Josephus suggests that three of the four principal accounts that claim Pharisaic influence among "the multitude" stem from Nicolaus of Damascus, Herod's court historian. The phrase "a king and a high priest" in the account about John Hyrcanus and the Pharisees (*Ant.* 13.288) appears to be making a distinction. This does not appear to fit Hyrcanus, who had not declared himself king as well as high priest, but it would fit the situation under Herod, the patron of Nicolaus. The linguistic as well as thematic parallels between that passage and Alexander Jannaeus's instruction to Salome Alexandra (*Ant.* 13.401–402: *pisteuesthai, para to plethei, phthonon/phthonountes*) suggest that Josephus is again following

28. Flusser, "Pharisees, Sadducees, and Essenes in Pesher Nahum."

Nicolaus, whose patron the Pharisees did scheme against (according to *Ant.* 17.41–45). Finally, the comment about the Pharisees having the support of the multitude (again *plethos*, when other terms were available) that closes the long passage about their break with Hyrcanus (*Ant.* 13.298) appears to have been influenced by if not taken from Nicolaus.[29]

In all of these accounts the Pharisees' influence pertains to (potentially) injuring the ruler, even supposedly by active agitation. Besides stemming probably from Nicolaus, who had witnessed Pharisaic resistance to Herod, these accounts focus on the open conflict that erupted between Alexander Jannaeus, one of Hyrcanus's sons, and the Pharisees (known from the combination of *Ant.* 13.372–273 and 4QpNah 1–2). Moreover, considering that the "urban crowd" or "mob" was about the only part of the people at large that could have much influence on the ruler in traditional agrarian societies[30]—the vast majority of the population being peasants in villages and towns at varying distance from the capital city, where politics was made—"the multitude" in these accounts must refer to the people in Jerusalem. Josephus mentions just such a protest by the Jerusalem crowd at the feast of tabernacles, when they pelted Alexander with citrons as he sacrificed at the altar (*Ant.* 13.372). The terms used with regard to the contrasting social base of the Sadducees (that they have the confidence of the *euporous* but not the *demotikon*), the latter term usually indicating either the nonpriestly elements, the citizen body of Jerusalem, or both, confirms the reading. "The multitude" must be the crowd in Jerusalem.

Thus the three accounts in *Antiquities* book 13 do not make the claim that the Pharisees have general influence and support among the whole Judean populace, but only that the Pharisees can (and did) make trouble for the Hasmonean or Herodian rulers when they disagreed strongly with the rulers' actions. These three texts do not pertain necessarily to the Pharisees' influence through their legislation for public life or their contacts with people in villages and towns. But they do indicate that the Pharisees were an active political force who could take their case to the Jerusalem crowd in a struggle with the rulers. That the Pharisees should have had influence with the people, especially in the capital city Jerusalem, is all the more credible when we take into account both the basic political-economic structure and the particular policies of the Hasmonean rulers and of the Roman client Herod. Besides the increasing Hellenistic influence in the Hasmonean court, John Hyrcanus and his sons Aristobulus and Alexander conducted nearly continuous wars of expansion for two generations. Although we can

---

29. See further Schwartz, "Josephus and Nicolas on the Pharisees."
30. Discussion in Horsley, *Jesus and the Spiral of Violence*, 90–93.

imagine the possible existence of a kind of popular imperialism in ancient Judean as well as in modern European history, it is more likely that these wars, conducted with foreign mercenary troops, were unpopular as an economic burden on the people—Jerusalemites and the Judean peasantry alike. Herod, of course, whose reign was forcibly imposed by the Romans, was unpopular generally. The Pharisees, whose social location and functions mediated between rulers and ruled, were in a position to utilize the popular alienation against a ruler, which they did at least in the case of Alexander Jannaeus.

Beyond these passages in *Antiquities* 13, there is only one other account that mentions the influence of the Pharisees generally. Josephus indicates that the individual Pharisees Sammaias and/or Pollion had great influence with the people of Jerusalem in their advice to submit to Herod's rule (*Ant.* 14.176; 15.3). The general portrayal of the three forms of Judean "philosophy" in *War* says only that the Pharisees are the leading party and most accurate expounders of the laws (*War* 2.162). The concluding statement that "the Pharisees are affectionate with one another and cultivate harmonious relations with the community," in contrast with the Sadducees, who are rude to their peers, pertains to the inner-group relation, not their stance toward the society at large (*War* 2.166, which corresponds to the discussion of the inner-groups relations among the Essenes in *War* 2.120–127). The corresponding account of the three "philosophies" in *Antiquities*, however, does provide some (cryptic) comments on the Pharisees' influence.

> Because of these views they are, as a matter of fact, extremely influential among the townsfolk (*tois demois pithanotatoi*); and all prayers and sacred rites are performed according to their exposition (*exegesei*). This is the great tribute that the cities (*hai poleis*), by practicing the highest ideals both in their way of living and in their discourse/doctrines/teachings (*logois*) have paid to the excellence of the Pharisees ... The Sadducees accomplish practically noting, however, for whenever they assume some office, though they submit unwillingly, yet submit they do to the formulas of the Pharisees, since otherwise the masses would not tolerate them. (*Ant.* 18:15, 18)

Who, precisely, might "the citizenries" and "the cities" have been? If these were singular, the reference would clearly be to the Jerusalemites. Given the plural, is this just one more example of how Josephus is couching his account in terms typical of Hellenistic urban life in which various philosophies had influence across many cities (and among the Judeans it is no different)? The description as it stands does not appear to be intended as a concrete reference to Palestinian society in the same way as Josephus elsewhere refers to "cities and villages" or "villages and towns." It would be stretching the evidence therefore to claim that Josephus was here referring to social practice town by town. But it is clear that he is referring to collectives, to the public life of the "citizenries" and "cities," not to the conduct or lifestyles of individuals.

Thus if we cut through the apologetic formulation of the Pharisees and their influence on the populace in terms of a Hellenistic philosophical school, we can discern that the Pharisees' cultivation of the laws and promulgation of additional regulations had evidently become institutionalized in public life. Public rituals, vows, etc., have come to be conducted according to the Pharisees' exposition.

Once we have recognized that with the inseparability of religion and politics in such a traditional society the offices that the Sadducees might assume were by no means only cultic, then there is no need to think that the rulings of the Pharisees had come to govern only temple rituals. In a temple-state, the offices were what might be called high civic offices, the highest of which, such as the temple captain and temple treasurers, were held by members of the high priestly families. Josephus is thus saying that the Pharisaic regulations had come to dominate public life to such a degree that they affected even the conduct of certain high offices. This corresponds to the repeated statements that the Pharisees were the most accurate concerning the laws, and with the information that the *nomima* had been official state law, at least under John Hyrcanus and Salome Alexandra. During those generations those *nomima* would have gained a good deal of authority as from a succession of ancestors.

We should again, finally, take into account the perspective from which Josephus writes: that of a wealthy aristocrat who was a member of the governing circles before the great revolt and was well-connected with the imperial court afterwards. It is thus simply not possible to deduce from his accounts that either the Pharisees themselves or the regulations that they established for public life were popular with the people. All that we can say on the basis of Josephus's reports is that insofar as the *nomima* that the Pharisees promulgated for the people had been official state law and policy for a few generations, they may well have come to influence political affairs in Jerusalem. But Josephus does not inform us, at least directly, about the degree to which the populace's response may have been willing acceptance or grudging acquiescence.

5

THE PHARISEES IN THE POLITICS OF THE JUDEAN TEMPLE-STATE

THE PHARISEES FIRST EMERGE as an identifiable group in Judea under the Hasmonean high priests in mid-second century BCE. They evidently disappear from history after the Roman destruction of Jerusalem temple following the great revolt against Roman rule in 66–70 CE. Because the four principal sources for the Pharisees focus on different aspects of their views and activities, it is virtually impossible to gain a fuller picture of them or to trace their history. Partly because modern interpreters focused on the Pharisees as one of the sects of Judaism (as a religion) and partly because of uncertainties about how to take Josephus's accounts, scholars have debated whether the Pharisees were in fact engaged in politics. The discovery of the Dead Sea Scrolls has provided some clarity with new evidence that confirms Josephus's portrayal of the Pharisees' political engagement under the Hasmoneans.

Since Josephus is the principal source on the political role of the Pharisees through the contingencies and conflicts of a sequence of historical contexts, we will proceed by examining his accounts in literary and historical contexts. Josephus's accounts cannot be taken at face value, given certain legendary features and Josephus's own historiographic agenda. Yet when combined with supplementary sources they provide important information and clues about the Pharisees' roles and relationships that we can analyze fruitfully.

THE PHARISEES AND THE HASMONEAN REGIME

The historical context in which the Pharisees first appeared and achieved considerable prominence and influence in Judean affairs was that of the Hasmonean power consolidation and territorial expansion in the aftermath of the Maccabean Revolt. Conflict between factions within the regime and between the regime and the people became more pronounced as the Hasmoneans expanded their military forces with foreign mercenaries, extended their conquests over nearby peoples, and imitated the style and practices of the Hellenistic imperial regimes that they replaced in Palestine. It is only in this context that we now attempt to understand Josephus's representation of the Pharisees as one of the factions in the shifting balance of power in the Hasmonean regime in Jerusalem.

Origins of the Pharisees and Other Factions under an Upstart High Priesthood

Allusions in certain Dead Sea Scrolls along with Josephus's accounts now make it possible to trace the origins of the Pharisees and the Sadducees as well as the Essenes (thought to be related to the Qumran community) to the beginnings of the Hasmonean dynasty in the mid-second century BCE.

Under the interventionist Seleucid emperor Antiochus Epiphanes, the Zadokite priestly family of Oniads lost control of the high priesthood to a Hellenizing reform faction who offered more revenue to the imperial regime. Following the extreme turmoil of resisting Hellenizing reform and the prolonged guerrilla struggle led by Judas the Maccabee against the imperial armies' attempts to subdue the resistance, either the high priesthood remained vacant, or its incumbent was ineffectual. In the imperial power vacuum following the death of Antiochus Epiphanes, Judas's brother and successor Jonathan, maneuvering between rivals for power in the Seleucid Empire, managed to get himself appointed to the high priesthood in 152 BCE (1 Macc 10:18–21). The ordinary priestly family of Hasmoneans thus usurped the high priestly office previously held by a hereditary Zadokite family. Jonathan's acceptance of the office from the imperial regime would surely have been seen by many engaged in the struggle against the Seleucid armies alongside the Hasmonean (Maccabean) leadership as a reversion to the imperial dependency and manipulation they had rebelled against.

It is surely significant that Josephus interrupts his narrative of Jonathan's maneuvering among the great powers of the time (roughly from 161 to 143 BCE) for his first brief account of the three main "ways of life" among the Judeans.

> Now at this time there were three schools of thought (*haireseis*; ways of life) among the Judeans, which held different views concerning human affairs; the first being the Pharisees, the second the Sadducees, and the third the Essenes. (*Ant.* 13.171–173)

At this point he briefly mentions only their different views on the Greek philosophical issue of fate versus free will. His placement of this reference to the three *haireseis* at this point in his narrative, however, suggests that some or perhaps all three of these "ways of life" or "schools of thought" came into existence in response to Jonathan's assumption of the high priesthood and consolidation of power in Judea (1 Macc 10:15—11:37; Josephus, *Ant.* 13.80–170).

Allusions in key texts from the Dead Sea Scrolls confirm these historical origins and potentially explain the roles and positions at least of the Pharisees and the group that produced the Scrolls. Archaeological analysis of the site where the Scrolls were discovered dated the origin of the dissident movement in the mid-second century, just about the time that Jonathan and then his brother Simon had ascended to the high priesthood. The Damascus Document (CD) dates the beginning of a movement related to the Qumran community to the "age of wrath," 390 years after the conquest of Jerusalem by Nebuchadnezzar, king of Babylon. This would bring us roughly into the early second century, when the crisis of reform and resistance evolved in Jerusalem.[1] The *pesher* (interpretation or application) of Hab 2:5–6 refers to

> the Wicked Priest who was called by the name of truth when he first arose. But when he ruled over Israel his heart became proud, and he forsook God and betrayed the precepts for the sake of riches. He robbed and amassed the riches of the men of violence who rebelled against God . . . and he took the wealth of the peoples . . . (1QpHab 8:4–13; cf. 9:5–12; 12:2–9; trans. Vermes)

This evidently refers to Jonathan's move from leader of the people to "ruler of Israel" as the new high priest, now expropriating the wealth of the previously exploitative Hellenizing reformists and plundering and taking spoil from the nearby cities that he attacked.[2] Because of his persecution of the teacher and his covenantal community he would "be delivered into the hand of the violent of the peoples" (4Q171 4:6–12). Indeed, Jonathan

---

1. Vermes, *Dead Sea Scrolls*, 58.
2. Vermes, *Dead Sea Scrolls*, 60–62.

was eventually defeated, captured, and killed by Trypho, one of the usurpers and pretenders to the tottering Seleucid regime. Other passages in the scrolls vilify the new high priestly incumbent for abandoning the proper way of running the temple cult and for persecuting their group of "the sons of Zadok," that is "Zadokites." The "righteous teacher" (who is apparently a priest, and probably a Zadokite, as in 1QpHab 2:8; 4Q171 3:15) and his followers might well have been some of the (Zadokite) priests and associated scribes who were displaced when Jonathan and his faction took over the high priesthood.[3]

The *pesher* (interpretation/application) of passages in Nahum (4Q169) and other texts castigate "the seekers of smooth things" or "smooth interpreters," and "Ephraim," which are thought to be code names for the Pharisees.[4] These allusions in the Dead Sea Scrolls, apparently produced by the community at Qumran, thus provide several references that confirm the impression from Josephus's first mention of the three Judean "ways of life" or "schools of thought": that the Pharisees, Sadducees, and Essenes all originated early in Hasmonean times, perhaps in response to Jonathan's assumption of the high priesthood.

Josephus's and Related Accounts of the Pharisees under Hasmonean Rulers

A survey of Josephus's accounts of the Pharisees' relations with three key Hasmonean rulers, supplemented by parallel sources, provides the basis for an assessment of their political role and activity under the Hasmonean regime. We can examine each of them in the context of Josephus's broader narrative of this watershed period of Judean history.

Hasmonean expansion began under the warrior-chieftains who usurped the high priesthood, Jonathan and Simon, with their takeover of three toparchies in Samaria and key fortresses toward the Mediterranean. From their years of military struggle, moreover, they had established a professional army of Judeans, with which they could at points tip the balance between rival Seleucid imperial factions, further consolidating their own power in Palestine (1 Macc 10:36–37; 11:42–51; 15:26). Simon's son and successor, John Hyrcanus (135–104 BCE), dramatically escalated Hasmonean expansion. He bolstered the army, already the basis of Hasmonean power,

---

3. Schiffman, *Reclaiming*, 87–95.

4. It may well be that "Manasseh" and his dignitaries in the *pesher* (interpretation/application) on Nahum are references to the Sadducees. Vermes, *Dead Sea Scrolls*, 62; Schiffman, *Reclaiming*, 84–87.

with foreign mercenaries, an addition he funded initially by plundering the tomb of David (*War* 1.261; *Ant.* 13.249). As Josephus comments, the further decline of the Seleucid imperial regime "gave Hyrcanus the leisure to exploit Judea undisturbed, with the result that he amassed a limitless amount of resources" (*Ant.* 13.273). Using his professional army, he subdued the Idumeans to the south, allowing them to remain on their land if they became circumcised and observed "the laws of the Judeans" (*War* 1.63; *Ant.* 13.257). In a sustained campaign he conquered Samaria and Gerizim to the north, destroying the city and the Samaritan temple, and subjugating the people (*War* 1.64–65; *Ant.* 13.255, 275–279). He also conquered several cities to the east of the Jordan and took over Scythopolis and the fertile lands of the Great Plain, thus further enhancing his revenues from those traditionally royal estates. At the end his account of Hyrcanus in both the *War* and the *Antiquities*, Josephus eulogizes him as the high point of the Hasmonean dynasty, having combined three of the greatest privileges: rule of the people, the office of high priest, and prophecy (*War* 1.68; *Ant.* 13.299).

This is the context in which Josephus places his account of the clash between Hyrcanus and the Pharisees, with its important implications for the central political role they had come to play prior to the falling-out. In his earlier account in the *War* he wrote that Hyrcanus and his sons' successes "provoked an insurrection among of the people (*epichorion*, i.e., native Judeans/Jerusalemites, in contrast to the peoples and cities that he and his sons had just been subduing), large numbers of whom held meetings to oppose them and continued to agitate, until the smoldering flames burst out in open war and the rebels were defeated" (*War* 1.67). At the corresponding point in his narrative in the *Antiquities* (13.288), Josephus elaborates in more precise terms with a story (13.289–296) and a comment (13.297–299). Note that the story Josephus repeats in 13.289–296 does not fit his framing (13.288), which even contradicts it.

> The envy of the Judeans was aroused against him ... Especially hostile to him were the Pharisees, one of the schools of thought among the Judeans, as we have explained above. So strong is their influence among the populace that even when they speak against a king and against a high priest they are immediately believed. (*Ant.* 13.288)
>
> Now Hyrcanus was also a disciple of theirs, and he was greatly loved by them. And he invited them to a feast and entertained them hospitably. When he saw how delighted they were, he started telling them that they knew he wished to be righteous and to do all things so as to please God and them (for the

Pharisees pursue a certain way of life [*hoi gar Pharisaioi philosophousin*]); nevertheless, he requested that if they noticed him doing anything wrong and veering from the path of righteousness, they were to lead him back and restore him to it. But they attested to his consummate virtue and he was pleased by their compliments.

However, one of the guests, named Eleazar, who was malicious by nature and took pleasure in dissension, said, "Since you have asked to know the truth, if you want to be righteous, then relinquish the high priesthood and be content with ruling the people (*to archein tou laou*)." When Hyrcanus asked him the reason why he should relinquish the high priesthood, he replied, "because we hear from the elders that your mother was a captive in the reign of Antiochus Epiphanes." But the story was false, and Hyrcanus became furious with the man and the Pharisees were all very indignant.

Then someone from the school (*hairesis*) of the Sadducees, who espouse a view/way of life opposed to that of the Pharisees, a certain Jonathan, who was among the most intimate friends [advisers/confidants] of Hyrcanus, began to say that Eleazar had uttered his slanders in agreement with the collective opinion of all the Pharisees. And this would become clear to him, Jonathan said, if he asked them what punishment was appropriate for what had been said.

When Hyrcanus asked the Pharisees what they considered a worthy punishment, . . . they proposed lashes and chains; for it did not seem right to punish someone with death on account of verbal abuse and, in any case, the Pharisees are naturally merciful in the matter of punishments. At this response, Hyrcanus became very angry and assumed that the man had slandered him with their approval.

Jonathan exacerbated his anger greatly and achieved the following result: he induced Hyrcanus to join the party of the Sadducees, to abandon the Pharisees, to repeal the ordinances that they had established for the people (*ta te hup' katastathenta nomima te demo katalusai*), and to punish those who observed these ordinances. This is the reason, then, that hatred developed among the populace toward him and his sons. (*Ant*. 291–296)

Now I want to explain here that the Pharisees passed on to the people certain ordinances from a succession of the fathers, which are not written down in the laws of Moses. For this reason the group [*genos*] of the Sadducees dismisses these [ordinances], holding that it is necessary to observe only those ordinances (regulations) that are written, but not to observe those from the tradition of the fathers. Also concerning these issues the two parties came to have conflicts and major differences, the Sadducees persuading only the wealthy but with no following among the people, while the Pharisees have the support of the populace. But of these two groups and of the Essenes, an accurate account has been given in the second book of my *Judaica*. (*Ant.* 13.297–298; translation adapted from Mason, who adapted from LCL)

A very similar story in rabbinic literature was told about Hyrcanus's son, Alexander Jannaeus, suggesting that the main part of Josephus's account here was a standard story about the Pharisees' relations with Hasmonean kings that continued to be told centuries later.

It is taught: The story is told that Yannai [Jannaeus] the King went to Kohalit in the wilderness and conquered there sixty towns. When he returned, he rejoiced greatly, and invited all the sages of Israel.

He said to them, "Our forefathers would eat salt fish when they were engaged in the building of the Holy House. Let us also eat salt fish as a memorial to our forefathers."

So they brought up salt fish on golden tables. And they ate.

There was there a certain scoffer. Evil-hearted and empty-headed, and Eleazar ben Poirah said to Yannai the King, "O King Yannai, the hearts of the Pharisees are [set] against you."

"What shall I do?"

"Test them by the plate that is between your eyes [the high priest's medallion]."

He tested them by the plate that was between his eyes.

There was a certain sage, and Judah b. Gedidiah was his name. Judah b. Gedidiah said to Yannai the king, "O King Yannai, let suffice for you the crown of sovereignty [kingship]. Leave the crown of the [high] priesthood for the seed of Aaron." For people said that his [Yannai's] mother had been taken captive in Modin [and was therefore suspected of having been raped]. The charge was investigated and not found [sustained]. The sages of Israel departed in anger.

Eleasar b. Poirah then said to Yannai the king, "O King Yannai, That is the law [not here specified, as the punishment inflicted on Judah] even for the ordinary folk in Israel. But you are King and High Priest—should that be your law too?"

"What should I do?"

"If you take my advice, you will trample them down."

> "But what will become of the Torah?"
>
> "Lo. It is rolled up and lying in the corner. Whoever wants to learn, let him come and learn."
>
> The evil blossomed through Eleazar b. Poirah. All the sages of Israel [= the Pharisees] were killed.
>
> The world was desolate until Simeon b. Shetah came and restored the Torah to its place. (b. Qiddushin 66a)[5]

Since the basis of the challenge to the Hasmonean high priestly ruler, that the mother had been a captive in wartime, is more likely for Hyrcanus's mother than for Jannai's, it seems somewhat more likely that Josephus tells the story about the appropriate Hasmonean. On the other hand, Josephus has unnamed opponents of Alexander Jannaeus's charge that he was descended from captives and therefore unfit to hold the high priestly office and officiate at sacrifices (*Ant.* 13.373), paralleling the rabbinic legend. In any case, since the Hasmonean ruler's power in Judea itself was rooted in his occupying the office of high priesthood, the challenge to the legitimacy of the ruler, who had to be born of a properly virgin mother, threatened to undermine his rule.

Whether or not the Pharisees' break with the Hasmonean rulers began under John Hyrcanus, both Josephus and the Dead Sea Scrolls, like the rabbinic legend, portray sharp opposition between the Pharisees and Hyrcanus's son Alexander Jannaeus (103–76 BCE). Like his brother Aristobulus, who had expanded Hasmonean rule into Galilee, Jannaeus assumed the title King as well as High Priest. The son also continued the expansionist wars of his father, attacking and taking many of the Hellenistic cities around the perimeter of Judea, Samaria, and Galilee, again depending heavily on his mercenary troops (now Pisidians and Cilicians, i.e., "Greeks"). As noted in Chapter 1 above, his own people arose in revolt, even pelting him with citrons as he sacrificed at the altar at the festival of Tabernacles. In retaliation, says Josephus, "he killed some six thousand of them" (*War* 1.88–89; *Ant.* 13.372–374). In the resulting civil war, his opponents called in one of the rival Seleucid pretenders, Demetrius III of Damascus. After Jannaeus prevailed, he "ordered some eight hundred of the Judeans to be crucified, and slaughtered their children and wives before the eyes of the still living wretches" (*Ant.* 13.376–380; *War* 1.96–98), whereupon some eight thousand of his opponents fled and remained in exile for the rest of his reign (*Ant.* 13.383).

Although he never mentions the Pharisees in these accounts of opposition to Jannaeus, Josephus does suggest that they were involved. He has

---

5. Translation from Neusner, *From Politics to Piety*, 59–60.

Jannaeus, at the end of his further sequence of wars of conquest, advise his wife and successor, Salome Alexandra, to "yield a certain amount of power to the Pharisees" as the political strategy that will assure her own hold on power.

> These men, he assured her, had so much influence with the people (*ethnos*) that they could injure those whom they hated and help those to whom they were friendly; for they held the complete confidence of the masses . . . And he himself, he added, had come into conflict with the people because he had treated these men so badly/arrogantly. (*Ant.* 13.401–402)

References in the Dead Sea Scrolls now confirm that the Pharisees, indicated in the code-name "seekers of smooth things," were opponents and victims of Jannaeus, indicated by "the young lion" in the text of Nahum.

> Demetrius king of Greece sought, on the counsel of those who seek smooth things, to enter Jerusalem. [But God did not permit the city to be delivered] into the hands of the kings of Greece . . . *The lion tears enough for its cubs* . . . (Nah 2:12a). Interpreted, this concerns the furious young lion [who executes revenge] on those who seek smooth things and hangs men alive, . . . [a thing never done] formerly in Israel. Because of a man hanged on [the] tree . . . (4QpNah 1:3–8)

The same *pesher* (interpretation) of Nahum from the priestly-scribal community at Qumran points to the political role of "those who seek smooth things" as advisers to rulers:

> (after citing Nah 3:4) Interpreted, this concerns those who lead Ephraim astray, who lead many astray through their false teaching, their lying tongue, and deceitful lips—kings, princes, priests, and people, together with the stranger who joins them. Cities and families shall perish through their counsel; honourable men and rulers shall fall through their tongue's [decision]. (4QpNah 2:7–10)

Salome Alexandra apparently took her husband Jannaeus's advice and restored the Pharisees to a prominent role in the Hasmonean regime. Josephus presents closely parallel accounts in his two histories that reveal his or his source's disdain for both the Pharisees and a woman as ruler.

Growing up around her [Salome Alexandra] into power [*exousia*] were the Pharisees, a troop/company of Judeans purportedly/seeming to be more religiously observant and more accurate exponents of the laws than the other [Judeans]. To them, being herself intensely religious, she listened with too great deference; while they, gradually exploiting/taking advantage of the ingenuous woman, became at length the real administrators of the whole [state], at liberty to banish and to recall, to loose and to bind, whom they would. In short, the enjoyments of royal authority were theirs; its expenses and burdens fell to Alexandra . . . But if she ruled the nation, the Pharisees ruled her.

Thus they put to death Diogenes, a[n intimate] friend of Alexander [her husband], accusing him of having advised the king to crucify his eight hundred victims. They further urged Alexandra to make away with the other who had instigated Alexander to punish those men; and as she from superstitious motives always gave way, they proceeded to kill whomsoever they would. The most eminent thus imperiled sought refuge with Aristobulus . . . (*War* 1.110–114)

Alexandra permitted the Pharisees to do as they liked in all matters, and also commanded the people to obey them . . . [added from LCL: and whatever regulations/ordinances [*nomima*] the Pharisees introduced according to the ancestral tradition (*nomima . . . kata ten patroan paradosin*) had been abolished by her father-in-law, Hyrcanus, these she again restored/established (*apokatestesen*).] And so, while she had the title of sovereign (*to onoma tes basileias*), the Pharisees had the power (*ten dynamin*). For example, they recalled exiles and freed prisoners, and, in a word, in no way differed from absolute rulers [*despoton*] . . . And throughout the country there was quiet except for the Pharisees; for they worked upon the feelings of the queen and tried to persuade her to kill those who had urged Alexander to put the eight hundred to death. Later they themselves slaughtered one of them, named Diogenes, and his death was followed by that of one after another, until the *dynatoi* came to the palace . . . (to cry out for protection from the Pharisees). (*Ant.* 13.408–412)[6]

The Pharisees do not appear thereafter in Josephus's narrative of the struggle between rival brothers in the last generation of Hasmoneans, as the Romans moved decisively to take over the eastern Mediterranean.

---

6. From Mason's translation in *Josephus on the Pharisees*, 253.

THE PHARISEES IN THE POLITICS OF THE HASMONEAN REGIME

If we place credence in Josephus's accounts, as confirmed at points by references in the Dead Sea Scrolls, it is evident that the Pharisees were prominent in the politics of the Hasmonean regime for almost the whole of its ninety-year duration. The general picture one receives from Josephus's accounts, now confirmed by the *pesher* on Nahum found in cave 4 at Qumran, is that the Pharisees (or "smooth interpreters") functioned basically as advisers to "kings, princes, priests, and people, . . . honorable men and rulers." Their position and role in the political-economic-religious structure of Judea closely resembles how Ben Sira represented that of scribes/sages (Sir 38:24—39:4). The Pharisees appear to have been scribal retainers of the Hasmonean temple-state. At the beginning (perhaps through most) of Hyrcanus's reign and again in the reign of Salome Alexandra, they were in favor at court, their legal traditions being included in state law. For three or four decades in-between, at the end of Hyrcanus's reign and through all of Alexander Jannaeus's reign, they were out of power. Far from simply withdrawing from Judean politics, however, they apparently figured prominently in the active opposition to the regime, its policies and practices, particularly those of Alexander Jannaeus.

During the time they were in favor with the Hasmonean rulers, they were far more than simply advisers to the rulers or mere custodians of Judean cultural and legal traditions. Josephus's accounts make fairly clear that they were vested with considerable political authority. By tradition the priesthood had authority over Judean Torah, and the high priesthood exercised that authority (Sir 45:6-22). Judging from the terms Josephus uses, John Hyrcanus or his Hasmonean predecessors who established themselves as high priests after the Maccabean Revolt had established the *nomima* that the Pharisees received from the ancestors as part of official state law. That is what we must assume to make sense of the term Josephus uses when Hyrcanus breaks with them. He "abrogated" or "rescinded" (*katalusai*) the *nomima* which the Pharisees had promulgated/established for the people. Later, when Salome Alexandra restored them to power, she "restored/reestablished" (*apokatestesen*) the Pharisees' legal traditions, apparently as state law. Not only that, but Josephus indicates that the power of the temple-state stood behind the Pharisees' regulations. Salome Alexandra, says Josephus, "commanded the people to obey them as having authority" (*peitharchein*). Correspondingly, when Hyrcanus had replaced the Pharisees with the Sadducees, the power of the state was used against their influence, as he rescinded "the regulations the Pharisees had established for the people" (*Ant.* 13.296).

The terms Josephus uses in description of the *nomima* of the Pharisees makes sense precisely in that context. The term *nomima* usually refers to a people's customs, that is, social customs or norms that had become standard and traditional from social practice, not by means of legislation (again in *Life* 191 it is the Pharisees' *nomima*). That they were "handed down from a succession of the ancestors" fits this sense of "customs." In his representation of the Pharisees at Hyrcanus's court, however, Josephus says that the Pharisees had "established" these *nomima* "for the people" (*demos*), i.e., in the sense of "constituting" the customs as regulations or ordinances for public life. Similarly, when Salome Alexandra reestablishes the Pharisees in power, Josephus refers to those rulings from the tradition of the fathers that Pharisees "had introduced" (*eisenegkan*). The Pharisees thus apparently exercised legal authority under Hyrcanus and again under Salome Alexandra, as both delegated and backed up by the head of state.

When in favor with the Hasmonean rulers, the Pharisees also appear to have wielded a certain amount of power generally, not only in "establishing rulings for the people." This is not simply an application of the concepts of modern-day political science, but is indicated in the terms of Josephus's accounts as well as in the relationships he portrays between the Pharisees and Hyrcanus and Salome Alexandra. For a ruler such as Hyrcanus to be a "disciple" of the proponents of a "philosophy" ("school of thought"/"way of life") in the Hellenistic world, and for his philosophical mentors to "love him," meant that they were his closest advisers and that he was following their political policy. And that is exactly what Josephus suggests in Hyrcanus's statement to the Pharisees at the banquet scene (*Ant.* 13.289). Changing policy and changing advisers were two aspects of the same political shift, as Josephus's account of Hyrcanus's break with the Pharisees and shift to the Sadducees suggests.

Under Alexander Jannaeus, the Pharisees were not only alienated from the regime but were apparently prominent in the widespread opposition. The *pesher* on Nahum found in cave 4 at Qumran now confirms the previous hypothesis that the Pharisees were (among) Jannaeus's opponents that the king killed so brutally. It seems clear from Josephus's accounts that opposition was prolonged and widespread, escalating into full-scale civil war, hence involving other elements of the populace as well as the Pharisees. It also appears that the opposition was at least partly in reaction against Alexander Jannaeus's persistent expansionist wars. It is also clear that Alexander became brutally repressive, deploying his Pisidian and Cilician mercenaries against his own people (*War* 1.88–89; *Ant.* 13.372–374). Both Josephus and the Nahum Pesher indicate explicitly that "the furious young lion's" vengeful crucifixion of hundreds of his opponents was unprecedented and shocking. "As a result of his excessive cruelty he was nicknamed 'the Thracian' by the Judeans" (*Ant.* 13.382; the Thracians were known for their ferocity). The Nahum Pesher presents the horrific crucifixion explicitly as vengeance on the "seekers of smooth things." It seems likely also that Pharisees who escaped this mass crucifixion were among the thousands who, says Josephus, fled into exile for the rest of his reign (*War* 1.98; *Ant.* 13.383).

In Josephus's accounts of the Pharisees' return to favor under Salome Alexandra, it is even clearer that they wielded a certain power in the regime. He has Alexander Jannaeus say explicitly to his queen and designated successor: she should "yield" or "hand over" a certain amount of authority/power (*exousia tina paraschein*). Josephus is surely exaggerating that Salome Alexandra placed in their hands "all . . . things concerning the kingdom/royal power" (*panta . . . ta peri tes basileias*). We probably get more of the sense of their authority, derivative from the queen's, when he writes that she made them her "friends" (*philous*, 13.405), that is, intimate confidants and advisers. The Pharisees may well have become the "real administrators of the whole (kingdom)," that is, in domestic affairs (*War* 1.111). It is surely rhetorical hyperbole when Josephus says that "while she had (only) the title of sovereign, the Pharisees had the power" (13.409; cf. "the royal prerogatives were theirs, while the expenses and burdens were Alexandra's"; *War* 1.111).

Just how powerful they were and were not with Salome Alexandra, however, is indicated fairly clearly in the ensuing account of the power struggle between the Pharisees and the *dynatoi*, the high (military) officers of the recently deceased Alexander Jannaeus and their champion, Salome Alexandra's son Aristobulus (*War* 1.113-114; *Ant.* 13.410-417). Particularly under Alexander Jannaeus, the Hasmonean regime consisted primarily of military forces, whose commanders were also the king's top advisers. The Pharisees tried to persuade Salome Alexandra to kill/execute "those who had urged Alexander to put the eight hundred to death." They themselves, says Josephus, "slaughtered" Diogenes and then others. But the Pharisees could press their revenge only so far against the countervailing forces of the regime. Through Aristobulus's intervention with Salome Alexandra, Alexander Jannaeus's former high officers, still apparently important figures in Jerusalem, persuaded the queen to deploy them in the garrisons of the fortresses around the country. Power was thus somewhat delicately balanced, and it was not difficult for Aristobulus to make a move to seize power even before his mother's death by mobilizing his father's military officers (*dynatoi*), an alternative power base in waiting in those nearby fortresses (*Ant.* 13.422–429; *War* 1.117).

Of course there may have been other groups, such as the Sadducees, also playing a role in the balance of power in, or against, the Hasmonean regime during Alexander's and Salome Alexandra's reigns. We shall never know for sure, because our principal source, Josephus, tends to mention only the major political players at the center of power. Yet given that tendency, it is surely a significant indicator when he does give the Pharisees such a prominent role in his narrative: this suggests that they were indeed one of the principal forces in Judean politics at the time, whether as high-ranking advisers with authority in domestic matters under Salome Alexandra, or as opponents of the regime, when earlier "they suffered many injuries" at the hands of Alexander Jannaeus.

One thing that is quite clear from Josephus's accounts is that there was conflict, sometimes flaring up into virtual civil war: on one side Hasmonean rulers, their high military retainers, and the Sadducees; and on the other side, the Pharisees and apparently others—for fifty years, from John Hyrcanus to Aristobulus II. What policy and practices of the Hasmoneans were so objectionable to the Pharisees, and what concerns did the Pharisees have that the Hasmoneans found unacceptable? It may be possible to discern some of the reasons for conflict between the Pharisees and Hasmoneans.

From the story Josephus tells of the break between Hyrcanus and the Pharisees, it appears that the initiative came from Hyrcanus, particularly if Eleazar, who criticized the high priest to his face, was not a Pharisee (Josephus's account does not identify him as such). If the initiative did come from Hyrcanus, he must have had reason or motive for the break. Josephus's accounts attribute the envy or uprising/insurrection/sedition (*stasis*) of the people against Hyrcanus to his (and his sons') "success(es)" (*eupragia*; *War* 1.67; *Ant.* 13.288). That suggests a very likely combination of related issues that the Pharisees and others were concerned about.

One would have been simply the Hasmoneans' consolidation of power, especially their assumption of the high priesthood. The so-called Maccabean brothers came to power as popular leaders of a coalition of ordinary priests, scribes, and peasants against (usurping) high priests who had attained power by manipulation of and collaboration with the Seleucid imperial regime. That coalition apparently fell apart, however, when Jonathan and Simon made themselves high priests through their skillful maneuvering with rival Seleucid pretenders. That was precisely what the Maccabees and their allies had fought against, that is, ambitious Judean strongmen gaining power over temple and people by special arrangements with the imperial regime that violated tradition and worked to the people's detriment. The upstart

Hasmonean high priests, moreover, expanded their now-professional army with mercenary troops and repeatedly used it to further consolidate their power in a steadily expanding Judea.

Second, the Hasmoneans also quickly broadened the scope of the high priest's power. As long as the Jerusalem high priesthood was sponsored by the empire, in effect constituting a subdivision of the imperial administration, the power of the Jerusalem rulers was checked by imperial constraints, their prerogatives confined to administration of the temple-state limited to the tiny territory of Judea. However, with the demise of imperial power, and Hasmoneans moving to fill the void, they emerged with a certain degree of imperial power themselves. In the second and third generations of their rule, the Hasmoneans made two dramatic moves. They expanded their rule far beyond the tiny area of Judea to include Idumea as well as Samaria, the Great Plain, and Galilee. And both of Hyrcanus's sons were so bold as to assume the imperial, royal title of king in addition to that of high priest. This proved a striking contrast to the sensitivity to public opinion that their grandfather, Simon, and his advisers had felt it necessary to exercise in the grand ceremonial consolidation of centralized power toward the end of Simon's reign as high priest roughly thirty-five of so years earlier (and in the Maccabean propaganda of 1 Maccabees). At the Great Assembly of priests and people and rulers of the people and the elders from the countryside, Simon was proclaimed "high priest" and "leader" and "(military) governor" (i.e., carefully avoiding "king"), in charge of the weapons and strongholds and administration of the country as well the temple. After Hyrcanus's break with the Pharisees and alliance with the party of priestly aristocrats, Aristobulus and Alexander Jannaeus both took the title of king. Opposition to this consolidation of power and its imperial symbolization as kingship persisted throughout the Hasmonean period. This is evident in the delegation that appealed to the Roman warlord Pompey, as the Hasmonean regime fell apart, that "the people" (*ethnos*) did not want to be ruled by a king, the ancestral tradition being rule by the priests.

Third, the objection to the "success" of Hyrcanus and his sons suggests that the people and the Pharisees also opposed their military conquests of surrounding areas and peoples. The almost continuous warfare, through several decades, would have meant a considerable economic and manpower drain on and hardship for the people of Judea, offsetting whatever pride may have accompanied Judea's new international prominence. The prominent role of foreign mercenaries in the regime and its continuous conquests can hardly have been popular.

Fourth, the later Hasmoneans' transformation of their regime in the direction of a Hellenistic kingdom must have seemed to utterly contradict the traditional Judean way of life that their ancestors had been fighting for in the Maccabean Revolt. Although we can no longer view that revolt only or even primarily in terms of an essentialist Judaism against an essentialist Hellenism, conflict between traditional Judean and Hellenistic political-religious forms was involved. Under the later Hasmoneans, however, Greek became the dominant language at court, the Cilician and Pisidian mercenaries were presumably Greek-speaking, and Aristobulus even took the nickname of Philhellene.

In connection with the Pharisees' continuing conflict with the Hasmonean regime, we should consider their relations with the people. Josephus's accounts of their break with Hyrcanus and their return to power under Salome Alexandra in the *Antiquities* are two of only three passages where he mentions explicitly their relation with the people (*Ant.* 13.288, 298, 401). A comparison with the third (*Ant.* 18.15) is immediately instructive. In the third passage, in one of his presentations of the Pharisees as a "philosophy," he says that "they happen to be credible among the townspeople" (*kai di' auta tois te demois pithanotatoi tygchanousin* . . .), which is connected directly with their views on matters such as fate and free will, rewards and punishment. And he immediately explains that prayers and sacred rites are performed according to their interpretation/rulings. Their popular credibility here is far removed from the rough-and-tumble of political conflict and civil strife. In the two passages about their conflict with the Hasmoneans, where the wording is as similar as it is different from that in *Ant.* 18.15, their "credibility" with "the populace" (*malista gar pisteuesthai para to plethei*) is a direct threat to the regime.

Given the sweeping claims that previous generations of interpreters have made for the Pharisees having been popular with or having had the backing of the people on the basis of these three passing comments by Josephus,[7] it is significant to note what Josephus is not saying in any of them. He does not say that they are leaders of the people or that the people believe, obey, and practice what they teach or legislate. His passing comments in the passages concerning Hyrcanus, Alexander, and Salome Alexandra are specific to their conflict with the Hasmoneans. And he suggests that under the Hasmoneans the Pharisees had sufficient credibility with the people that they could make the difference in the stability and survival of the regime.

What is specific to Josephus's passing comments about the Pharisees' role under the Hasmonean regime can be comprehended in terms of recent studies of the political-economic structure of pre-industrial "royal" or

---

7. These claims were repeated again and again in Mason, *Flavius Josephus on the Phariseess*.

"capital" cities. Ancient Jerusalem as the site of the Hasmonean temple-state was certainly not a large royal or imperial metropolis, but it had many of the characteristics of such urban centers of power.[8]

First, as Josephus's accounts of the Hasmoneans—and again later of Herod the Great and the high priestly aristocracy under the Roman governors—indicate, it was important, indeed essential, for the regime to have the support, or at least the acceptance, of the "common people" or "populace" (*plethos*). The "populace" or "people" (as opposed to the priests and/or the "nobles/powerful" in Josephus's narratives) would have been primarily the Jerusalemite artisans and laborers who basically served the needs of the temple, court, and government operations. The vast majority of Judeans, like the vast majority of people in any traditional agrarian society, would have been preoccupied in agricultural pursuits and village life at some distance from the capital, where politics was made. With the annual pilgrimage festivals such as Passover, Pentecost, and Tabernacles, of course, Judean peasants were in an unusual situation of potentially playing a political role as part of the urban crowd at festival times. And they could have been among those who pelted Alexander Jannaeus with citrons as he sacrificed at the altar during the festival of Tabernacles. Ordinarily, however, it was the urban populace (the "mob") itself that the regime needed to satisfy minimally in order to carry out its designs, such as foreign conquest.

Second, the Hasmonean rulers and their high-ranking staff would have had little or no direct contact with the common people (except their personal servants at court). The public role of the high priest was ceremonial. Otherwise the high priestly aristocracy and their high officers enjoyed their perks and privileges, from revenues derived from the peasantry and perhaps warfare, in the isolation of their mansions, which became increasingly elaborate during the Hasmonean and Herodian periods. Reliance on the Sadducees did little to mitigate the polarization since, as Josephus points out, the Sadducees had the confidence of the wealthy alone, but no following among the populace (*Ant.* 13.298). Moreover, the Hasmonean rulers were engaged in military expeditions much of the time. As the regime became increasingly repressive under Alexander Jannaeus, of course, relations between regime and the Jerusalem crowd took the form of riots countered by military violence, beatings, and executions.

Third, the people in the middle were the Pharisees, perhaps along with other scribal circles and to a degree the ordinary priests, many of whom apparently lived in the city. These constituted the only possible mediating force

---

8. Rudé, *The Crowd*; Hobsbawm, *Primitive Rebels*, chap. 7; applied to Jerusalem under Roman rule in Horsley, *Jesus and the Spiral*, 90–93.

between regime and the urban common people. Economically dependent on the regime, they carried out certain governing functions. As representatives of the regime, they came into direct contact with the populace (at least the Jerusalem populace), although it is difficult to discern the specific ways in which this contact happened. In this connection it is significant to take another look at Ben Sira's teaching. On the one hand, he is clearly uneasy about the designs and arbitrary power of the rulers above him, for whom he works. He sees clearly that there is no love lost between the rulers and the people. Yet he exhorts the people to faithfully render up their tithes and offerings to the temple and high priesthood, on which he is economically dependent. At the same time, he is sympathetic with the plight of the poor people and teaches his students that it is part of the role of the scribe/sage to mediate between the powerful and the powerless, in order to mitigate the worst effects of abuse on the poor by powerful rulers and their officers. The series of woes against the wealthy and powerful in the Epistle of Enoch suggests similarly that a scribal circle adopted a mediating position between the rulers and the people whom they exploited.

These features of the structural division in Judea between rulers and people in the Jerusalem temple-state, increasingly polarized by the Hasmonean wars of conquest, suggest that the mediating role of the Pharisees could well have been an important factor. They had at least some contact with the Jerusalem populace. In their mediating role they could well have become a decisive factor in whether the Jerusalem populace would acquiesce in or oppose the regime.

To conclude this analysis, in the Judean temple-state before the Maccabean Revolt, scribal circles played a mediating role between the high priestly rulers and the people of Jerusalem and Judea. This can be seen both in the teachings of Ben Sira, who apparently collaborated with the incumbent Oniad priests, and in literary remains of the dissident Enoch circle, whose members condemned aristocratic abuses. Within a generation after the Maccabean Revolt, the Pharisees were playing a similar role under the Hasmoneans. Josephus's accounts of the Pharisees' roles under John Hyrcanus and Salome Alexandra, however, indicate a far more important administrative function and more effective political power than anything that Ben Sira suggests for earlier scribes/sages. The Pharisees' mediating role, in fact, appears to have become one of the keys to the regime's ability to control the populace, as Josephus has Alexander Jannaeus say to his wife and successor, Salome Alexandra. The serious conflicts between Hasmonean rulers and the Pharisees suggest that if the Pharisees were on the outs with the regime, they might well be drumming up support for their own position and trouble for the regime. But if they were given an active role in the regime, then they themselves would have had an interest in ensuring support among the populace.

PHARISEES UNDER HEROD

For the period of Herod's reign Josephus offers only accounts of individual figures named as Pharisees and a few brief accounts of incidents in the Pharisees' relation with Herod and his court. These references suggest that Pharisees no longer played anything like the influential political role they exercised under the Hasmonean regime. This should not be surprising, however, once we recognize that the Romans and Herod imposed a new political structure on greater Judea. While Herod retained the temple and the high priesthood as integral instruments of his rule, he also installed his own royal administration above the apparatus of the temple-state. As scribal retainers of the temple-state, the Pharisees thus underwent a dramatic "demotion" in rank, function, influence, and prestige. Yet by no means did they withdraw from political affairs. Instead we find them involved in politics, particularly with regard to Herod's rise to power and his later autocratic measures.

Early in his rise to power, the arrogant and petulant young Herod had a major confrontation with the governing council in Jerusalem (*Ant.* 14.158–176) that involved one or more figures who were apparently Pharisees. His father, the Idumean strongman Antipater, who was really ruling Judea behind the façade of the figurehead king and high priest, Hyrcanus II, appointed Herod military governor of Galilee. In that capacity he captured and killed the brigand-chief Hezekiah and many of his large band who had been raiding on the Syrian frontier in the aftermath of the frequent Roman and Hasmonean civil wars that had swept through the area. His "pacification" of the area brought him into favor with Julius Caesar's relative Sextus, then governor of Syria. But the relatives of the murdered men protested to Hyrcanus and the people (*demos*) of Jerusalem to bring Herod to trial before the governing council (*synhedrion*). The "men" (high priestly officers) of the Judeans, moreover, apprehensive about the rapid rise to power of Herod, his father and brother, military governor of Jerusalem, urged action against Herod for killing the men in violation of the law. Hyrcanus finally summoned Herod to trial, while Sextus Caesar signaled to the king that he had better make sure Herod was acquitted. The brash young Herod appeared before the court "clothed in purple" and surrounded by a bodyguard of his troops, effectively intimidating the members of the court.

At that point, says Josephus, Shemiah, "an upright man and for that reason superior to fear," admonished the king and the council for their cowardice, and warned: "God is great, and this man, whom you now wish to release for Hyrcanus's sake, will one day punish you and the king as well" (*Ant.* 14.172–176). Referring back to this episode later in his narrative, Josephus says that it was Pollion the Pharisee, whose disciple was Shemiah, who "reproachfully foretold to Hyrcanus and the judges that if Herod's life were spared, he would (one day) persecute them all" (*Ant.* 15.3–4). It is indeed more likely that the teacher Pollion rather than the disciple Shemiah participated in this council in 47 BCE. In any case, Josephus clearly associates the prophetic warning with a Pharisee and apparently assumes that Shemiah, the disciple of a Pharisee, was also a Pharisee.

According to two brief accounts by Josephus, this Pharisee, his disciple, or both played a significant role again several years later. After being declared "king of the Judeans" by the Roman Senate in 40 BCE (*War* 1.282–285; *Ant.* 14.381–385), Herod launched what would be a three-year military campaign to conquer his realm. While he was besieging Jerusalem, Samaias, or Pollion and Samaias, "advised the people/citizens to admit Herod" to the city, and "said that on account of their sins they would not be able to escape him" (*Ant.* 14.176; 15.3). For this reason, says Josephus, when Herod began almost immediately to purge those who had opposed him, including eventually Hyrcanus II and all the other members of the council before whom he had been brought to trial earlier, he not only spared, but "greatly honored Pollion the Pharisee and his disciple Shemiah" (*Ant.* 14.176; 15.3–4).

These two incidents indicate that Pharisees continued to be involved at a high level in the politics of the Hasmonean regime during its declining years. These two at least would appear to have viewed the rise of the Idumean strongman Antipater and his sons as a threat to Judean societal life under the ancestral laws—and were prepared to say so publicly, in the councils of state, even when others were intimidated. They also appear to have been political realists who saw at a certain point that Herod would inevitably take over Jerusalem and Judea anyhow, so were prepared to make their compromises with the realities of Roman-determined rule in Palestine.

Modern scholars have commonly identified Samaias and Pollion with Shemaiah and Abtalion, cited in the Mishnah tractate Abot, as one of the pairs of "fathers" among the sages. This identification goes beyond what the fragmentary evidence allows.[9] The saying "Love work, hate authority, don't get friendly with the government" (m. Abot 1:10), attributed to Shemaiah, whom the sequence of pairs in tractate Abot places roughly at the

---

9. Neusner, *Rabbinic Traditions about the Pharisees*, vol. 1, 5.

beginning of Herod's reign, does parallel the caution evident in Samaias's and Pollion's stance toward Herod, as represented in Josephus's narrative. The theology implicit in the Pharisee's prophecy that Herod would become God's instrument of punishment for the sins of the Jerusalem council parallels the near-contemporary Psalms of Solomon 17 (previously thought to be Pharisaic), which has Pompey as God's instrument, punishing the Judeans for the corrupt Hasmoneans who usurped the throne of David (see esp. Pss Sol 17:5–20).

Far from withdrawing from politics under Herod's reign, the Pharisees remained active in the only way left for Judeans and Jerusalemites with any pretense to influence on political affairs: at Herod's court. The point of Roman indirect rule in the East, through client rulers such as Herod, was to keep traditional indigenous social-political structures in place as a way to maintain order. The Romans had thus propped up the Hasmonean high priesthood for a time, then opted for the military strongman because of the perceived threat of the Parthians to the Roman imperial order on the eastern frontier. Accordingly, Herod kept the temple-state apparatus with its high priesthood intact and used that structure as an instrument of his own rule. Before long, in fact, he launched the massive rebuilding of the temple complex in grand Hellenistic-Roman style, which added to his prestige as the builder of one of the wonders of the (ancient) world. The high priesthood, whose incumbents he now appointed, simply did his bidding. Real political power was exercised by his own regime, and his royal court was the center of power. If the Pharisees wanted to have any serious influence, it would have to be at court. And sure enough, that is where the Pharisees crop up during Herod's reign, at his court, and heavily implicated in court intrigue.

Whatever their maneuvering and machinations at court, the Pharisees seem to have kept a certain critical distance from Herod himself and the Roman imperial order that he established in real and symbolic terms. Josephus sometimes states explicitly and otherwise indicates by his narrative sequencing that certain events and incidents are interrelated. In his account of affairs toward the middle of Herod's reign (in the 20s BCE), he juxtaposes Herod's massive building projects in honor of Caesar and Rome, such as imperial temples and whole cities named for the emperor (Caesarea and Sebaste), in which he departed from or altered the customs and laws of the Judeans (*Ant.* 15.326–231, 365, etc.), on the one hand, and opposition among the Judeans, which led Herod to take repressive measures, on the other (*Ant.* 15.365–368). In addition to forbidding meetings, deploying spies, and condemning suspects to death in one of the royal fortresses, he forced the populace to take an oath of loyalty to his rule.

> Now most of the people yielded to his demand out of complaisance or fear, but those who showed some spirit and objected to compulsion he got rid of by every possible means. He also tried to persuade Pollion the Pharisee and Samaias and most of their disciples [those who spent much time/lived with them], but they would not agree; and yet they were not punished as were the others who refused, for they were shown consideration on Pollion's account. And . . . the Essenes were also excused . . . (15.368–371)

Much later in his extensive account of Herod's long reign, Josephus again mentions a/the loyalty oath, this time of loyalty to Caesar as well as Herod himself.

> There was also a certain segment (*morion*) of Judeans that prided itself greatly on its extremely precise adherence to the ancestral heritage, claiming [to observe] laws with which the Deity is pleased; by them the female faction [at court] was directed. Called Pharisees, these men were entirely capable of issuing predictions for the king's benefit, and yet, evidently, they rose up to combat and injure [him]. At least when the whole Judean people affirmed by an oath that it would be loyal to Caesar and the king's government, these men, over six thousand in number,[10] refused to take this oath, and then the king punished them with a fine, Pheroras's wife paid the fine for them. (*Ant.* 17.41–42)[11]

These accounts could possibly refer to the same oath. But the different points in Josephus's narrative, separated by many years of Herod's reign, and the quite different circumstances and results of the incidents recounted, suggest that these were two separate incidents. In any case, they indicate that the Pharisees were not only still politically active, but active in a way that brought them into almost direct contact with Herod and his court. Moreover, these accounts indicate that the Pharisees were engaged in carefully calculated resistance to Herod. And they indicate that the Pharisees' resistance had something to do with Herod's close collaboration with the

---

10. Josephus surely exaggerated the numerical strength of the Pharisees. Six hundred would be an appropriate number if indeed the Pharisees provided a substantial percentage of the scribal-legal retainers of the temple-state for a population of several hundred thousand Judeans and Galileans, but not those resident in or subject to the non-Judean cities and towns under the control of Herod but not of the temple-state.

11. The first sentence of this uncertain text adapted from Mason, *Flavius Josephus on the Pharisees*, 263, with discussion of terms, 264–67.

Romans as their client ruler who was implementing the Roman imperial order in Judea and the rest of his realm.[12]

The incident that follows Josephus's second account of a loyalty oath suggests that the Pharisees' repertoire included far more than expertise in the ancestral laws of the Judeans, even as it indicates their engagement in court intrigue aimed at subverting Herod's rule. Having already mentioned that the Pharisees had come to control some women at court revolving around the wife of Herod's brother Pheroras, who had paid the fine levied for their refusal of the loyalty oath, Josephus expands on the intrigue.[13]

> In return for her friendliness they foretold—for they were believed to have foreknowledge of things through God's appearance to them—that by God's decree Herod's throne would be taken from him, both from himself and his descendants, and the royal power would fall to her and Pheroras and to any children that they might have ... The king put to death those of the Pharisees who were most to blame and the eunuch Bagoas and a certain Karos who was outstanding among his contemporaries for his surpassing beauty and was a darling (lover) of the king. He also killed all those of his household who approved of what the Pharisees said. (*Ant.* 17.43–45; cf. *War* 1.571)

We must be careful not to jump to conclusions on the basis of this account, for Josephus would not hesitate to portray the Pharisees in a bad light as scheming behind the scenes against Herod, particularly with a juicy tidbit that would make Herod and the ambitious family members also look bad. Given the contemporary parallels, however, including Josephus's own claims about his own precocious gifts, this account is credible.[14]

The learned scribe Ben Sira had claimed not only to be learned in prophecies but to have prophetic gifts (Sir 39:1, 6). Scribal circles produced not only didactic wisdom but mantic wisdom as well, which led, in crises of imperial oppression, to visions that prophesied deliverance (e.g., Dan 7). Josephus himself claimed to be a prophet, indeed the one who prophesied that Vespasian was the fulfillment of Judean messianic prophecies.[15] Judging from Josephus's account, the Pharisees' prophecy stood squarely in

---

12. See Alon, who argued this in *Jews, Judaism and the Classical World*.

13. For a critical defense of Josephus's authorship of this passage, see Mason, *Flavius Josephus on the Pharisees*, 274–80.

14. Blenkinsopp, "Prophecy and Priesthood"; van Unnik, *Flavius Josephus*, 41–52.

15. The closely contemporary Pss Sol 17 presents a prophecy of a messiah, son of David, who would restore the people of Israel on their land in righteousness, a prophecy that appears to be a direct response to a situation of the wrong king, i.e., Herod, being in power.

Israelite tradition (by God's decree) and was messianic in content (a new god-designated king, appointed from above), even fantastic in its imagery (the messianic agent offering extraordinary new life, including reproductive power to a eunuch). Whatever manipulation, conspiracy, and wishful fantasy may have been involved on the part of the Pharisees, Pheroras's wife, and/or others at court, many aspects of Josephus's account fit the historical cultural context rather well. If it is a credible story about the Pharisees, then their repertoire, like that of Josephus himself, included prophecy rooted in ancient Israelite tradition that applied directly to contemporary historical circumstances, as well as a claim to expertise in the ancestral laws of the Judeans.

These accounts of the delicately balanced relations between the Pharisees and Herod indicate clearly that the Pharisees had not withdrawn from politics at all under Herod, as has been supposed in recent decades. Given their opposition to the loyalty oath, for which Herod killed others, we must wonder why Herod left them intact, and even perhaps honored some of them. This is especially puzzling when we consider that Herod generally did not hesitate to take severe repressive measures against opposition, real or imagined (see esp. *Ant.* 15.173–178, 247–252, 262–266, 280–289, 365–369; 16.235–237). One possibility is suggested by Josephus's parallel comment that Herod also exempted the Essenes from the loyalty oath: they were simply politically innocuous. That seems unlikely, however, because according to Josephus's accounts of Pharisees, their political engagement is how Herod came into contact with them and why he honored them, and some were even active at court. Certainly the Pharisees' machinations and conspiracy at court later in Herod's reign were not politically innocuous. Yet although Josephus says that Herod executed those "who were most to blame," he does not give any indication that the rest suddenly went into exile, as had several thousand opponents of Alexander Jannaeus, who exercised far more severe repression than did Herod.

Perhaps we should consider just the opposite explanation. Perhaps, like the temple-state centered in the high priesthood and temple ceremonies and apparatus, the Pharisees were important in the functioning of the state in maintaining order in the society. As Josephus says later about the Sadducees and himself, those who filled an office and otherwise participated in public life had to follow the Pharisees' school of thought and exposition of the laws because they had become integral to the functioning of the temple-state in Jerusalem and, by extension, Judean society. This would in no way suggest that all or most Judeans agreed with or practiced a Pharisaic Judaism. That would be a projection of a modern way of thinking about religion. Perhaps, rather, the Pharisees had come to constitute something like an infrastructure for the temple-state that Herod and later the Roman governors left intact. Such a hypothesis would fit Herod's toleration of the Pharisees' politics as well as Alexander Jannaeus's recommendation to his queen and the Pharisees' operations under Salome Alexandra.

We may also wonder why, from their side, the Pharisees did not simply withdraw from politics during the repressive reign of a Rome-sponsored king whom they opposed and perhaps detested—in some way short of forming a communal utopian enclave in the wilderness like the scribal-priestly community at Qumran. It is conceivable that the Pharisees viewed it as their responsibility to continue their mediating functions in the political order. Another factor may be that they had little alternative, since they had no independent economic base. We now realize that there is little or no evidence that they were economically independent urban artisans who also happened to be torah scholars and "associates." Their role, social location, and function in Judean society were traditionally fixed, "ascribed," as sociologists would say. They were also apparently attached and committed to the tradition of laws and legal interpretation which it was their role to cultivate (see the next chapter). Like scribal circles before them, they were playing a mediating role in the overall political structure and therefore were sometimes "caught in the middle," depending on the orientation, policy, and practices of the rulers under whom they worked.

Other sages in addition to the Pharisees were also active during Herod's reign. Josephus recounts in both histories that near the end of Herod's reign, as he lay dying, two prominent teachers led their students to cut down the golden Roman eagle that Herod had erected above the great gate of the temple (*War* 1.648–650; *Ant.* 17.148–160). In neither account does he identify them as Pharisees, but he characterizes them in the same terms he uses elsewhere for the Pharisees—that is, they are known for accuracy in the ancestral laws. They and their students must have been keeping a fairly low profile during Herod's repressive reign. But as he lay dying they were emboldened to declare that this was the time to pull down the structures that he had erected in violation of the ancestral laws. The bedridden Herod had the teachers and those who cut down the golden eagle burned alive. Josephus emphasizes that these two sages had been prominent teachers of the ancestral laws. Apparently they had previously opposed Herod publicly. But Josephus does not place them in an ongoing political role/function the way he does the Pharisees.

PHARISEES UNDER THE HIGH PRIESTS IN THE FIRST CENTURY CE

The Pharisees continued to play an active role in Judean political affairs during the decades before the destruction of the temple, judging from the limited references in Josephus. He refers to the Pharisees only in connection with events in 6 CE and in 66–67 CE (as discussed in Chapter 2, above). But these references suggest that both at the beginning of direct Roman rule and still at the outbreak of the great revolt, the Pharisees played an important role in Judean politics—indeed in the councils of the temple-state as well as in the conduct of political-religious life. Their general position, moreover, was still as mediators of the Roman-sponsored political-religious order in Judea. And the structural conflicts that were strained to the breaking point under direct rule by the Roman governors in collaboration with the high priestly aristocracy found the Pharisees at times "caught in the middle."

In both histories, Josephus places his most substantial sketch of the three Judean schools of thought at the beginning of his account of Judea under Roman governors. The ostensible occasion is to contrast the main schools of thought in the Judean philosophy (way of life) with the "intrusive" "fourth school of thought," which he blames for the great revolt (particularly in the *Antiquities*). He is also explaining, however, that the others were still very much alive. Here are his most positive representations of the Pharisees, particularly in comparison with the negative representation of the Sadducees.

> The Pharisees, who are considered the most accurate interpreters of the laws (*ta nomima*) and hold the position of the leading school of thought/way of life/party, ... are affectionate with each other and cultivate harmonious relations with the community. The Sadducees, on the contrary, are, even among themselves, rather boorish in their behavior, and in their intercourse with their peers are as rude as to aliens. (*War* 2.162–163, 166)

> The Pharisees simplify their standard of living, making no concession to luxury. They follow the guidance of that which their doctrine has selected and transmitted as good, attaching the chief importance to the observance of those commandments which it has seen fit to dictate to them. They show respect and deference to their elders, nor do they rashly presume to contradict their proposals. Though they postulate that everything is brought about by fate, still they do not deprive the human will of the pursuit of what is in man's power, since it was God's good pleasure that there should be a fusion and that the will of

man with his virtue and vice should be admitted to the council-chamber of fate. (*Ant.* 18.12–14; LCL trans.)

On account of these (views) they happen to be the most persuasive to the peoples; of prayers and sacred rites, whatever is considered divine happens to be conducted according to their interpretation. This much of their influence the cities have demonstrated, in both manner of life and discourse, by their pursuit of [or "adherence to"] the way that prevails over all. (*Ant.* 18.15; Mason trans.)[16]

The Sadducees hold that the soul perishes along with the body. They own no observance of any sort apart from the laws; in fact, they reckon it a virtue to dispute with the teachers of the path of wisdom that they pursue. There are but few men to whom this doctrine has been made known, but these are men of the highest standing. They accomplish practically nothing, however. For whenever they assume some office, though they submit unwillingly and perforce, yet submit they do to whatever the Pharisee says, since otherwise the crowd/masses would not tolerate them. (*Ant.* 18.16–17; LCL trans.)

Particularly noteworthy in these accounts, midst the analogies to Greek philosophy, are several indications of just how integral the Pharisees' interpretations of the laws are in the functioning of political-religious affairs. "All prayers and sacred rites are performed according to their interpretation." "The cities" follow their guidelines "in both manner of life and discourse" (*Ant.* 18.14–15). Even the Sadducees who assume some office in the temple-state find it necessary to submit to "whatever the Pharisee says lest the ordinary people not tolerate them" (18.17). Although these accounts of Josephus start out speaking of seemingly abstract philosophical doctrines, they move into the Pharisees' important function in the conduct of public social-religious life.

After these general accounts placed at the beginning of direct Roman rule in Judea, Josephus does not refer again to the Pharisees until his narratives of the beginning of the great revolt in 66. At that point, however, he represents the "leading" or "most notable" Pharisees as operating at the highest level of politics They are engaged in close cooperation with prominent high priestly figures in attempting to retain control of a society slipping into political turmoil and outright revolt, in the summer of 66. First they attempted to head off the revolt they sensed was brewing. "The nobles came together with the high priests and the most notable Pharisees to deliberate

---

16. Translation from Mason, *Flavius Josephus on the Pharisees*, 305.

on the whole state of affairs . . . Deciding to try the effect of an appeal to the revolutionaries, they called the people (the Jerusalem *demos*) together before the bronze gate, that of the inner temple facing eastward" (*War* 2.411). When soon thereafter the revolt erupted in Jerusalem, Josephus and the others took refuge in the inner court of the temple.

Then after the messianic pretender Menahem and his cohorts among the Sicarii had been killed later in the summer, "I ventured out of the temple and once more consorted with the chief priests and the leading Pharisees" (*Life* 21). Being "powerless to check the revolutionaries," they pretended to go along. But they formulated a provisional government that consisted mainly of ranking high priestly figures. Similarly they delegated mainly prominent high priestly and other priestly aristocratic figures such as Josephus himself as commanders to take control of the various districts, while excluding the popular leaders who had led the revolt during the previous summer (*War* 2.562-568). The strategy was to restore public order and to buy time to negotiate with the Romans, partly in order to save their own positions of power and privilege. (In modern political terms this might be called a counterrevolution.) The "leading Pharisees" here acted in concert with the high priestly and other rulers in Jerusalem and were evidently already situated in a position to do so well before events began to escalate toward revolt.

Later, in Josephus's account of his campaign to control the turmoil in Galilee, he reveals the integral role that those "leading Pharisees" were playing in the provisional government in Jerusalem that was trying to reestablish order. His rival in Galilee, John of Gischala, sought the help of Simon son of Gamaliel to "induce the *koinon* of Jerusalemites (the provisional government headed by the high priests Ananus and Jesus) to deprive me of the command of Galilee and to vote for his appointment to the post."

> This Simon was a native of Jerusalem, of a very illustrious family, and of the school of the Pharisees, who have the reputation of surpassing the others in accuracy concerning the ancestral laws (*nomima*). A man highly gifted with intelligence and judgment, he could by sheer genius retrieve an unfortunate situation in affairs of state (*pragmata*). (*Life* 190-191)

Although Josephus smears him with a charge of bribery in the next paragraph, he obviously has high regard for Simon's powerful position and considerable ability and influence in "affairs of state." Simon was clearly a high-ranking participant in the Jerusalem *koinon* (or provisional government) headed by the two high priests. But he was not the only Pharisee involved in its political operations. The delegation sent to relieve Josephus of his command in Galilee consisted of a high priest, named Simon, and three Pharisees, one a priest named Jozar, and two laymen, Ananias and Jonathan, who was apparently the leader (196–197). These were no mere messengers carrying a dispatch. Although not as accomplished and high ranking as Simon son of Gamaliel in the provisional government, they were "men of affairs," envoys sent with the important mission of replacing one of the district commanders.

Simon son of Gamaliel and these other three Pharisees had not suddenly jumped back into politics after a lifetime of pious devotion in a religious association. Like the high priestly members of the *koinon,* they were already engaged in public affairs and able to respond to the emergency of the revolt by participating in the provisional government and its attempt to restore order. The book of Acts represents Simon's father Gamaliel as having occupied a prestigious political position similar to his son's a generation later: "A Pharisee in the council, a teacher of the law, respected by all the people" (Acts 5:34). Acts portrays Gamaliel, moreover, as playing a mediating role between the high priestly rulers, ready to take sharp, repressive measures against a movement they viewed as a threat to the established order, and the populace among which movements emerge and then disappear again (5:35–38). Such participation in political affairs, in a mediating role, had apparently been the Pharisees' role for generations.

A few additional references in Josephus and other literature confirm this picture of the Pharisees as still centrally involved in political affairs in Jerusalem under the Roman governors. One of the original leaders of the "fourth school of thought," says Josephus in the *Antiquities* (18.4–5), was a Pharisee named Saddok (Zadok). But not only did the leadership of this "intrusive" school involve Pharisees as well as other "teachers" such as Judas of Gamla. Except for its intense passion for liberty, its views "in all other respects agreed with the position of the Pharisees" (18.23). Josephus may well have been trying to further tarnish the image of the Pharisees here. But in order for that to work rhetorically, his representation had to be grounded in historical memory and to fit what he had already written about the Pharisees in *Antiquities.* The Pharisees' views obviously had serious implications for the conflictual situation of Judeans trying to live according to their ancestral laws under Roman imperial rule. And as Saddok the Pharisee and Judas the sage/teacher claimed, in agreement with the views of the Pharisees, those laws that forbade them to have no lord and master other than God had obvious implications for payment of the tribute to Caesar, honored as divine throughout the empire as well as in Herod's building projects. The Pharisees and other scribes/sages were caught in the middle. Some, such as Saddok and Judas of Gamla, acted on the implications of their views, while most apparently pursued the greater political realism of continuing to mediate the Roman imperial order in Judea.

A critical examination of Josephus's works thus shows the Pharisees as originating as a party of intellectual-legal retainers of the restored temple-state under the early Hasmoneans. At least by early in John Hyrcanus's reign they served as his "friends" (that is close advisers), engaged in promulgating regulations for public life that they derived from a succession of ancestors. These would have been ancestral customs, laws, and practices presumably particularly relevant to the operation of the temple-state. At some point, however, Hyrcanus broke with them and pushed them out of temple-state operations in favor of the Sadducees, a party more closely aligned with the newly established priestly aristocracy, as Hyrcanus gained fuller control of Judea and conquered nearby areas with his newly hired foreign mercenaries. The Pharisees evidently remained out of operations of the temple-state under Alexander Jannaeus, who even more aggressively expanded Jerusalem's control of cities on the periphery of the extensive territory already taken over by the Hasmoneans. But the Judean populace was now in full-scale revolt against the arrogant high priests who had taken the title of king in imitation of the Hellenistic kingdoms after which they were patterning their pursuit of greater territory and power. Certain passages in the scrolls from Qumran confirm the hint in Josephus's histories that the Pharisees were involved in the revolt, and may well have suffered from Jannaeus's extreme brutality.

In a reversal of policy, however, Salome Alexandra brought the Pharisees back into service of the temple-state, reapproving their regulations as enforced state law and placing most domestic affairs under their administration. From the period of the Pharisees' service as retainers under Hyrcanus and then again under Salome Alexandra, the Pharisees and their regulations derived from ancestral tradition probably became integral to the operations of the temple-state. With the political chaos of battles between rival Hasmoneans, compounded by the spillover of the empirewide (un)civil war between rival Roman warlords, the Pharisees may well have been influential in the continuing the operations of the temple and its political-economic-religious functions. This would help explain the Pharisees' continuing presence and political realism during Herod's ruthless, relentless rise to power. Even though they maintained their semi-independence under Herod, refusing the oaths of loyalty he required of the populace, Herod honored them because of the political realism of Pollion and Samaias in advising the people to submit to his rule. After Herod, the Pharisees must have continued to serve in the operations of the temple-state, apparently trying to check the worst abuses by high priestly families who became ever more predatory against their own people. Although splinter groups of dissident retainers undertook acts of resistance, evidently the majority of Pharisees persisted in a moderating role. And at the beginning of the great revolt the leading Pharisees collaborated with the high priests who had not fled Jerusalem, in an attempt to control the revolt until they could negotiate their own continuation as the Roman client-rulers of Judea and Galilee. Without the direct presence of Roman military forces, however, the provisional government of high priestly figures and leading Pharisees could not withstand the revolt by a coalition of peasant forces who entered Jerusalem, or were driven into Jerusalem by Roman troops, as their last hope for resisting Roman reconquest.

6

THE PHARISEES AS RETAINERS
OF THE TEMPLE-STATE AND JESUS' WOES IN Q

ANTHONY SALDARINI AND OTHERS of his generation, particularly those who specialized in late second-temple Judean and early rabbinic sources, could not avoid recognizing two prominent features of their subject matter: There was considerable diversity among the literatures and groups or movements that were usually lumped together as Judaism. And what later emerged as "normative" rabbinic Judaism was not yet a historical reality at the time of Jesus and Paul. Still assuming that the standard "philosophies" or "sects" of Pharisees, Sadducees, and Essenes constituted the important groups—and perhaps focused on the newly discovered Dead Sea Scrolls—many scholars moved to the concept of "sectarian Judaism." Jacob Neusner, who pioneered the new critical study of rabbinic literature and has profoundly influenced our generation of scholarship, suggested that, since what later emerged as a normative rabbinic Judaism was still undergoing a process of formation, the appropriate term was "formative Judaism." And he and some of his students also suggested that, considering the diversity within Judaism, it was only appropriate to think in terms of "Judaisms" prior to the emergence of "formative Judaism."

Although he continued to use the term "Judaism," Saldarini pushed our fields to rethink the literature, groups, and history that constituted our subject matter in other key respects. In contrast to the historically distinctive separation of religion from political-economic affairs in modern Western societies, "in traditional society, including the Roman empire and Jewish Palestinian society, religion was embedded in the political and social fabric of the community. Religious belief and practice were part of the family, ethnic, and territorial groups into which people were born."[1] In studying texts, groups, and movements in late second-temple Judea, therefore, we are dealing with a whole society, in the same way that other fields deal with a whole society. It is an obvious step, therefore, to borrow and adapt disciplines such as sociology and anthropology in approaching Judean history and literature and their embedded religious dimension. In much of his seminal scholarship of the 1980s and 1990s, this is what Saldarini pioneered, particularly with regard to the Pharisees, scribes, and Sadducees and the Gospel of Matthew and its Christian Jewish community.[2] And in challenging and replacing the old paradigm in biblical studies, Saldarini virtually reversed the dominant previous understanding of the historically most influential Gospel, that of Matthew. Far from presenting the good news of the new religion of Christianity that condemned and superseded the old religion of Judaism, the composers of Matthew were among the diverse groups and movements struggling to chart a path of social renewal in the aftermath of the Romans devastation of Israel in Palestine in their suppression of the great revolt of 66–70.

With Saldarini having already laid out definitive analysis of the Pharisees and the Gospel of Matthew, I would like to honor his path-breaking scholarship by slipping underneath Matthew's Gospel to one of its sources, the sequence of Jesus speeches called Q, to investigate its representation of Jesus' attack on the Pharisees. In pursuing this investigation, moreover, I would like to proceed further along the lines of investigation that Saldarini pioneered on the Pharisees.

PHARISEES AND SCRIBES AS RETAINERS OF THE JERUSALEM TEMPLE-STATE

In a systematic analysis of the sources, Saldarini laid out a convincing case that the Pharisees, along with the scribes, were intellectual-legal *retainers* deployed by and dependent on the governing class of the ancient agrarian society in Judea (Palestine). More precisely, we might say that the Pharisees and scribes were scribal retainers of the Jerusalem temple-state that ruled Judean and other Israelite peoples in Palestine, prior to and later in cooperation with the Roman imperial regime and their client Herodian rulers This conceptualization offers a far more historically precise replacement for

1. Saldarini, *Pharisees*, 5.

2. I cite only the two principal books from the late 1980s and early 1990s: *Pharisees*; and *Matthew's Christian-Jewish Community*.

the vague and historically questionable concept of protorabbis as normative interpreters of the Torah and for the anachronistic concepts of sect and religion.

Saldarini's case in *The Pharisees, Scribes and Sadducees* is based on a well-reasoned critical analysis of the sources, among which Josephus's histories are of particular importance. He finds that the thesis about Josephus's *Antiquities*, in contrast with *War*, presenting a brief for the Pharisees' recognition by the Romans as the appropriate leaders of post-70 Judea lacks plausibility. His own and others' careful critical analysis of key sources, particularly legends of Yohanan ben Zakkai and the council of Yavneh, suggested that the Romans did not recognize the Pharisees or any other body as leaders of Judean society for several generations after the destruction of Jerusalem and the temple.[3] "The emerging rabbis did not immediately take over and receive recognition from the people and the Romans"[4]—perhaps until the time of Judah the Prince. Therefore, "Since Josephus' accounts of Pharisaic disruptive and revolutionary political involvement in the *Antiquities* do not derive from or especially serve his political purposes, these accounts are to be trusted as representative of Pharisaic political involvement."[5] That also pulls the rug out from under much New Testament scholarship on Jesus, the Synoptic Gospels, and the synoptic tradition, which was based on the assumption that soon after 70, from Yavneh on, the Romans had placed the Pharisees in charge of Palestinian Jewish society.

Saldarini's social location of the Pharisees and scribes as retainers in an ancient agrarian society uses the widely influential comparative historical-sociological scholarship of Gerhard Lenski and other studies, such as John Kautsky's on "aristocratic empires." "Agrarian societies . . . are constituted by two major classes separated by a wide gulf and unmediated by a middle class . . . a large peasant class which produces . . . and a small, elite governing class which . . . lives off the agricultural surplus . . . [T]he peasants are forced to produce a surplus which can be extracted from them, usually by burdensome taxes."[6] "The governing class maintained its position with the assistance of what Lenski calls retainers, whose roles in society were military, governing, administrative, judicial and priestly."[7]

---

3. Review of the evidence in Levine, 'The Jewish Patriarch"; Levine, *The Rabbinic Class*, chap. 4; and Cohen, "The Significance of Yavneh," 36–38.

4. Saldarini, *Pharisees*, 131.

5. Saldadini, *Pharisees*, 131.

6. Saldarini, *Pharisees*, 36, drawing on Lenski, *Power and Privilege*; Kautsky, *Politics of Aristocratic Empires*; and others.

7. Saldarini, *Pharisees*, 37.

Saldarini finds a vivid illustration of his argument in Josephus's account of the confrontation between the Pharisees and the Hasmonean high priest John Hyrcanus, when he angrily rescinded the Pharisees' rulings not found in the law of Moses as state law and replaced them in the state administration with the Sadducees. "The Pharisees are pictured as part of Hyrcanus's circle of retainers and as a group they have achieved considerable influence . . . Any power they have is based on influence with Hyrcanus."[8] Again Josephus portrays the Pharisees as retainers of the temple-state when Salome Alexandra reinstates them into governmental administration and their rulings as state law.[9] Sociologically, the Pharisees are part of Lenski's retainer class, in the service of the ruling class as bureaucrats, educators, and officials.[10] These are not merely squabbles about religious interpretation of the Torah. Rather, "the views of these groups affect the running of the Jewish state."[11]

Neusner had already noted the prominent political role that the Pharisees played under the Hasmoneans.[12] Most influential in the fields of Jewish history and New Testament studies, however, was his thesis that under Herod's iron-fisted rule, the Pharisees had more or less withdrawn from political affairs and focused mainly on a set of religious issues such as table fellowship, purity, and tithing. Saldarini argued instead that "the Pharisees remained influential actors at the highest levels of society, both in Herod's court and in the Sanhedrin . . . The Pharisees, like all upper classes, were controlled by Herod and failed to attain any real power while he lived, yet they did not withdraw, but remained active participants in political life."[13] In fact, they had "considerable influence on the opponents of Herod."[14] Moreover, again on the eve of the revolt, "the Pharisees are in the thick of things as part of the 'governing class.'"[15] "That the Pharisees did survive after the reign of Herod as a political force is attested to by the presence of Pharisees among the Jerusalem leaders at the beginning of the war with Rome and on the delegation sent from Jerusalem to Josephus in Galilee."[16]

---

8. Saldarini, *Pharisees*, 87–88.
9. Saldarini, *Pharisees*, 91.
10. Saldarini, *Pharisees*, 94.
11. Saldarini, *Pharisees*, 117.
12. Neusner, *From Politics to Piety*, chap. 3.
13. Saldarini, *Pharisees*, 95.
14. Saldarini, *Pharisees*, 100.
15. Saldarini, *Pharisees*, 102.
16. Saldarini, *Pharisees*, 133.

About the scribes as well Saldarini concludes that they were retainers of the temple state in Jerusalem. This is evident, for example, even in early sources such as Antiochus III's letter to Ptolemy, governor of Coele-Syria (c. 200 BCE), where "the scribes of the temple," mentioned along with the senate, the priests, and the temple singers, are "concerned either with the financial and organizational functions of the Temple or with the recording and teaching of sacred traditions and laws."[17] Scribes are dependent on temple revenues and subordinate to the priests who control the temple. Indeed, scribes appear in the same or similar position in Ben Sira's teaching of scribal proteges, in Josephus's historical accounts, and in the Gospels, among other sources, where they "are associated with Jerusalem and the chief priests as part of the government, high officials and advisors, thus typical members of the retainer class."[18] That is, like the Pharisees, the scribes based in the temple were not just or even primarily interpreters of the Torah, but were advisors, administrators, and aides in the religiously constituted political economy of the temple-state.

Saldarini's determination, by careful examination of the sources (separately), that the Pharisees, like the scribes, were retainers of the Jerusalem temple-state enables us to locate them in the overall political-economic structure of ancient Judean society and to discern their social role or function. Although still regnant for most in the New Testament field, the dominant older picture of the scribes and Pharisees as *Schriftgelehrte*[19] was no longer credible to those with closer knowledge of the sources. Neusner had already decisively challenged this standard old picture, suggesting that Scripture interpretation was not even their primary activity. Saldarini was able to inscribe the Pharisees and scribes on the sociological map of Judea and to explain their function as administrators of the temple-state, one that continued through the significant changes in the governing class from Hasmoneans to Herod to priestly aristocracy under Roman governors and eventually to the provisional government of the great revolt. This allows us to take seriously not only Josephus's statements that they had once cultivated extrascriptural rulings that had been part of state law and were unrivaled interpreters of the laws, but also the Qumranites' complaints that they were "smooth interpreters," and the Gospels' representations of them

17. Saldarini, *Pharisees*, 249–50.

18. Saldarini, *Pharisees*, 254–55, 261–66. See further Horsley and Tiller, "Ben Sira and the Sociology of the Second Temple," for a critique of Lenski's sociological model and close analysis of evidence in the book of Sirach on the political-economic structure and social roles in second-temple Judean society.

19. Standardized by Emil Schürer, *Geschichte des Jüdischen Volkes*; perpetuated in standard scholarly works through Martin Hengel, *Judaism and Hellenism*.

as challenging Jesus on questions of the laws. But their activity in legal interpretation and promulgation can no longer stand as the be-all and end-all of their function as scribal retainers, administrators and representatives of the Jerusalem temple-state, instrumental to and politically-economically dependent on their high priestly patrons.

JESUS AND JESUS-MOVEMENTS AMONG THE PEASANTRY

Saldarini's sociological location of the Pharisees and scribes as retainers in the Jerusalem temple-state that headed the traditional agrarian society of Judea/Palestine has obvious implications for the conflicts between the Pharisees and Jesus as represented in the Gospels. In such a society divided between the rulers and the peasants, Jesus and his followers obviously belonged to the productive peasantry who constituted the vast majority of the people governed with the assistance of the Pharisees and scribes. The conflict between Jesus and the Pharisees portrayed in Mark and other Gospel materials was rooted in the religiously sanctioned political-economic structure of the historical situation. As Saldarini explained briefly at certain points, on the basis of the standard comparative historical-sociological studies on which he was drawing, "The activities, interests and outlooks of the governing and peasant classes totally differed from each other. The peasants ... lived in a world apart from the upper classes and the townsfolk who were dependent on the governing class."[20]

Although such information was not necessary for his analysis of the social position and function of scribes and Pharisees, Saldarini was already aware of some key aspects of the class division that previous scholarship had tended to ignore, which some of us in conversation with him here in Boston were beginning to explore. He mentioned in passing that peasant villages were basically semiautonomous communities in charge of conducting their own affairs. Although he was not quite sure how to take Gospel accounts that seemed to portray the Pharisees as active in Galilean villages, he was clear that "the leaders of a village were the elders ... who were the leaders of prominent families"[21]—and not the Pharisees, as often supposed. He was one of the first to recognize that insofar as all but one or two of the synagogue buildings that archaeologists had explored dated from the third century CE and after, the synagogues mentioned in the Gospels must refer not to religious buildings but to local village assemblies. "It is likely that the town assembly for business and celebration was coextensive with the

20. Saldarini. *Pharisees*, 37.
21. Saldarini. *Pharisees*, 51–52.

assembly for prayer on Sabbath and feasts."[22] Subsequent studies argued that the synagogue was indeed the form of local community governance, i.e., the village assembly.[23] Gospel texts such as Mark 13:9 and Luke 1:11 suggest that local synagogues/assemblies had political jurisdiction and authority to keep the peace and to discipline troublemakers. In the Mishnah (e.g., m. Shebuot 4:10) it is assumed that the village assembly or certain members thereof constituted themselves as a court ("house of judgment"). Tosefta passages indicate that the assembly of a village (*'ir*) was competent to regulate its own local economic affairs, such as the wages of workers.[24]

In fact, far from being a unified, homogeneous "society," late second-temple Judea and Galilee consisted of communities at two different levels.[25] The economic base was composed of hundreds of semi-independent, self-governing, and economically self-sufficient village communities. The vast majority of Judeans and Galileans were thus largely defined and determined by their membership in village communities, the component families of which were relatively continuous over many generations. The hundreds of village communities were subject to and taxed by the "governing class" of the priestly aristocracy and Herodians located in urban communities of their retainers and the artisans and others who served their needs, mainly in Jerusalem, but also, after the Romans placed Antipas in charge of Galilee and Perea, in the cities he (re)built, Sepphoris and Tiberias. So long as taxes and tithes and offerings were paid regularly, rulers interfered very little in village affairs. We have the impression, however, that Herod and Antipas were quite rigorous in their revenue collection, and both Josephus and certain rabbinic passages suggest that by the mid-first century high priestly families had become downright predatory (Josephus, *Ant.* 20.206–207; b. Pesahim 57a). Saldarini is clear also about the potential conflict inherent in this political-economic structure: "Representatives of the government, such as bureaucratic officials and tax collectors, . . . if they were foreign or

---

22. Saldarini. *Pharisees*, 52.

23. Kee, "The Transformation of the Synagogue after 70 CE"; Goodman, *State and Society in Roman Galilee*; Horsley, *Galilee*, chap. 10. In the synoptic Gospels and Acts, only two uses of *synagoge*, Luke 7:5 and Acts 18:7, clearly and unambiguously refer to a building. In all of the Markan occurrences (e.g., 1:21, 23, 29; 3:1; 6:2; and the Matthean and Lukan parallels) the assumption is that the *synagogai* are local *assemblies*, with nothing in the texts to suggest that buildings might be involved.

24. Goodman, *State and Society*, 120; Horsley, *Galilee*, 227–33.

25. Discussed briefly in Horsley, *Sociology and the Jesus Movement*, chap. 4; more fully in Horsley, *Galilee*, chaps. 8–10.

perceived as hostile to the villagers, were [seen as] adversaries of the village leaders."[26]

Historical, Political, and Cultural Factors in the Relationship of Pharisees and Jesus

Regional Differences Compounding the Division between Rulers and Peasantry

Since Saldarini's foundational analysis of the social positions and roles of the Pharisees and scribes, a number of other factors have emerged that impinge decisively on interpretation of Jesus and the Pharisees. Most significant perhaps is the difference in regional historical experience between Galilee and Jerusalem/Judea that compounded the class difference between ruling cities and subject villages. According to biblical narratives, most of the tribes of Israel, originally independent of any kingship, had rebelled against Davidic rule from Jerusalem after Solomon's death (1 Kgs 12). Then Galilean villages remained part of a separate imperial province for centuries, while Judean villagers had for centuries been subject to the Jerusalem temple-state under the Persian and Hellenistic empires and participated in the successful war of liberation against Antiochus Epiphanes. Not until 104 BCE were the Galileans subjected to Jerusalem rule by the Hasmoneans. The Galileans remained under the Jerusalem temple and high priest during the rule of Rome and Herod the Great. After Herod's death, however, while Judea proper continued directly under the temple/high priestly administration and Roman governors, Galilean villagers were subject to the regime of Antipas, then to various Herodian or Roman jurisdictions, with the temple/high priests apparently left to exert whatever influence they could from Jerusalem (but without direct jurisdiction).

These divergent histories combined with a temporary subjection of Galilee to Jerusalem rule resulted in serious cultural divergences and political-religious tensions between Galileans and the ruling institutions in Jerusalem. While most Galileans were presumably Israelite, they were not Judeans. There is simply no evidence of a mass migration of Judeans northward in the generations immediately following the Hasmonean takeover of Galilee. Previous claims that prominent priestly families resided in Sepphoris during the first century CE appear to be projections from later

---

26. Saldarini, *Pharisees*, 52.

sources.²⁷ The consensus among Jewish historians is that the migration of sages northward to Galilee happened well after the disaster of 70 CE, and probably mainly following the further Roman devastation of Judea in suppressing the Bar Kokhba Revolt. I have argued that the most compelling reading of the fragmentary evidence from earlier centuries is that most Galileans in second-temple times were the descendants of northern Israelite peasants who were left on the land by the Assyrians who deported the ruling class in Samaria. Therefore Galileans were not forcibly converted by the Hasmonean army, as were the Idumeans.²⁸ They were already Israelites, living out of Israelite traditions parallel to or shared with Judeans and, to a degree, the Jerusalem temple-state (to be explored momentarily).

The inhabitants of Galilee, however, previously subject to the Itureans, and before that under a separate Persian or Ptolemaic or Seleucid imperial administrative district that separated them from Judea, were required by the Hasmonean regime to become subject to "the laws of the Judeans," according to Josephus's accounts (*Ant.* 13.318). Josephus does not clarify precisely what is meant by "the laws of the Judeans." We may presume that it included the laws of Moses (Torah) in some form or another. We would be hard-pressed to find any evidence that Galilean villagers used or even knew of a written form of the Torah (in five books, say) prior to coming under Hasmonean rule. Because source material is so limited and fragmentary, taking a leaf from Saldarini's notebook, we may seek help from social sciences in attempting to understand what the subjection of the Galileans to "the laws of the Judeans" may have meant in concrete social-historical terms.

Great Tradition and Little Tradition

In striving to understand the cultural variations found among the peasantry versus what prevails in ruling circles in agrarian societies, anthropologists have developed the distinction between the "little tradition," cultivated and lived by ordinary people and the "great tradition," the official version of a cultural tradition maintained by professional custodians and interpreters, often partly in written forms.²⁹ These traditions, moreover, both popular and official, are not simply free-floating culture, but are the stories and

---

27. Miller, *Studies in the History and Tradition of Sepphoris*, 62–88, 120–27.
28. Horsley, *Galilee*, chap. 2.
29. The treatment most useful for ancient Judean and Galilean materials is Scott, "Protest and Profanation. On Israelite popular tradition, see further Horsley, *Galilee*, 148–56; Horsley, "Israelite Traditions in Q"; and Horsley, *Hearing the Whole Story*, 156–61.

customs and laws by which people live or by which rulers and their retainers organize and control social life. The little and the great traditions may well have much of the same content, and there is regular interaction between them, as when the official tradition might finally recognize and take into itself stories and even dissident figures who had emerged from the popular tradition or when oral transmission of the popular tradition might be altered under influence by the textually based great tradition as pressed on the people by official interpreters. But there can be differences in content and certainly differences in emphases between the popular and the official traditions, even to the point that they would appear to be different patterns of belief and practice. It is significant that the variation between popular and official traditions depends partly on the distance between the village communities and the ruling elite.

There is historical basis for both common content and divergent understanding and emphases between an official tradition based in the ruling institutions in Jerusalem, on the one hand, and Galilean popular tradition(s), on the other. Both were rooted in Israelite history, from Abraham, Isaac, and Jacob/Israel through Moses, the exodus, and the covenant, to at least David and Solomon. Thereafter the Israelites, except for Judah and Benjamin, rejected Jerusalem (Solomonic) rule, and continued under different Israelite or foreign imperial rule for eight centuries—all the while developing distinctive traditions of their own, such as stories about Elijah and Elisha. Yet even during the period of divergence, some popular Northern Israelite traditions, such as the Elijah-Elisha cycle in 1–2 Kings and the prophecies of Amos and Hosea (along with popular Judean traditions, such as the prophecies of Micah), were taken up into the great tradition established in the postexilic temple-state centered in Jerusalem. Neither the Jerusalemite great tradition nor the Judean and Galilean little traditions would have been frozen, fixed in permanent form, but would continue to develop for centuries prior to the Hasmonean takeover of Galilee.

Indeed, there is increasingly widespread debate in the interrelated fields of Jewish history and biblical studies about just when the biblical tradition of the Jerusalem temple-state assumed more or less fixed form as written literature. And that debate must inevitably come to grips with yet another issue that is only beginning to emerge in these fields focused on what most biblical scholars have simply assumed: an ethos of literacy.

Oral Communication

One of the most striking and distinctive aspects of late second-temple Judea must surely be its amazing level of literary productivity. The discovery of the Dead Sea Scrolls has further illuminated both the remarkable variety and sheer quantity of literature produced in Hebrew and Aramaic by Judean scribal circles during the Hellenistic, Hasmonean, and early Roman periods. Nevertheless, oral communication, not literacy, was still dominant in Judea as well as Galilee, as in the ancient Near East and Mediterranean world generally. A few pioneers in Jewish history and biblical studies have outlined the basically oral communication environment, while most scholars in these fields resist the obvious—understandably since our professional "bread and butter" focuses on the analysis and interpretation of texts, understood and practiced on the assumptions and procedures of print culture.[30] Recent studies by classics scholars have made clear that at most fifteen percent of the people in the Roman Empire generally were even minimally literate.[31] And even if we had still relied on special pleading about how literate the "biblical" people of "Judaism" were, a comprehensive recent study has made unavoidably clear that literacy was not more prevalent and practiced in Judea than in the rest of the Roman Empire.[32] Rabbinic scholars, of course, have known for some time that scripture itself as well as rabbinic learning was memorized, recited, and cultivated and debated orally. Neusner, as usual, was one of the leaders in exploring this issue as it came to the fore, and other rabbinic scholars have furthered the discussion, particularly by focusing on the "oral Torah," or "Torah in the mouth."[33]

The implications of oral communication having been dominant in Judea and Galilee has serious implications for exploring issues such as the conflict between Jesus and the Pharisees, as represented in Gospel literature. Galilean and Judean villagers were basically non-literate. But that does not mean that they were ignorant, for such villagers cultivated their revered Israelite traditions orally in families and village assemblies, from generation to generation. Covenant commandments and customs constituted the basis for family and village community life, social-economic as well as religious. Previous scholarly arguments that the (written) Torah was known in Galilee have focused on matters such as observance of the Sabbath and the practice of circumcision. But Galilean villagers hardly needed to be literate to know

---

30. Kelber, *Oral and Written Gospel*; Botha, "Graeco-Roman Literacy as Setting for New Testament Writings"; and Niditch, *Oral World and Written Word*.

31. See especially Harris, *Ancient Literacy*.

32. See especially Hezser, *Jewish Literacy*.

33. See especially Neusner, *Oral Tradition in Judaism*; and Jaffee, *Torah in the Mouth*.

about and observe the Sabbath, circumcise their male infants, honor their father and mother, refrain from stealing from their neighbors, set aside tithes, leave their fields fallow on the seventh year for the sake of the poor, recite traditional prayers, sing the psalms of Miriam and Deborah, celebrate the Passover, and recite stories about Elijah. Israelite popular tradition was cultivated and practiced orally in village communities, which had little need of writing (except perhaps in dealing with officials of the state). Judean and Galilean peasants may well have held written texts, particularly sacred scrolls, in high regard. Written texts laid up in the temple may well have been surrounded by an almost divine aura in the popular mind. But parchment scrolls were extremely expensive and beyond the reach of most village communities. In this connection Saldarini was far ahead of most in the field when he wrote the book on the Pharisees and scribes: "It is doubtful that small poor villages had their own Torah scroll or a teacher learned in more than the basics of the law."[34]

Equally difficult for us moderns who assume print culture, perhaps, is that oral communication also dominated in scribal circles, despite their literacy. In his book of wisdom, Ben Sira writes about how the scribe/sage devotes himself "to the study of the law of the Most High, . . . and seeks out the wisdom of all the ancients." Yet he does not cite specific laws and sapiential sayings from written texts. Rather, it is by memorization and oral cultivation that "he preserves the sayings of the famous and penetrates the subtleties of parables; seeks out the hidden meanings of proverbs" as he "serves among the great and appears before rulers" (Sir 38:34—39:4). It is not by accident that we do not possess literature written by Pharisees. In a predominantly oral society, including in the court of the ruling elite, scribal retainers such as Ben Sira and Pharisees such as Gamaliel were valuable because they had—not at their fingertips, but stored up in their mind for the right situation and moment—the appropriate proverbs, parables, and prophecies, as well as the ancestral "laws of the Judeans"—whether they were also written in the laws of Moses or were the rulings/regulations handed down by the fathers/elders, as in the dispute between the Pharisees and John Hyrcanus (*Ant.* 13.297; cf. 408). Nothing in those accounts of Ben Sira and Josephus suggest that the scribes/sages or Pharisees concerned were engaged in reading written texts, even though such texts existed and part of their function was their ability to read them.

---

34. Saldarini, *Pharisees*, 52–53.

The Status and Presence/Absence of Scripture

And this predominance of oral communication even in scribal circles leads to yet another, related issue bearing on the conflict between Jesus and the Pharisees, as represented in Gospel texts. Another contribution of the Dead Sea Scrolls to current discussions of biblical materials is the evidence they provide for the state of the development of the text of biblical literature. Colleagues who have devoted the better part of their careers to poring over scrolls of the books of the Torah are finally able to report on some of their systematic study of text types and their development.[35] As I understand it, two or three different text types were present simultaneously at Qumran, and all were still developing. Such evidence suggests that we are not at all certain that a standard text of the Torah prevailed in Judea, much less in Galilee, in late second-temple times. Josephus writes that the Pharisees were the unrivaled and accurate interpreters of the laws. But what version of the laws, and in what mode, written or oral, were they the accurate expounders? And given the general nonliterate knowledge of Israelite tradition among Galilean villagers such as Jesus and his followers and the probable unavailability of costly scrolls in villages such as Nazareth and Capernaum, it seems highly unlikely that Jesus and the Pharisees were, as it were, on the same page when it came to disputes about the law.

The Possible Role of Pharisees in Galilee

All of these complications of class and regional historical and cultural differences, however, may at least frame the way we might approach one of the principal conundrums of the conflict between Jesus and the Pharisees. The Gospels are the only sources that place the Pharisees in Galilee for more than a short single mission as envoys of the Jerusalem government (Josephus's account of the largely Pharisaic delegation sent by the provisional government in 67 CE to relieve him of his command in Galilee). The Gospel stories of Mark and Matthew represent the scribes and Pharisees as making frequent trips to Galilee. But are the Gospel accounts persuasive and sufficient to evoke confidence that the Pharisees did, in fact, historically operate in Galilee? The Lukan story is the only source that once presents the Pharisees as "from the villages of Galilee" (5:17, my translation), and this appears to be a later projection. In his analysis of Gospel sources for the Pharisees, Saldarini saw the problem clearly, and judging from his tentative

---

35. See especially Ulrich, "Bible in the Making"; and Tov, "Biblical Texts as Reworked."

observations on key Gospel passages had not yet arrived at a solution with which he felt confident. It is likely that no such solution will be possible given our limited sources. Meanwhile, many Gospel interpreters, also recognizing the problem, have seized on that component of the old paradigm that had the Romans recognizing the Pharisees soon after the destruction of the temple as the new leaders of Palestinian Judaism. As noted already above, however, it is now apparent that the Romans did not so recognize the Pharisaic and other leaders at Yavneh and their immediate successors, and that proto-rabbinic circles did not migrate to Galilee until after the Bar Kokhba Revolt and even then had questionable authority among the people—in an emerging consensus to which Saldarini and other critical scholars contributed.[36]

There is a more appropriate way to state the question, however. Can we imagine, on the basis of the more precise sketch of the multifaceted history of the relations between Jerusalem rulers and the Galilean people, historical circumstances in which the Pharisees may have played a role in Galilee that would have provided a possible historical basis for the emergence of the Jesus-traditions that appear in Mark and the other sources of Matthew and Luke? I can think of two possibilities, one of which Saldarini suggested, at least briefly and in passing.

The Hasmoneans, says Josephus, required the inhabitants of Galilee to become subject to "the laws of the Judeans." If we trust Josephus's accounts, the Pharisees played a significant role as legal-scribal retainers in the Hasmonean regime (under John Hyrcanus) well before the takeover of Galilee and were reinstated in that role (by Salome Alexandra) in the first generation of Jerusalem rule in the area (*Ant.* 13.295–297, 408–409). In that capacity, among other things, they promulgated regulations/rulings not contained in the (written) laws of Moses that were handed down by the(ir) ancestors. And they were supposedly experts in the interpretation of the laws. They would seem to have been the obvious candidates for the Hasmonean regime to delegate to represent "the laws of the Judeans" to the Galileans.

Two important factors, however, make such a "missionary" program unlikely given what we know of Hasmonean history and the division of an agrarian society into village communities, on one level, and the ruling elite in Jerusalem, on another. First, the sixty-some years of Hasmonean rule over Galilee were filled with turmoil that would have kept the regime preoccupied with its own survival and less attentive to the consolidation of its

---

36. Saldarini, "Johanan ben Zakkai's Escape"; Schäfer, "Die Flucht Rabban Johanan b. Zakkai"; Levine, "The Jewish Patriarch"; Levine, *The Rabbinic Class*, chap. 4; and Cohen, "The Significance of Yavneh."

rule in Galilee (following Josephus's account in *Antiquities* 13). Alexander Jannaeus was preoccupied with wars of expansion and, far from deploying the Pharisees and other intellectuals, fell into virtual civil war with them, viciously executing a great number. After the Pharisees were restored to power under the short reign of Salome Alexandra, civil war erupted among rival Hasmonean factions, the Romans took over Palestine, and civil war erupted again periodically between rival Hasmoneans. Thereafter, the Pharisees experienced a demotion of status and lessening of influence and role, insofar as the Romans' client-king, Herod, installed his own political-economic administration, while keeping the temple-state in a subordinate position. That makes it all the more unlikely that in subjecting the Galileans to "the laws of the Judeans" the Hasmonean regime could possibly have attempted a thorough "resocialization" of Galilean village communities, i.e., attempting to replace Galilean popular tradition with Judean scribally cultivated tradition. Rather they were imposing "the laws of the Judean temple-state" on the Galileans, laws pertaining to political economic relations between village communities and the temple and high priesthood on such matters as revenues (including tithes and offerings) and related matters in which the official Jerusalem-based "great tradition" would have differed from the Galilean Israelite popular tradition. Both of these considerations considerably lessen the scope in which the Pharisees or other Jerusalem retainers would have attempted to influence political-economic-religious practices among Galilean villagers. But in this limited way, as the retainers who cultivated the scribal tradition according to which the temple-state operated, the Pharisees could well have played a role that affected Galilee and Galileans for the century of Jerusalem rule—that is, from the Hasmonean takeover in 104 BCE until the end of Jerusalem's direct jurisdiction over Galileans after Herod's death in 4 BCE.

Second, in the new situation after Herod's death there would have been even less of a role for the Pharisees in Galilee than before. The Romans placed Antipas over Galilee along with Perea, thus ending Jerusalem's direct jurisdiction. And Antipas, who pursued massive building programs of two new cities, would presumably have been concerned to guard his revenue base against serious competition for peasant produce. In building Tiberias, moreover, or at least his palace overlooking the new, presumably Roman-style city, he virtually thumbed his nose at the Jerusalem-based guardians of official Judean tradition (Josephus, *Life* 65). Nevertheless, it is at least conceivable that, with or without Antipas's tacit permission, the Jerusalem high priesthood delegated some of the Pharisees to represent Jerusalem's interest in continuing tithes, offerings, and other income from Galilean Israelites. In fact, the Gospel of Mark gives us a specific example: Pharisees and scribes from Jerusalem are accused of pressing Galileans to devote (*qorban*) property and/or the produce from it to the temple, to the detriment of Galilean family subsistence. That the provisional government in Jerusalem in the summer of 66 CE immediately sent envoys (including Josephus) to take charge of affairs in Galilee and that the priests among them thought they were entitled to collect tithes from the Galileans suggests that the Jerusalem priesthood believed that it had a rightful claim to jurisdiction over Galilee (*Life* 63, 80; *War* 2.562–569). If both possibilities are credible, then the Pharisees might have played a minor role after Jerusalem lost jurisdiction over Galilee. More likely is that the Jesus-movements that produced the Gospel stories knew of the Pharisees in the Jerusalem temple-state as those who cultivated and pushed the laws and customs and policy. Simply this could have been the basis of the Gospels portrayal of the Pharisees as representatives of the Jerusalem temple-state in Galilee, a basis for the controversy stories in Mark and the woes in Matthew and Luke, both of which concern the effects of the Pharisees role as retainers of the temple-state.

While envisioning the possibilities of Pharisees' role as representatives of and advocates for the Jerusalem temple-state's interests in Galilee, however, it would be well to be explicit about what that did not include. There is no evidence that Pharisees were resident in Galilee (Luke 5:17b is simply not credible historically), much less members of village communities, on which basis they might have been leaders of village assemblies.[37] It has now been made clear that the later rabbis did not become influential in synagogues until centuries later. It is extremely difficult to say how much and what kind of influence the Pharisees exercised in Galilee. Some, or they would not be subject to attack in Gospel materials that presumably derive from Galilean origins. In the first possibility sketched above of their possible role, of course their influence would have been backed up by the coercive power of the state. But they cannot be said to have held power or authority over Galileans, as those words are normally understood. Further, it seems inappropriate to say that Pharisees were in competition with Galilean leaders such as Jesus, since their conflict is based in the prevailing structural conflicts in Roman Palestine. In any case, directly contrary to the conclusions he is arguing, the evidence Freyne presents indicates fairly clearly that Galileans tended to resist the demands of the temple authorities and official interpretation of the Torah.[38] As Saldarini saw clearly, if they played a role at all in Galilee during the time of Jesus, the Pharisees were hardly a leading

---

37. The pronouncement stories in which the Pharisees challenge Jesus in Mark are simply not connected with the synagogues, contra Mack, *A Myth of Innocence*.

38. Freyne, *Galilee*, chaps. 7 and 8.

political or religious force there. They would have been outsiders, representatives of the Jerusalem temple-state. And that "would explain their small numbers in Galilee, their lack of mention in other sources, [and] their hostility to Jesus"[39]—and Jesus' hostility to them, rooted in the very structure of the historical situation.

JESUS' WOES AGAINST THE PHARISEES AND SCRIBES IN Q 11:39–52

Having ascertained the Pharisees' limited role in Galilee, albeit somewhat tenuously, we can investigate Jesus' pronouncements against them in Q. The latter is commonly understood as the "Source" from which Matthew and Luke drew the "sayings" of Jesus that they present in a strikingly parallel sequence and wording, often virtually verbatim. In the case of these woes against the Pharisees and scribes/lawyers, the sequence and wording are sufficiently different that it may be impossible to reconstruct the source with much confidence. Attending to the variations in wording may actually be helpful in sensing the possible range of rhetoric and meaning anyhow, making the reconstruction of the source less important.

Many recent interpretations of Q still work with the standard old Christian theological paradigm of the emergence of early Christianity from Judaism, which thus determines the reading. Since Pharisees were by definition the principal spokesmen for normative Judaism, conflict with the Pharisees is broadened into conflict with Judaism generally. Since the woes against the Pharisees include condemnation of "this generation" and "Jerusalem" as well, Q scholars conclude that the condemnation must be a rejection of "all Israel."[40] Since the focus of the conflict was the law, with which the scribes and Pharisees were integrally linked as its official interpreters, Q interpreters have tended to find the struggle over the law at several points in Q whether it is referred to or not, but particularly in the woes against the Pharisees and scribes/lawyers.[41]

Particularly important for those reading through the lenses of the standard old paradigm are the woe against cleansing the outside of the cup (Luke/Q 11:39–41) and the woe against the tithing of mint, dill, and cumin (Luke/Q11:42). (It is now standard to refer to Q passages according to their order in Luke.) On the assumption that these issues lay at the

---

39. Saldarini, *Pharisees*, 296.

40. E.g., Kloppenborg, *Formation of Q*, 167, etc. I choose this illustration because of the influence of his book on Q studies in the United States and Canada.

41. E.g., Tuckett, *Q and the History of Early Christianity*, 404–24.

heart of Pharisaic interpretation, and keying particularly on the phrase at the end of 11:42 ("these [i.e., justice and mercy] you ought to have done, without neglecting the others [i.e., tithing the herbs])," some have argued recently that cultic laws such as those concerned with purity and tithing were not being rejected but rather set within a broader context of divine demands.[42] In contrast with Paul, Q did not break with or reject the Torah but radicalized it. The Q community was thus in effect another Jewish sect in competition with the Pharisees. Another reading through the same standard lens finds a three-stage development behind the woes against the Pharisees.[43] In the first stage, reflected in 11:39-41 and 42 the Q community is still Torah-observant. But in 11:46, where "loading people with heavy burdens" is understood as referring to the practice of scribal interpretation that multiplies rules, the Q community rejects Pharisaic interpretation and leadership of the synagogues. Finally, in the more vituperative woes of 11:44, 47-48, 52 the Pharisees are condemned as the very enemies of God's purpose. Yet another reading according to the old paradigm, noting that in 11:39-41 Q understands the vessels as metaphors for ethical, not ritual, purity, and that in calling the Pharisees "unmarked graves" in 11:44 Q is utilizing corpse-pollution as a metaphor for moral failing, finds that purity is indeed important for the Q community but is redefined in ethical terms.[44]

Before proceeding it is important to establish appropriate principles for analysis and interpretation of biblical and other ancient texts. Along with the standard Christian theological paradigm went the isolation of text fragments from their literary as well as historical context so that they could be examined closely for their theological content and/or the historical evidence they could be made to yield. In recent years, however, as we have stepped away from the old practices, we have learned to view texts as wholes, in this case to take our Gospels whole and the speeches in the Gospels whole. In his book on Matthew, Saldarini consistently worked with the Gospel as a whole as he explored various aspects. Neusner has shown the way for a whole generation of students and colleagues to dealing with the Mishnah in terms of whole tractates, attending further to the sequence of conceptual units and steps within the whole. Indeed he holds himself to the high standard of dealing with the Mishnah as a whole system. In recent books I have attempted to adhere to the same principle in reading/hearing the Gospel of Mark and Q as a source used by Matthew and Luke.

---

42. Wild, "The Encounter"; Schultz, *Q—Die Spruchquelle.*
43. Kloppenborg, "Nomos and Ethos in Q"; Schürmann, "Die Redekomposition."
44. Kloppenborg, "Nomos and Ethos in Q."

In the case of a nonnarrative text such as Q, which is also uncertain in its reconstruction, this is unusually difficult. Nevertheless, by relying on the highly sophisticated recent compositional criticism of Kloppenborg, we can discern the contours of a text very different from its previous conception in the field. Ironically, perhaps, as part of his elaborate stratigraphical analysis of Q, Kloppenborg has convincingly demonstrated that Q is not a collection of sayings but a sequence of speeches or discourses.[45] Again ironically perhaps, unlike the Gospel of Thomas with which it has been compared, and which does present a mere collection of isolated single, double, or triple sayings of Jesus, Q consists of a whole series of Jesus-speeches on various topics and with particular functions. What's more, if we further assume that like most ancient texts, Q was repeatedly recited in a group context, then the discourses appear to be addressed to the concerns and needs of communities of a Jesus-movement.[46]

Q even has a certain structure and sequence. It opens with John's promise of baptism by the Spirit and threat of baptism with fire and closes with the assurance of the twelve liberating (not judging) the tribes of Israel in a renewal or restoration of the people (Q/Luke 3:7-9; 22:28-30).[47] Jesus' opening discourse (6:20-49) offers the kingdom of God to the poor and hungry and provides covenantal instructions for intracommunity social and economic relations in what appears to us as apparently performative speech; i.e., it is an enactment of covenant renewal (as evident in 1QS from Qumran). Jesus' last full discourse concerning the suddenness of the judgmental "day of the son of man" (17:23-37) provides sanction on the exhortation to the community in the rest of the speeches. In between are several speeches on such matters as the respective roles of John and Jesus (7:18-35), the mission to expand the movement (9:57—10:16), prayer (11:2-4, 9-13), bold confession when apprehended by the authorities (12:2-12), anxiety about the basic necessities of food and shelter (12:22-31), and community discipline (17:1-6). In the two speeches with the sharpest language of judgment, Jesus ostensibly addresses outsiders: the Pharisees, in 11:39-52, and the Jerusalem rulers, in 13:28-29, 34-35; 14:16-24. That is, the sequence of speeches in Q presents a renewal of Israel combined with an outright condemnation of the rulers and their representatives.

---

45. Kloppenborg, *Formation of Q*.

46. I have attempted to lay out the case for the contours of Q as a "text" consisting of a sequence of speeches, based on, but coming to conclusions different from, those of Kloppenborg and others in *Whoever Hears You Hears Me*, chap. 4.

47. See further, Horsley, in *Whoever Hears You*, 84-90. On Luke/Q 22:28-30, see my earlier analysis and interpretation in *Jesus and the Spiral*, 199-208.

Simply on the basis of this literary survey of Q it is possible to establish an important corrective to readings of Q based on the old Christian theological paradigm. Contrary to what many recent studies of Q have been claiming, Q represents not a rejection or condemnation of "all Israel" but a renewal of the people Israel. Particularly once we recognize the division between rulers and villagers in Judea and Galilee that Saldarini and others have been pointing out, it is unmistakable that the prophetic woes and laments in Q are directed not at Israel generally, but are specifically targeted at the Pharisees and the Jerusalem ruling house.

Prominent in recent North American interpretation of Q has been the practice of classifying individual sayings according to one of the standard dichotomies of established New Testament scholarship, sapiential and apocalyptic—mainly as the key to sorting out different strata in the document. Quite aside from there being virtually no apocalyptic sayings in Q, this has blocked recognition of traditional Israelite forms taken by the larger speeches of which the sayings are components. If we have ears to hear, on the other hand, it is evident not only that the speech in Q 6:20–49 is a renewed covenant, but that the woes against the Pharisees cohere as a sequence of prophetic woes climaxed by a declaration of sentence familiar from the classical Israelite prophets and from the Epistle of Enoch, closer to the time of Jesus.[48] In several prophetic books, besides individual woes coupled with statements of sentence, there are sequences of two to four woes followed by a statement of punishment, clearly against injustices by the rulers or their officers (Amos 6:1–3, 4–6 + 7; Isa 5:18–19, 20, 21, 22–23 + 24; Hab 2:9–11, 12, 15 + 16–17, 19 [another woe]). In the Epistle of Enoch the woes all appear in sets of three to eight, sometimes with each woe having an attached declaration of sentence, sometimes with series of four or five woes capped by a sentence/punishment directed against the wealthy and powerful oppressors of the people (96:4, 5, 6, 7, 8 + sentence; 97:7, 8, 9, 10 + sentence). That is, far from isolating on individual sayings of woe, interpretation must take the woes in Q 11:39–52 as a whole sequence of woes-plus-sentence that draws upon and resonates with other such sets of woes in Israelite prophetic tradition.

It seems evident, furthermore, that the woes are prophetic indictments coupled with the corresponding declaration of sentence. The very monograph that decisively delineated the development of the form of the woes in Israelite prophets ironically also seriously downplays the degree to which those woes (including the sequences) indict the wealthy and powerful rulers and/or their officers (not the people!) for exploiting and oppressing their

---

48. Horsley in *Whoever Hears You Hears Me*, chaps. 9 and 13 respectively.

people.[49] While the prophetic rhetoric is rather general in Isa 5:18–24 (except for 5:23), Amos 6:1–3, 4–8 and Hab 2:6–8, 9–11, 12 specify "those who are secure in Zion/Samaria," the idle rich, those who load up on goods taken in pledge, who get evil gain, and who build a city by bloodshed. Nickelsburg has noted that the woes in the Epistle of Enoch continue the "overtones of a vengeful curse, again indicting the wealthy and powerful "sinners" for exploitative practices against the poor in violation of covenantal principles, in rhetoric that is often reminiscent of the specific language of Amos and other prophets.[50] Exploring the implications of Nickelsburg's work, I have suggested that the social location and social conflict of the woes in 1 Enoch can be specified even more precisely: the scribal authors of the Epistle, dissident (former?) retainers of the Jerusalem temple-state in the (late third or) early second century are indicting the incumbent aristocracy in no uncertain (prophetic!) terms for exploiting the people (and apparently persecuting the dissident scribal circle).[51] It is thus an intriguing possibility that the spokesperson(s) for Jesus in Q 11:39–52, aware that scribal circles had long since, in certain circumstances, employed prophetic woes against the ruling aristocracy, turned precisely these woes against the scribes and Pharisees.

If in considering the Q speech of woes against the Pharisees we abandon the old paradigm and read again closely, a picture very different from the previous focus on the law quickly appears. It is highly questionable, in fact, whether the woes are about the law at all, even about the supposed Pharisaic/Jewish obsession with purity codes. Only one of the woes (11:42) even refers to the law, and only two others mention issues of purity (11:39 and 44), and then in a rhetorical mocking of the Pharisees rather than as the main issue of indictment. The second woe begins with reference to tithes, which while not a matter of ceremonial law is surely a matter of law, concerns taxes. The reference to "mint, dill, and cumin" is surely hyperbole and caricature, probably full of sarcasm or ridicule (were such herbs even tithed?). The focus, however, quickly moves from the law about tithes to an exhortation about justice and compassion. The first woe (11:39–41) does indeed refer to the Pharisees' concerns about ritual purity (as Neusner has documented and explained)[52] but quickly shifts the vessels into metaphors, explicitly in Luke's version, implicitly in Matthew's. With that shift, however, the issue is no longer on purity. In what may be the most clever woe of all, the accusation that the Pharisees are like "unmarked graves" surely alludes

---

49. Janzen, *Mourning Cry and Woe Oracles*.
50. Nickelsburg, *1 Enoch 1*, 416–17, 460–511.
51. Horsley, "Social Relations and Social Conflict."
52. Neusner, "First Cleanse the Inside."

to the concerns of the Pharisees/scribes about purity, but again purity functions metaphorically. In the only three woes that mention either an issue of the law or of purity codes, the focus is on something else. We must take a closer look.

The (rhetorical) charge in Luke 11:42 that the Pharisees were obsessed with even the minor items, not even cultivated, such as mint and herbs, serves to indicate how rigorous they were about the principal cultivated products subject to tithes/taxes such as grain, on which the very survival of subsistence producers themselves depended. If the Pharisees or scribes/lawyers, as representatives of Jerusalem, were still insisting on payment of tithes in addition to the taxes that Galilean peasants were paying to the government of Antipas or Agrippa and the tribute they were rendering to Caesar, they were indeed neglecting justice and compassion. The latter indictment alludes to prophetic covenantal exhortation demanding *mišpat, ḥesed, ṣedeq, 'emet*, known in the great tradition from such texts as Hos 4:1; 12:7; Mic 6:8; and Zech 7:9–10: "Thus says the Lord of hosts: Render true judgments, show kindness and mercy to one another; do not oppress the widow, the orphan, the alien, or the poor." Presumably villagers were also fully aware of this tradition of prophetic call for economic justice. The charge that the Pharisees neglect justice and compassion, with its allusion to the tradition of prophetic exhortation, in connection with the rhetorical mocking of how rigorous they are in enforcing the tithing laws, makes this woe not so much a dispute about the laws as it is an indictment of the Pharisees for merciless injustice in their role as administrative retainers.

The two woes that appeared to earlier readers to focus on purity rather use the Pharisees' concerns about purity in a metaphorical way. How the metaphor works is simplest and clearest in Luke 11:44, which surely represents Q more directly, and Matthew's version (23:27–28) spells the analogy out explicitly. Drawing on the Pharisees' concerns with purity, this woe compares them to unmarked graves, which people do not see, meaning fairly clearly that they are dangerous to the people in ways that the people cannot see or detect. The simple simile in 11:44 then aids us discerning what is intended in 11:39–41 and Matt 23:25–26. Again mocking their concerns about purity—peasants would hardly have shared those concerns!—this woe charges the Pharisees with nothing less than extortion and rapacity. This is an ominous indictment, pertaining evidently to how they operate in their political-economic role as retainers of the temple-state. Insofar as this is the first in the series of woes, moreover, this sets the tone for the whole series. Woes are being pronounced over the Pharisees because of their extortion!

The remaining four woes do not allude to the law or purity in any way. But they do focus on yet other aspects of the behavior of the Pharisees and scribes/lawyers in carrying out their roles as retainers of the temple-state. It would have been galling for villagers if the representatives of the temple who pressed them mercilessly to pay their tithes and squeezed them to the limits of their subsistence productivity then presumed to expect honor and deference in public places, the indictment in Luke 11:43//Matt 23:6 (paralleled in the episode in Mark 12:41-44). The "heavy burdens" in Luke 11:46 //Matt 23:4 were surely not the multiplication of rules by scribal interpretation, but the burdens of tithes and other dues. One of the functions of the scribes and Pharisees was evidently instruction about, perhaps even administration of, tithes and other dues. The reference to the Pharisees or lawyers not touching those burdens with one of their fingers is thus an allusion to how such interpreters-administrators responsible for interpretation and application of laws and regulations concerning revenues could help alleviate the burdens of the peasant producers through their scribal role, if only they would. As for building the graves/tombs of the prophets in Luke 11:47-48//Matt 23:29-32, the custodians of such memorials or monuments would have been precisely the retainers of the temple-state, such as Pharisees and scribes/lawyers. It is heavy hypocrisy and irony, however, as well as ideological mystification, for the representatives of the current rulers to be cultivating the sacred memory of those who had protested against earlier rulers, and sometimes paid with their lives. The final woe is a comprehensive indictment that sums up all the previous ones. Matthew's phrase, "shutting the kingdom of heaven" (23:13), and Luke's accusation of "taking away the keys of knowledge" (11:52) are parallel, equivalent expressions. As in key prophetic passages (e.g., Isa 1:2-3), "knowledge" here refers to covenant keeping, which would be synonymous with living under or according to the kingdom of God/heaven. The Pharisees are accused of blocking the way in their role as retainers so that the people cannot enter the kingdom (now being proclaimed and manifested in Jesus' mission).

Pulling these observations about each of the woes together, it is clear that the focus in the series is not on the law and/or purity at all but on the social-political-economic role of the Pharisees and scribes/lawyers. In fact, the whole set of woes constitutes a series of prophetic indictments, deeply grounded in Israelite prophetic tradition, for the ways they, only partly related to their role as interpreters of the Torah, were contributing to the exploitation of the people.

The declaration of sentence with which the prophetic indictments in the woes climax in Luke 11:49-51//Matt 23:34-36 is strikingly harsh in tone, like those in Israelite prophetic tradition in which this Q speech is rooted. It indicates just how seriously the indictments were intended. This is no mere dispute or debate about the laws, but a prophetic pronouncement of judgment. The charge of killing the prophets is repeated from the immediately preceding woe (11:47-48), providing the link between indictments and sentence. It repetition in the prophetic lament over Jerusalem in 13:34-35 suggests that the killing of the prophets was a serious issue for the Q speeches and the movement they addressed. One suspects that the Q people understood John and Jesus as the latest in the long line of martyred Israelite prophets and understood themselves as their successors, also undergoing persecution (see the last beatitude in Luke/Q 6:22-23).

That the blood of the martyred prophets is required of "this generation" has led many to imagine that "all Israel" or "Judaism" in general stands condemned here. But that is hardly the thrust of the declaration. "This generation" (or "this kind") was probably a contemporary idiomatic expression, the meaning of which must be determined from immediate context and other contexts in Q and other Gospel literature. Mark uses the term in a broad general reference, pejoratively in 8:38, neutrally in 13:30. Mark refers the term more specifically to the disciples in 9:19 and to the Pharisees in 8:12, which is the Markan parallel to Luke/Q 11:29-32. Especially if Matt 12:38 represents the order of Q,[53] then Q as well as Mark uses "this generation" in reference to the (scribes and) Pharisees in connection with seeking a sign. Significantly, the only other use of "this generation" in Q occurs in a court context of adversarial address, suggesting figures such as scribes and Pharisees. Q thus appears to be fairly consistent in using "this generation" with direct or indirect implicit reference to scribes and Pharisees.[54] "All Israel" is hardly implicated. As in most prophetic uses of woes plus sentences, the targets are specific, usually the rulers and/or their representatives.

The seeming exaggeration of the persecution of prophets may appear to be mere rhetoric, since few of the "canonical" prophets included or mentioned in the Hebrew Bible were persecuted and killed. We should keep in mind, however, that neither the "great tradition" in Jerusalem nor the "little traditions" of Judean and Galilean village communities were stable, much less canonized, in the first century CE. It is clear from such literature as the Martyrdom of Isaiah and the Lives of the Prophets that legends of the prophets' persecution and martyrdom were being actively cultivated.[55] Of the five prophets said to have been martyred under kings, the three said to be in Jerusalem were Isaiah, Amos, and Zechariah son of Jehoiadas, who is

---

53. So Kloppenborg, *Q Parallels*.

54. See further Horsley, "Social Conflict," 49.

55. See further Satran, *Biblical Prophets*, who argues that the *Lives of the Prophets* is a much later, largely Christian document; and Schwemere, *Studien*, esp. 1.65-71, who makes compelling arguments that most material in the *Lives* stems from prior to 70 CE.

the last prophet to appear in the Lives. According to the legend, moreover, he was supposedly killed "near the altar" (23:1).[56]

Memory of the prophets, moreover, was being cultivated in monuments as well as in literature. Contemporaries claimed to know the burial places of the prophets. And it is not hard to imagine that the building of memorials to the prophets was part of the wider program of building under Herod and his successors. The ostentatious religious-cultural renaissance of buildings and monuments inaugurated by Herod, such as the entrance to David's tomb (*Ant.* 7.392–94; 16.179–88), was sustained by wealthy diaspora Jews and prominent proselytes from abroad (*Ant.* 20.95; *War* 5.55, 119, 47).[57] If the temple-state was responsible for supervising these monuments, who more obvious to place in charge but the scribes and Pharisees. The whole program of later rulers and their representatives building memorials to prophets who had condemned ancient rulers and been killed by them, however, appeared as the height of hypocrisy and callous attempt at self-legitimation and mystification to the Galilean peasantry for whom "Jesus" is the spokesperson in Q 11:39–52. And this issue may have been of special poignancy to the movement that produced Q, which contains nothing that corresponds to the narrative of arrest, trial, and crucifixion in Mark, but apparently did understand Jesus as a prophet like Moses and Elijah, with a program of restoration and renewal of Israel.

I hope to have illustrated how the sociological approach to the Pharisees that Tony Saldarini pioneered, supplemented by the borrowing of other comparative historical studies of agrarian societies, can also begin to illuminate the conflict between Jesus and the Pharisees represented in Gospel literature. The resulting picture is a far more credible sense of the historical structural division between what Saldarini identified as the governing class and their retainers, on the one hand, and the productive peasantry, on the other. Far from Jesus and the earliest Gospel traditions having articulated a condemnation of Judaism or Israel, they rather articulated a program of renewal of Israel, but in opposition to the incumbent Jerusalem rulers and their representatives. And that should be a credible reconstruction of the development of the Jesus movement represented by Q, one of the sources used by the Gospel of Matthew, which Saldarini explained as a gospel within, not opposed to, the varied spectrum of groups and movements that constituted Israel in the aftermath of the Roman destruction of Jerusalem.

---

56. Schwemer, *Studien*, vol. 2, 283–321.

57. Still useful is Jeremias, *Heiligengraeber in Jesu Unwelt*; up to date is Roller, *Building Program*; cf. Richardson, *Herod*, chap. 8.

7

PHARISEES AND SCRIBES
IN THE GOSPEL STORIES

DRAWING ON THE GOSPEL stories as sources for fuller understanding of the Pharisees and their conflict with Jesus has been blocked by two self-imposed limitations of New Testament studies. One is the deeply rooted scholarly habit of focusing narrowly on particular text fragments and not considering the broader literary context of the overall Gospel narratives. In the 1970s and 1980s, however, Gospel scholars (re)discovered that the Gospels are sustained narratives, whole stories with dominant plots and interlocking subplots.[1] Moreover, the overall story of a Gospel is the best guide to the historical context of the story as a whole and of its particular episodes. And this leads to the second limitation deeply rooted in the field. The historical context is conceptualized synthetically as Judaism, a construct that lumps together a variety of regions and movements and institutions, and simply blocks recognition of significant regional differences of historical experience, shifting and conflictual political relations, and movements of different forms.

Studies of the historical Jesus and of the Pharisees and their conflict with Jesus have not yet moved beyond these limitations. By considering more fully the overall Gospel stories and their broader portrayal of the Pharisees, however, it may be possible to discern how the Gospel stories'

---

1. Among the early explorations of whole Gospel stories, see Kelber, *Mark's Story of Jesus*; helpful and incisive reflection on the explorations of the Gospels as narratives in Moore, *Literary Criticism of the Gospels*.

broader portrayal of the position and role of the Pharisees fits into the historical context as known from extra-Gospel sources.

The Gospel stories locate the mission of Jesus of Nazareth mainly in the villages of Galilee. Presumably it would be important to understand as much as possible about the historical situation in Galilee in the first century CE. This is all the more important for an approach that attempts to consider the Pharisees relationally, in their political-economic position and role, particularly insofar as the works of Josephus, perhaps the most important source for the Pharisees, has them located in Jerusalem, including during the time when the high priestly rulers took control of Galilee, which had not been under Jerusalem rule for many centuries. During the lifetime of Jesus, moreover, the Jerusalem high priesthood no longer had jurisdiction over Galilee. The historical context of Galilee and Galileans in late second-temple times, however, has been obscured by the controlling construct of Judaism in the fields of New Testament studies.

The concept of Judaism has historically meant rabbinic Judaism. And rabbinic culture did not develop in Galilee until the second century and after. The rabbis did not locate in Galilee until after the Roman devastation of Judea in suppression of the second revolt of 132–135 CE, and did not gain much influence among the people until the third century. It is estimated that the rabbis did not gain decisive influence in the synagogues until the seventh century.[2] The historical regional experience of the people living in Galilee in the previous centuries, however, had been very different from that of the people of Judea, especially the Jerusalemites in the Second Temple Period. Because ancient empires did not generally deport the peasantry when they conquered an area, we can probably surmise that many people in Galilee were descendants of former Israelites, primarily of the tribes of Naphtali, Issachar, and Zebulun. After the northern tribes rebelled against the Davidic monarchy in Jerusalem in 921 BCE (if there was such a monarchy then), these Israelites lived under a separate monarchy for nearly two centuries. After the Assyrians conquered the area in 732 BCE, ten years before the fall of Samaria itself, Galilee was under a separate imperial provincial administration from Judea through the succession of Assyrian, Babylonian, Persian, and Hellenistic empires. Galilee did not come under Jerusalem rule until, in the expansionist wars by the Hasmonean regime, Aristobulus took control of the area from the Itureans in 104 BCE. As they did to the Idumeans to the south of Judea, the Hasmonean regime compelled the inhabitants of Galilee "to live in accordance with the laws of the Judeans," according to Josephus (*Ant.* 13.318; cf. 13.257). But what did that mean?

---

2. Cohen, *From the Maccabees to the Mishnah*, 221.

Despite the shared cultural traditions from ancient Israel, one must question just how rapidly and deeply the "Judaization" of the Galileans went, given the different regional histories. Josephus provides an intriguing parallel case of Idumeans who effectively resisted the assimilation of/to "the laws of the Judeans" for nearly a century in the story of Costobar, governor of Idumea under Herod and married to Herod's sister Salome. If such a prominent family involved in the network of imperial political relations resisted assimilation to Judean customs (and Hellenization as well?), villagers in the hill country of Galilee likely clung to their traditional (presumably Israelite) ways all the more. The process of adjustment to "the laws of the Judeans" must have been slow at best, and raises the question of what the mechanism may have been through which the Hasmonean regime pressed their rule in or administered Galilee.

That the Jerusalem temple-state had apparently not enforced "the laws of the Judeans," so that Costobar and other Idumeans had not adopted the customs of the Judeans in family and community life, suggests that requiring the Galileans to live "according to the laws of the Judeans" did not mean their resocialization. Replacing the Galilean Israelite customs and way of life with the laws and customs devised by scribes and Pharisees based in Jerusalem would have taken a concentrated program staffed by hundreds if not thousands of priests and scribal teachers. From what we know of traditional agrarian societies, their rulers did not interfere with local village life except to collect taxes and tithes from the threshing floors and olive and wine presses. If the Jerusalem temple-state had been devoted to pressing Judean customs and traditions into village life, such a program would have been spasmodic and intermittent. Ordinary priests, many of whom lived in villages around Jerusalem, were hardly mobile and available for reassignment. The situation of the Hasmonean state, including for the Pharisees and any other scribes, moreover, would have made any "missionary" effort virtually impossible. The Hasmonean agenda was conquest of other territory and nearby cities with their mercenary troops. Immediately after Galilee had been taken over by Aristobulus in 104 BCE, the Jerusalem populace and other Judeans, evidently joined by the Pharisees whom King and High Priest Hyrcanus had expelled from the administration, came into intense and prolonged civil conflict with Alexander Jannaeus (103–76 BCE). Then for nearly thirty years in the mid-first century BCE, Jerusalem and outlying areas were embroiled in a series of civil wars between rival Hasmonean rulers and conquests by the Romans until the military strongman Rome designated as king finally imposed his rule effectively, in 37 BCE. When Salome Alexandra (r. 76–67 BCE) brought the Pharisees back into the temple-state administration, according to Josephus's accounts, they focused primarily on regaining equilibrium in domestic affairs after the intense armed conflicts and sought to bring to justice the military officers who had participated in the brutal treatment of Alexander Jannaeus's opponents. Under Herod, when the Pharisees had in effect been demoted with the temple-state subordinated to the king's administration, Josephus suggests, they were focused on opposing the worst effects of Herod's repressive rule. It is difficult to discern when the temple-state might have devoted serious attention to pressing Judean customs onto local village life in Galilee. Thus for Galileans, being required "to live according to the laws of the Judeans" probably pertained primarily to accepting Jerusalem rule, including particularly its taxation.

After the death of Herod the Romans imposed his son Herod Antipas as ruler of Galilee (from 4 BCE to 39 CE), so that the priestly aristocracy in Jerusalem, now under the oversight of a Roman governor in Caesarea, no longer had jurisdiction there. Thereafter the Galileans lived directly under the rule of a Roman governor or one of the Agrippas. It is thus unclear just what kind of authority or influence any representative of the temple and high priesthood in Jerusalem could have exerted in Galilee. So it is striking, in Josephus's accounts, that the council (*koinon*) of high priests and leading Pharisees that formed a provisional government in Jerusalem was quick to assert its jurisdiction and authority over Galilee and the Galileans in the late summer of 66 CE. This suggests that the authorities in Jerusalem had attended to affairs in Galilee right along, even though they had not held official political jurisdiction during the first century CE.

Whatever degree of moderating intention one might attribute to them, the high priests and leading Pharisees who formed a provisional government in Jerusalem at the end of the insurrectionary summer of 66 moved immediately to assert their control of Galilee, even though it had not been under Jerusalem jurisdiction for seventy years. Despite Josephus's self-serving apology in the *Life* and his self-portrait as the ideal general in the *War*, it is clear from a close reading of both accounts that the real agenda of the provisional government in Jerusalem as well as of their commander in Galilee was to regain effective control over the insurrectionary populace (see esp. *War* 2.562–568).[3]

The Pharisees were integral participants in their operations. The leading Pharisees in Jerusalem moved quickly to the fore in governing councils (*Life* 190–196). In terms of political roles, when the Jerusalem *koinon* formed a delegation for the purpose of removing Josephus from his "command" in Galilee, three out of four members were Pharisees.

---

3. In 1990 I had already begun the close examination of Josephus's accounts that was published later in "The Power Vacuum and Power Struggle in 66–67 CE."

> The scheme agreed upon was to send a deputation consisting of men different in rank but equal in education. Two of them, Jonathan and Ananias, were regular citizens and Pharisees by party, the third, Joazar, also a Pharisee, was of priestly lineage, and the youngest, Simon, was descended from the high priests. (*Life* 196-197; cf. *War* 2.628)

Because this was an important mission, a high priest was included in the delegation. But the inclusion of three Pharisees suggests that missions of the provisional government, and perhaps those of the high priestly regime before the revolt, were carried out by Pharisees. Thus Pharisees or other scribes may have served as representatives of the high priesthood in outlying districts such as Galilee in the first century. It remains to be seen if the Gospel stories provide any further specification of the function of Pharisees and scribes in Galilee.

THE MARKAN STORY

The Markan Story is considered the earliest Gospel by consensus among Gospel scholars, its composition usually dated to just before or after the great revolt in 66-70. Because of early Christian tradition that Mark was supposedly Peter's companion and interpreter and the tradition of Peter as the first bishop in Rome, the Markan Gospel is assumed to have originated in Rome. Critical reexamination of the Markan story (in which I am involved), however, leads to an alternative hypothesis that it developed in Galilee and nearby areas of Syria and to its present form before great revolt. This makes for a considerable difference in the way the Gospel is read and interpreted, as Gospel specialists are learning to appreciate that it is a sustained narrative, a whole story with a conflictual main plot and subplots.

Before the consideration of the Gospels as stories was more fully developed, Anthony Saldarini examined the number of appearances the Pharisees make, where they appear geographically, and the issues with which they are concerned in Mark. Thus without the benefit of considering the overall Markan story, his principal conclusion was that as in Josephus, so in Mark the Pharisees (and the scribes) can be placed in the retainer class, at the edges of the governing class. They are "a political interest group," yet are somehow "out of power."[4] Nevertheless, "the Pharisees were recognized leaders in the Galilean community, according to Mark . . . , [with] high standing in the community and influence, if not power, with the people and

---

4. Saldarini, *Pharisees*, 146-57.

other leaders."[5] Burton Mack, using the pre-Markan pronouncement stories to trace the social history of the group from which the Gospel eventually emerged, suggested that the Pharisees were religious authorities who, in effect, won out over the "synagogue reform movement" that produced the pronouncement stories. The Pharisees were thus active in the synagogues that the Jesus people were attempting to reform.[6]

If, on the other hand, we start with the overall narrative, the Markan story portrays the Pharisees and scribes as representatives of the high priestly heads of the temple-state, more or less as do Josephus's works. They "come down from Jerusalem," where they are evidently based (3:22; 7:1), to Galilee to keep Jesus under surveillance. They lack authority with the Galileans in the synagogues in villages such as Capernaum. Early in the story, when Jesus heals on the Sabbath in a synagogue, the Pharisees conspire with the Herodians (evidently representatives of Herod Antipas, the ruler of Galilee) to destroy Jesus (3:6). Not many episodes later (3:22), they charge Jesus with "having Beelzebul, and casting out demons by the prince of demons" (which, in modern terms, would be like a combination of political subversion and religious blasphemy). In the middle of the story they again "come down from Jerusalem" and charge that Jesus' disciples are violating "the tradition of the elders" in not washing their hands before eating (7:1–5). But Jesus changes the subject to the temple-state's economic drain on local family resources, charging the Pharisees with countermanding the fundamental commandment of "honoring one's parents" by urging them to "devote" some of their land or its produce to God (i.e., to support the temple, 7:9–13). Then in Jesus' sustained confrontation with the Jerusalem rulers (chapters 11–12), after he has pronounced a prophetic parable against the high priests (12:1–12), they send the Pharisees again with the Herodians to entrap him over the issue of paying tribute to Caesar (12:13–17), which would enable them finally to destroy him.

In the narrative prior to the Pharisees and scribes appearing in tandem with the high priests in Jerusalem, the Pharisees and scribes always appear in *controversy stories*. That is, they are almost always portrayed challenging Jesus or his disciples and usually being bested by Jesus, on one issue after another. This means that it is difficult to discern their location and its significance. Almost always their location is utterly indeterminate, even in "Levi's house" in 2:15–17 and "Judea beyond the Jordan," in the transition to the story in 10:2–9. Otherwise, that they appear mostly in Galilee during Jesus' mission there and once in Jerusalem at the climax of the story depends

5. Saldarini, *Pharisees*, 151.
6. Mack, *Myth of Innocence*, 192–98.

on the overall plotting of the narrative, and does not pertain directly to what the Pharisees are portrayed as doing or saying in particular cases. Thus the overall narrative is more telling as an indication of their role and function, that is, as the representatives of the temple-state who, in Galilee, conspire with the Herodians in an official capacity to attempt to destroy Jesus and, in Jerusalem, are delegated by the high priests to entrap Jesus on a capital political charge that would lead to his execution by the Romans.

Thus, while the Markan story as an overall narrative has a certain historical verisimilitude, with the high priests, elders, and scribes being the rulers and their retainers in Jerusalem itself, and the Pharisees and scribes ("down from Jerusalem") as a presence in the outlying districts of Galilee, Judea, and beyond the Jordan, we must be careful how we characterize that presence. Even to say somewhat vaguely that the Pharisees were *active in* Galilee stretches the literary evidence, for they appear almost always in a controversy story where their location is indeterminate. Any impression we get of the Pharisees and scribes having Jesus under surveillance probably stems from the combination of the overall narrative effect and the statement "they were watching him" in one episode (3:1–5). In contrast to modern governments that do place their citizens under surveillance, ancient governments paid little attention to the people as long as tax revenues were regularly forthcoming. Certainly to suggest that Mark or Markan materials locate the Pharisees in the synagogues (Mack) or that Mark's Pharisees have high standing and influence in the Galilean community (Saldarini) goes beyond the literary evidence. Only once in all the pronouncement stories do the Pharisees appear in a synagogue, and that by virtue of the narrative sequence (2:24; 3:1–2). There is nothing in Mark to suggest that the "their" of "their synagogues" in 1:23, 39 refers to the Pharisees (who do not appear in the narrative until 2:16). In 3:6 the Pharisees do collaborate with the Herodians. But nothing in the pronouncement stories, in which the appearance of the Pharisees occurs and to which it is confined, indicates that they have any sort of standing or influence with the people whom Jesus is addressing and healing (presumably mostly Galileans). The only possible basis for our imagining their social relationship with the people in Galilee would be by analogy with the scribes. That Jesus "taught them as one having authority, and not as the scribes," in 1:22, suggests that the scribes were teachers but (as official representatives?) lacked credibility or resonance with the people. Thus if we were to take the Pharisees as having social relations analogous to those of the scribes in Mark, then they (would) have (had) a rather negative standing or influence with the people.

Examination of the social function of the pronouncement stories in Mark may give further indications of the Pharisees' social function. As

Mack noted, the pronouncement stories feature Jesus as the authority for a Jesus-movement, articulating the movement's position on various issues. As the challengers or opponents in those stories, then, the Pharisees or the Pharisees with the scribes or Herodians function as the established authorities on the issues at stake. The issues range from table fellowship (who can eat with whom, 2:15–17) to Sabbath observance (2:23–28) to purity juxtaposed with the use of economic resources (7:1–13) to divorce/marriage (10:2–9) to the religious-political sanction of the Roman tribute (12:13–17). This is a wide range of issues in which the religious dimension cannot be separated from the political-economic dimensions (*qorban* and the tribute) or the social dimension (table fellowship, healing on the Sabbath, marriage/divorce). That is, the Pharisees' and scribes' social role or function in the Markan pronouncement stories is as authorities who attempt to define proper social relationships and codes of behavior and to control the people's behavior accordingly—and whose definitions and control Jesus resists on behalf of the people. This representation of the Pharisees (and scribes) in the Markan pronouncement stories, in terms of their social role or function, is much the same as Josephus repeatedly indicates: the Pharisees are the experts on the laws.

A closer look at the most elaborate pronouncement story, Mark 7:1–13, can lead us a step or two further. At the beginning and in the middle the issue appears to be purity (washing hands before meals). And much of the traditional discussion of the story has focused on the issue of purity, influenced by the gloss in 7:19c, which reshapes the issue in a later or a "Pauline" direction (cf. Acts 11:1–18; Gal 2). The story is richer and more complex, however, than the reading according to the purity issue has allowed. The introductory challenge by the Pharisees and scribes introduces "the tradition of the elders," which Jesus then makes into the focal issue in both 7:6–8 and 7:9–13, contrasting that tradition with the basic "commandment of God." The issue in is not "the oral law" *versus* "the written law." No mention is made of anything written. But "your tradition," "the tradition of the elders," would appear to be the same as what Josephus describes the Pharisees as having been promulgating for the people as part of their function in the Hasmonean temple-state. And from Josephus's subsequent accounts of the Pharisees (investigated in the chapters above), it is difficult to believe that the Pharisees had ever backed away from cultivating and perpetuating that ancestral tradition.

This conclusion seems confirmed by the particular illustration Jesus gives of the conflict between their "tradition" and "the commandment of God," in 7:9–13. It is difficult to find anything in the Torah proper that would correspond to the dedication of property to God as *qorban*; hence

Jesus would appear to have taken the illustration from "their tradition," which was not in the written books of Moses, which Josephus's Sadducees viewed as having sole authority. Furthermore, the substance of the issue in the conflict between the Pharisees'/scribes' "tradition" and "the commandment of God," in this case, was the question of the political control of economic resources. It is clear from 7:11–12 that if anyone actually dedicates (*qorban*) a certain property or resource to God, then that property could no longer be used for any other purpose, specifically the economic support of one's elderly parents (which Jesus asserts is the concrete meaning of the divine commandment to "honor your father and your mother"). The function or role of the Pharisees/scribes in this story lay in producing "tradition" that would serve to generate resources for the support of the temple—resources that in this case Jesus claims were intended by the commandment of God to be used for the support of one's family locally. Thus the interests of the Pharisees/scribes in this story coincide with the interests of the temple, indicating that implicit in the story is the information that the Pharisees/scribes are representatives of the temple and high priestly government in Jerusalem. This implicit information, moreover, is paralleled by the introductory statement in 7:1 that the scribes with whom the Pharisees are linked in the story "had come from Jerusalem."

The representation of the Pharisees as encouraging the people to devote their limited resources to the support of the temple is paralleled by Mark's representation of the scribes in 12:38—13:2 (i.e., in narrative sequence). The assumption of 12:38–39, similar to the assumption in the woe against the Pharisees and scribes in Q (Luke 11:43, on which see Chapter 6, above), is that the scribes periodically visit local assemblies or public places (with no indication just where). Then the next indictment, that "they devour widows' houses" (a house = one's household and fields, i.e. resources), is followed by the vignette of the poor widow giving her last two copper coins, pointedly all she had left to live on, to the temple treasury, which in turn is followed by the prediction of the destruction of the temple! Mark's Jesus considers the scribes' activities misguided and reprehensible. The point here is that this polemic provides us a window onto the scribes' role of encouraging support of the temple, which parallels the Pharisees' role implicit in Mark 7:9–13.

The political position and function of the Pharisees/scribes in the pronouncement story in Mark 7 thus parallels rather extensively their political position and function discerned in Josephus's accounts. Yet, as has been more regularly noticed, the portrayal of the Pharisees'/scribes' concerns for purity in this pronouncement story also parallels the representation of their concerns for purity in rabbinic tradition. As Neusner commented, "for all we know, all reports are correct"—because the different sources represent different yet overlapping facets of the concerns and activities of the Pharisees. They were clearly concerned with purity regulations (although less clear is to what extent they may have pressed those upon the populace at large), but their broader political role was, as representatives or retainers of the temple-state, to promulgate, cultivate, and apparently propagate regulations for public life.

THE MATTHEAN STORY

The Matthean story, with its long Jesus-speeches, has somewhat systematized and sharpened the picture of the Pharisees from the Markan story, presumably one of its two principal sources, the other being the Q speeches (discussed in the previous chapter). The Pharisees still appear in the pronouncement stories, but Matthew has added several "clarifying" touches. Most important are the more explicit connection of the Pharisees with Jerusalem (they along with the scribes come from Jerusalem to Jesus, 15:1) and their conspiring against Jesus, without the collaboration of the Herodians, both during the mission in Galilee and in Jerusalem (12:14, 22:15). Matthew presents a more schematic conflict between Jesus and the Pharisees, framed by the Pharisees' conspiring and fed by their arguments with Jesus in the controversy stories taken over from Mark, but also punctuated by the Pharisees' asking for signs and being rejected by Jesus as "blind guides" (e.g., 12:38; 15:12; 16:1). Most striking in Matthew's presentation of the Pharisees are three things unique to this Gospel. First, the Pharisees are included with the high priests as the object of condemnation in the prophetic parable of the wicked tenants (21:45; cf. Mark 12:1–12). Second, Matthew includes a lengthy speech against "the scribes and Pharisees" that incorporates but is three times the length of the speech in Q (Matt 23). And, third, by concluding this speech with the prophetic lament against the Jerusalem ruling house, Matthew associates the Pharisees closely with the high priestly heads of the temple-state (23:37–38). In Matthew the Pharisees are thus much more closely rooted in the temple-state and act as the authorities of the temple-state in conflict with and conspiring against Jesus.

As in Mark, so in Matthew the Pharisees are by narrative arrangement placed in Galilee, from their first appearance in 9:11 until the action moves to "Judea beyond the Jordan" in 19:1 and thence to Jerusalem. But nothing in Matthew suggests they are rooted in Galilee—i.e., "influential in the local village leadership."[7] It was previously imagined that the Pharisees as leaders of local congregations sat in seats that were a feature of later synagogue

---

7. So Saldarini, *Pharisees*, 172.

buildings. Archaeologists who have excavated the synagogue buildings in Galilean villages, however, have dated them to late antiquity. In Matthew as in Mark, the *synagogai* refer not to buildings but to village assemblies. As noted just above, moreover, the rabbis who have been imagined as the successors of the Pharisees had little to do with the synagogues even in the second and third centuries. So we can no longer imagine that "Moses's seat" on which "the scribes and Pharisees sit" in Matt 23:2 was a concrete place in which the Pharisees sat supposedly as leaders of local congregations. Rather "Moses's seat" must be a reference to the authoritative teaching office of the expert expounders of the laws of Moses—exactly the role in which Josephus portrays them. Even if "phylacteries and fringed garments" and titles such as "rabbi" and "teacher" were used by local Jewish leaders in later centuries, there is no justification for projecting that into the late first-century situation of Matthew's Gospel. In one of the sayings taken from Q, in Matt 23:6-7, the scribes and Pharisees are presumed to have visited the local assemblies and to have expected deference to their social position and authority. But in Matt 23 the scribes and Pharisees are clearly not local leaders in Galilee. They are rather the Jerusalem-based authorities on social-religious policy and practice, apparently with titles such as "teacher" or "rabbi," who know and expound regulations concerning such matters as oaths and tithing. They are also officials in charge of tombs memorializing the prophets and are influential in the courts that maintain public order (23:16-24, 29-38). The principal conflict portrayed in Matthew is not between the "Christian (Jewish)" assemblies and the "Jewish" synagogues, but between Jesus and the temple-state, in which the Pharisees were representatives of the temple-state whose role was known even in outlying villages in Galilee and towns in Syria to which the Matthean Jesus-movement may have spread. Again in Matthew the political position and functions of the Pharisees are much the same as they are in the accounts of Josephus.

THE LUKAN STORY

That Matthew, like Mark, is still portraying the Pharisees, their position in the political structure, and their social functions in ways similar to the portrayal in Josephus and certain Dead Sea Scrolls is all the clearer by comparison with the Lukan Gospel story. Luke's Pharisees are still Jesus' principal opponents during his mission in Galilee, but they virtually disappear after Jesus' so-called triumphal entry into Jerusalem (19:29-48). Luke does retain the woes against the effects of their political-economic role (11:37-52), but he drops the most developed and important controversy story, Mark

7:1–13, and other indications of the scribes' being "from Jerusalem." Luke's Pharisees are, shall we say, domesticated, particularly in the Gospel traditions special to Luke. Although "filled with fury" at his actions (6:11), they do little more than badger and admonish him. Far from plotting to destroy him, they even warn him against Herod Antipas's design on his life (6:11; 11:53; 13:31; 15:1–2; 19:39). Most strikingly, the Pharisees invite Jesus to dine with them—improbably so because Jesus then immediately opposes and even condemns them while ostensibly the recipient of their hospitality (7:36–50; 11:37–52; 14:1–24).

Recent treatments claim that Luke pictures the Pharisees as "the local leaders" with "power and wealth in the Galilean villages."[8] Except for 5:17, none of the texts cited suggest this—unless of course we imply from Luke's literary device of the Pharisees' invitations to Jesus that they had homes in Galilee. Two of those invitations, however, come while Jesus is on his famous Lukan literary journey toward Jerusalem, beginning in 9:51. It thus seems inappropriate to read Luke's Gospel as a representation of historical or social realities.

Thus none of the Synoptic Gospels can be read as representing the Pharisees or scribes as "local leaders" or as associating with, much less being leaders of, the synagogues. In the Gospel stories, the Pharisees and scribes are rather representatives of the Jerusalem temple-state in which they serve as the intellectual-legal retainers who cultivate and apply laws and customs for public life that include the provisions of revenues to support the temple's operations. Their portrayal in the Gospels parallels that in Josephus's histories with regard to the Pharisees' political position as retainers of the temple-state. There is a significant difference in the portrayals by the wealthy Judean priest Josephus and by the Gospels, however. Josephus mentions that in certain circumstances the Pharisees resisted the expansionist Hasmoneans and later King Herod, whose building projects in honor of Caesar were contrary to the laws of the Judeans. That suggests that the Pharisees, with their distinct role of cultivating and applying the laws and customs, had a sense of their own authority—an authority that transcended that of the incumbent rulers. In their position as retainers of the temple-state they evidently saw their role as mediating between the imperial order and its client rulers. The Jesus-movements that produced the Gospel stories, on the other hand, were evidently villagers subject to the rule of the temple-state and client kings that the Pharisees and scribes were mediating. In the Gospel stories Jesus, as the

---

8. E.g., Saldarini, *Pharisees*, 178, 175; Moxnes, *Economy of the Kingdom*, 18–19.

spokesperson for those subjected people, pronounced sharp condemnation of some of the effects of the Pharisees' mediating role. In Jesus' woes against the scribes and Pharisees this was prefaced by his mocking the Pharisees' concern about purity rules. It has been a deep tragedy historically that passages such as those woes became the basis for Christian anti-Judaism.

BIBLIOGRAPHY

Alon, Gedalia. *Jews, Judaism, and the Classical World: Studies in Jewish History in the Times of the Second Temple and Talmud.* Translated by I. Abrahams. Jerusalem: Magnes, 1977.

Attridge, Harry W. *The Interpretation of Biblical History in the Antiquitates Judaicae of Flavius Josephus.* Harvard Dissertations in Religion 7. Missoula, MT: Scholars, 1976.

Baumgarten, Albert I. *The Flourishing of Jewish Sects in the Maccabean Era: An Interpretation.* Journal for the Study of Judaism Supplements 55. Leiden: Brill, 1997.

———. "The Pharisaic *Paradosis*." *Harvard Theological Review* 80 (1987) 63–77.

Blenkinsopp, Joseph. "Prophecy and Priesthood in Josephus." *Journal of Jewish Studies* 25 (1974) 239–62.

Botha, Pieter J. J. "Graeco-Roman Literacy as Setting for New Testament Writings," *Noetestamentica* 26 (1992) 201–22.

Carr, David M. *Writing on the Tablet of the Heart: Origins of Scripture and Literature.* Oxford: Oxford University Press, 2005.

Chaney, Marvin L. "Bitter Bounty: The Dynamics of Political Economy Critiqued by the Eighth-Century Prophets." In *Reformed Faith and Economicsm*, edited by Robert L. Stivers, 15–30. New York: University Press of America, 1989. Reprinted in Chaney, *Peasants, Prophets, and Political Economy: The Hebrew Bible and Social Analysis*, 147–59. Eugene, OR: Cascade Books, 2017.

Cohen, Shaye J. D. *From the Maccabees to the Mishnah.* Library of Early Christianity 7. Philadelphia: Westminster, 1987. (3rd ed., 2014.)

———. *Josephus in Galilee and Rome: His Vita and Development as a Historian.* Columbia Studies in the Classical Tradition 8. Leiden: Brill, 1979.

———. "The Significance of Yavneh: Pharisees, Rabbis, and the End of Jewish Sectarianism." *Hebrew Union College Annual* 55 (1984) 27–53.

Collins, John J. *Daniel: A Commentary on the Book of Daniel.* Hermeneia. Minneapolis: Fortress, 1993.

Elliott, John H. "Social Scientific Criticism of the New Testament and Its Social World." *Semeia* 35 (1986) 1–33.

Flusser, David. "Pharisees, Sadducees, and Essenes in Pesher Nahum." In *Qumran*, edited by Karl Erich Grözinger et al., 121–66. Wege der Forschung 410. Darmstadt: Wissenschaftliche Buchgesellschaft, 1981. Reprinted in Flusser, *Judaism of the Second Temple Period*, vol. 1: *Qumran and Apocalypticism*, 214–57. Translated by Azzan Yadin. Grand Rapids: Eerdmans, 2007.

Freyne, Sean. *Galilee from Alexander the Great to Hadrian, 323 B.C.E. to 145 C.E.: A Study of Second Temple Judaism*. University of Notre Dame Center for the Study of Judaism and Christianity in Antiquity Series 5. Wilmington, DE: Glazier, 1980.
Goodman, Martin. *The Ruling Class of Judea: The Origins of the Jewish Revolt Against Rome A.D. 66–70*. Cambridge: Cambridge University Press, 1987.
———. *State and Society in Roman Galilee, A. D. 132–212*. Totowa, NJ: Rowman & Allanheld, 1983.
Harris, William V. *Ancient Literacy*. Cambridge: Harvard University Press, 1989.
Hengel, Martin. *Judaism and Hellenism: Studies in Their Encounter in Palestine during the Early Hellenistic Period*. 2 vols. Translated by John Bowden. Philadelphia: Fortress, 1974. Reprint, Eugene, OR: Wipf & Stock, 2003.
Hezser, Catherine. *Jewish Literacy in Roman Palestine*. Texts and Studies in Ancient Judaism 81. Tübingen: Mohr Siebeck, 2001.
Hobsbawm, Eric J. *Primitive Rebels*. New York: Norton, 1965.
Horsley, Richard A. *Galilee: History, Politics, People*. Valley Forge, PA: Trinity, 1995.
———. *Hearing the Whole Story: The Politics of Plot in Mark's Gospel*. Louisville: Westminster John Knox, 2001.
———. "High Priests and the Politics of Roman Palestine: A Contextual Analysis of the Evidence in Josephus." *Journal for the Study of Judaism* 17 (1986) 23–55.
———. "Israelite Traditions in Q." In Richard A. Horsley with Jonathan Draper, *Whoever Hears You Hears Me: Prophets, Performance, and Tradition in Q*, 94–121. Harrisburg, PA: Trinity, 1999.
———. *Jesus and the Spiral of Violence: Popular Jewish Resistance in Roman Palestine*. 1987. Reprint, Minneapolis: Fortress, 1993.
———. "The Pharisees and Jesus in Galilee and Q." In *When Judaism and Christianity Began: Essays in Memory of Anthony J. Saldarini*, edited by Alan Avery-Peck, Daniel Harrington, and Jacob Neusner, vol. 1, 117–45. 2 vols. Journal for the Study of Judaism Supplements 85. Leiden: Brill, 2004.
———. "The Political Roots of Early Judean Apocalyptic Texts." In *To Break Every Yoke: Essays in Honor of Marvin L. Chaney*, edited by Robert B. Coote and Norman K. Gottwald, 262–78. Social World of Biblical Antiquity Series 2/3. Sheffield: Sheffield Phoenix, 2007.
———. *Politics, Conflicts, and Movements in First-Century Palestine*. Eugene, OR: Cascade Books, forthcoming.
———. "Popular Messianic Movements around the Time of Jesus." *Catholic Biblical Quarterly* 46 (1984) 471–93.
———. "Popular Prophetic Movements at the Time of Jesus: Their Principal Features and Social Origins." *Journal for the Study of the New Testament* 26 (1986) 3–27.
———. "The Power Vacuum and Power Struggle in 66–67 C.E." In *The First Jewish Revolt: Archaeology, History, and Ideology*, edited by Andrea M. Berlin and J. Andrew Overman, 87–109. London: Routledge, 2002.
———. *Scribes, Visionaries, and the Politics of Second-Temple Judea*. Louisville: Westminster John Knox, 2007.
———. "Social Conflict in the Synoptic Sayings Source Q." In *Conflict and Invention: Literary, Rhetorical, and Social Studies on the Sayings Gosepl Q*, edited by John S. Kloppenborg, 37–52. Valley Forge, PA: Trinity, 1995.
———. "Social Relations and Social Conflict in the *Epistle of Enoch*." In *For a Later Generation: The Transformation of Tradition in Israel, Early Judaism, and Early*

Christianity, edited by Randal A. Argall et al., 100–115. Harrisburg, PA: Trinity, 2000.

———. *Sociology and the Jesus Movement*. New York: Crossroad, 1989.

Horsley, Richard, with Jonathan Draper. *Whoever Hears You Hears Me: Prophets, Performance, and Tradition in Q*. Harrisburg, PA: Trinity, 1999.

Horsley, Richard, and Patrick Tiller. *After Apocalyptic and Wisdom: Rethinking Texts in Context*. Eugene, OR: Cascade Books, 2012.

———. "Ben Sira and the Sociology of the Second Temple." In *Second Temple Studies III: Studies in Politics, Class, and Material Culture*, edited by Philip R. Davies and John M. Halligan, 74–107. Journal for the Study of the Old Testament Supplements 340. Sheffield: Sheffield Academic, 2002. Reprinted in Horsley and Tiller, *After Apocalyptic and Wisdom: Rethinking Texts in Context*, 19–55. Eugene, OR: Cascade Books, 2012.

Jaffee, Martin S. *Torah in the Mouth: Writing and Oral Tradition in Palestinian Judaism, 200 BCE–400 CE*. Oxford: Oxford University Press, 2001.

Janzen, Waldemar. *Mourning Cry and Woe Oracles*. Beihefte zur Zeitschrift für die alttestamentliche Wissenschaft 125. Berlin: de Gruyter, 1972.

Jeremias, Joachim. *Heiligengräber in Jesu Umwelt: Eine Untersuchung zur Volksreligion der Zeit Jesu*. Göttingen: Vandenhoeck & Ruprecht, 1958.

Karris, Robert J. "The Background and Significance of the Polemic of the Pastoral Epistles." *Journal of Biblical Literature* 92 (1973) 549–64.

Kautsky, John H. *The Politics of Aristocratic Empires*. Chapel Hill: University of North Carolina Press, 1982.

Kee, Howard Clark. "The Transformation of the Synagogue after 70 C.E.: Its Import for Early Christianity." *New Testament Studies* 36 (1990) 1–24.

Kelber, Werner H. *Mark's Story of Jesus*. Philadelphia: Fortress, 1979.

———. *The Oral and Written Gospel: The Hermeneutics of Speaking and Writing in the Synoptic Tradition, Mark, Paul, and Q*. Philadelphia: Fortress, 1983.

Kloppenborg, John S. *The Formation of Q: Trajectories in Ancient Wisdom*. Studies in Antiquity and Christianity. Philadelphia: Fortress, 1987.

———. "Nomos and Ethos in Q." In *Gospel Origins and Christian Beginnings: In Honor of James M. Robinson*, edited by James E. Goehring et al., 35–48. Forum Fascicles 1. Sonoma, CA: Polebridge, 1990.

———. *Q Parallels: Synopsis, Critical Notes, and Concordance*. Foundations & Facets: Reference Series. Sonoma, CA: Polebridge, 1988.

Laqueur, R. *Der Jüdische Historiker Flavius Josephus: Ein biographischer Versuch auf neuer quellenkritischer Grundlage*. 1920. Reprint, Darmstadt: Wissenschaftliche Buchgesellschaft, 1970.

Lenski, Gerhard. *Power and Privilege: A Theory of Social Stratification*. New York: McGraw, 1966. (2nd ed., Chapel Hill: University of North Carolina Press, 1984.)

Levine, Lee I. "The Jewish Patriarch (Nasi) in Third-Century Palestine." In *Aufstieg und Niedergang der römischen Welt* II.19.2, edited by Hildegard Temporini and Wolfgang Haase, 649–88. Berlin: de Gruyter, 1979.

———. *The Rabbinic Class of Roman Palestine in Late Antiquity*. New York: Jewish Theological Seminary of America, 1989.

Mack, Burton L. *A Myth of Innocence: Mark and Christian Origins*. Philadelphia: Fortress, 1988.

Mason, Steve. *Flavius Josephus on the Pharisees: A Composition-Critical Study*. Studia Post-Biblica 39. Leiden: Brill, 1991.

———. "Was Josephus a Pharisee? A Re-Examination of *Life* 10–12." *Journal of Jewish Studies* 40 (1989) 31–45.

Miller, Stewart S. *Studies in the History and Tradition of Sepphoris*. Studies in Judaism in Late Antiquity 37. Leiden: Brill, 1984.

Moore, Stephen D. *Literary Criticism and the Gospels*. New Haven: Yale University Press, 1989.

Moxnes, Halvor. *The Economy of the Kingdom: Social Conflict and Economic Relations in Luke's Gospel*. Overtures to Biblical Theology. Philadelphia: Fortress, 1988. Reprint, Eugene, OR: Wipf & Stock, 2004.

Neusner, Jacob. "'First Cleanse the Inside': The Halakhic Background of a Controversy Saying." *New Testament Studies* 22 (1976) 486–95.

———. *From Politics to Piety: The Emergence of Pharisaic Judaism*. 1973. Reprint, Eugene, OR: Wipf & Stock, 2003.

———. *Oral Tradition in Judaism: The Case of the Mishnah*. Garland Reference Library of the Humanities 764. New York: Garland, 1987.

———. *Rabbinic Traditions about the Pharisees before 70*. 3 vols. Leiden: Brill, 1971. Reprint, Eugene, OR: Wipf & Stock, 2005.

Nickelsburg, George W. E. *1 Enoch 1: A Commentary on the Book of 1 Enoch, Chapters 1–36, 81–108*. Hermeneia. Minneapolis: Fortress, 2001.

Niditch, Susan. *Oral World and Written Word: Ancient Israelite Literature*. Library of Ancient Israel. Louisville: Westminster John Knox, 1996.

Rajak, Tessa, *Josephus: The Historian and His Society*. London: Duckworth, 1983.

Richardson, Peter. *Herod: King of the Jews and Friend of the Romans*. Columbia: University of South Carolina Press, 1996. (2nd ed., London: Routledge, 2018.)

Roller, Duane W. *The Building Program of Herod the Great*. Berkeley: University of California Press, 1998.

Rostovtzeff, Michael. *The Social and Economic History of the Hellenistic World*. 3 vols. Oxford: Clarendon, 1941.

Rudé, Georg. *The Crowd in History: A Study of Popular Disturbances in France and England, 1730–1848*. New York: Wiley, 1964. (Rev. ed., London: Lawrence & Wishart, 1981.)

Saldarini, Anthony J. "Johanan ben Zakkai's Escape from Jerusalem: Origin and Development of a Rabbinic Story." *Journal for the Study of Judaism* 6 (1975) 189–220.

———. *Matthew's Christian-Jewish Community*. Chicago Studies in the History of Judaism. Chicago: University of Chicago Press, 1994.

———. *Pharisees, Scribes and Sadducees: A Sociological Approach*. Wilmington, DE: Glazier, 1988.

Satran, David. *Biblical Prophets in Byzantine Palestine: Reassessing the Lives of the Prophets*. Studia in Veteris Testamenti Pseudepigrapha 11. Leiden: Brill, 1995.

Schäfer, Peter. "Die Flucht Yohanan b. Zakkais aus Jerusalem und der Gründung des 'Lehrhauses.'" In *Aufstieg und Niedergang der römischen Welt* II.19.2, edited by Hildegard Temporini and Wolfgang Haase, 43–101. Berlin: de Gruyter, 1979.

Schiffman, Lawrence H. *The Halakhah at Qumran*. Studies in Judaism in Late Antiquity 16. Leiden: Brill, 1975.

———. *Reclaiming the Dead Sea Scrolls: The History of Judaism, the Background of Christianity, the Lost Library of Qumran.* Philadelphia: Jewish Publication Society, 1994. Reprint, Anchor Bible Reference Library. New York: Doubleday, 1995.
Schürer, Emil. *Geschichte des Jüdischen Volkes im Zeitalter Jesu Christi.* Leipzig: Hinrichs, 1886–1911. (various editions since 1874).
Schürmann, Heinz. "Die Redekomposition wider 'dieses Geschlecht' und seine Führung in der Redequelle (vgl. Mt 12,1–39 par Lk 11,37–54): Bestand – Akoluthe – Kompositionsformen." In *Studien zum Neuen Testament und Seiner Umwelt*, edited by Albert Fuchs, 33–81. Series A, 11. Linz: Studien zum Neuen Testament und Seiner Umwelt, 1986.
Schulz, Siegfried. *Q—Die Spruchquelle der Evangelisten.* Zurich: TVZ, 1971.
Schwartz, Daniel R. "Josephus and Nicolas on the Pharisees." *Journal for the Study of Judaism* 14 (1983) 157–71.
Schwemer, Anna Maria. *Studien zu den frühjüdischen Prophetenslegenden Vitae Prophetarum.* 2 vols. Texte und Studien zum Atiken Judentum 49, 50. Tübingen: Mohr Siebeck, 1995.
Scott, James C. "Protest and Profanation: Agrarian Revolt and the Little Tradition." *Theory and Society* 4 (1977) 1–38, 211–46.
Sievers, Joseph. "Who Were the Pharisees?" In *Hillel and Jesus: Comparative Studies of Two Major Religious Leaders*, edited by James H. Charlesworth and Loren L. Johns, 137–55. Minneapolis: Fortress: 1997.
Skehan, Patrick W., and Alexander A. DiLella. *The Wisdom of Ben Sira.* Anchor Bible 39. Garden City, NY: Doubleday, 1987.
Smith, Morton. "Palestinian Judaism in the First Century." In *Israel: Its Role in Civilization*, edited by Moshe Davis, 67–81. New York: Harper & Row, 1956.
Tcherikover, Victor A. *Hellenistic Civilization and the Jews.* Translated by S. Applebaum. 1959. Reprint, New York: Atheneum, 1977.
Thackeray, H. St. John. *Josephus: The Man and the Historian.* New York: Jewish Institute of Religion Press, 1929.
Theissen, Gerd. *The Sociology of Early Palestinian Christianity.* Translated by John Bowden. Philadelphia: Fortress, 1978.
Tiller, Patrick A. *A Commentary on the Animal Apocalypse of 1 Enoch.* Early Judaism and Its Literature 4. Atlanta: Scholars, 1993.
Tov, Emanuel. "Biblical Texts as Reworked in Some Qumran Manuscripts with Special Attention to 4QRP and 4Qpara Gen-Exod." In *The Community of the Renewed Covenant: The Notre Dame Symposium on the Dead Sea Scrolls*, edited by Eugene Ulrich and James VanderKam, 111–34. Christianity and Judaism in Antiquity 10. Notre Dame, IN: University of Notre Dame Press, 1993.
Tuckett, Christopher M. *Q and the History of Early Christianity.* Peabody, MA: Hendrickson, 1996.
Ulrich, Eugene. "The Bible in the Making: The Scriptures at Qumran," in *The Community of the Renewed Covenant: The Notre Dame Symposium on the Dead Sea Scrolls*, edited by Eugene Ulrich and James VanderKam, 77–93. Christianity and Judaism in Antiquity 10. Notre Dame, IN: University of Notre Dame Press, 1993.
Unnik, W. C. van. *Flavius Josephus als historische Schriftsteller.* Franz Delitzsch Vorlesungen, n.F. 1972. Heidelberg: Schneider, 1978.

Urbach, Ephraim E. *Class-Status and Leadership in the World of the Palestinian Sages.* Proceedings of the Israel Academy of Sciences and Humanities. Jerusalem: Central Press, 1966.

Vermes, Geza. *The Complete Dead Sea Scrolls in English.* New York: Penguin, 1997.

Wild, Robert A. "The Encounter between Pharisaic and Christian Judaism: Some Early Gospel Evidence." *Novum Testamentum* 27 (1985) 105–24.

Worsley, Peter. *The Third World.* The Nature of Human Society Series. Chicago: University of Chicago Press, 1964.

INDEX

Alexander Jannaeus (Hasmonean king/high priest), 92–93

Bellah, Robert N., 50–51
Ben Sira, 5, 12–13, 47–50

Christianity, construct of, 2
conflict, multilevel, 4

Daniel 7–12, 13, 18, 59–61
Dead Sea Scrolls / Qumran Community, 43–44
  polemical references attack Pharisees, 43–44, 87–88
  as sources for Pharisees and high priests, 43–44
Deuteronomy, and centralization in temple-state, 11

1 Enoch 85–90, 13, 18, 59–61

Fourth Philosophy, 73, 110, 113
  Pharisee(s) as leader(s), 110, 113
  resisting Roman rule, 73, 110, 113

Galilee/ Galileans, 123–24
  different regional history, 38–39, 123–24, 142–45
  ruled by Antipas not Jerusalem, 123, 130, 142
  subjected to "the laws of the Judeans," 124
Gospel stories, 5, 37–40
  and Christian stereotype, 37
  focus on impact of Pharisees' role, 39
  represent Pharisees and scribes based in Jerusalem, 142
  represent Pharisees and scribes as retainers, 152–53
  whole stories not fragments, 37–40, 141–42
  view from below, 38–40

Hasmonean dynasty, 13–15, 86–102
  conquered Idumea and Samaria, 14, 88–89, 98–99
  consolidation of power, 86–89, 98–99
  mercenary army, 14, 88–89
  resisted by people and Pharisees, 14, 92–93, 98–99, 101–2
  take-over of Galilee, 92
Hellenizing reform, 13, 58–59
  resisted by scribal circles, 13, 57–61
Hengel, Martin
  projection of modern commerce onto Judea, 45–46
Herod
  imposed as king by Romans, 15
  massive rebuilding of temple, 15
  subordinated temple to his rule, 18, 144
high priest(s)
  appointed by Roman governors, 7
  heads of the temple-state, 8, 48–49
  transformed Jerusalem into Hellenistic *polis*, 13

high priestly families (priestly aristocracy), 15, 34, 48–49, 84, 115
(John) Hyrcanus (Hasmonean high priest), 88–92

imperial rule, 2, 6–20, 50, 54
  Persian, 9–11
  unstable, 8–9

Jesus' woes against Pharisees and scribes, 132–40
  in old Christian theological scheme, 132–33
  memory of the prophets in, 139–40
  a prophetic speech in speech-collection, 133–34
  prophetic indictment of effect of Pharisees' role, 137–38
  purity laws not main concern, 135–36
  series of woes in prophets and 1 Enoch, 135–36
Jonathan (brother of Judas Maccabaeus)
  gained high priesthood, 13, 86
Josephus, Flavius
  broader historical accounts of, 5
  Josephus was not a Pharisee, 26–29
Josephus' works as sources, 24–37
  Judean Antiquities, 32–37
    Josephus' attitude in, 33–37
    Morton Smith's view of, 34
    not pro-Pharisee, 69–70
  Judean War, 29–32
    Josephus' attitude in, 31–32
  Life, 26–29
  steps of assessment of, 25
Judaism, construct of, 2, 6, 33, 37, 41–42, 142
  Christian theological scheme of, 21–22, 37
Judah the Prince, 66–67

Kee, Howard Clark
  synagogues as assemblies of Pharisees, 65–66

laws, 7–8

Lenski, Gerhard, 3–5, 45–47, 50–54, 75–77, 118–19
  propriety theory of the state, 53
  refining his theory, 51
Lukan story, portrayal of Pharisees in, 151–52
  badger and admonish Jesus, 152
  domestication not historically credible, 152
  invite Jesus to dine, 152

Maccabean Revolt, 13
Mack, Burton L.
  "synagogue reform movement," 65–66, 146
Markan story, portrayal of Pharisees in, 145–50
  Pharisees/scribes came down from Jerusalem, 146
  role as temple-state authorities on issues, 148–49
  urge economic support of temple, 148–49
maskilim, 5, 18
Mason, Steve, 5
  on Josephus' Flavian perspective, 23
Matthean story, portrayal of Pharisees in, 150–51
  based in Jerusalem, 150
  closely linked with high priests, 150–51
  not leaders in Galilean synagogues, 151
  role as Jerusalem authorities on issues, 150–51
Mishnah, 22, 24, 40, 63, 67, 104, 122, 133

Nehemiah 5:1–13, 10
Neusner, Jacob
  critical analysis of rabbinic traditions, 22, 64
  From Politics to Piety, 22, 34, 64
  development of Morton Smith's view, 34
  influence on New Testament scholars, 34, 64–66

oral communication, 125–28
    dominant among the people, 125–27
    also dominant in scribal circles, 127

Passover festival, 7
patriarchate, 66–67
peasants / villagers, 121–22
    exploitation of, 9–10
Pharisees, 8
    continuous involvement in politics, 70–74, 83–84
    effects of their role on the people, 5, 101–2
    experts on the laws, 77–81, 84, 95–96
    historical contexts of, 5, 86–115
    influence with the people, 81–84, 101–4
    leading Pharisees work to control revolt, 73–74, 110–13, 115
    mediated imperial rule, 15, 18, 101–2, 110, 114–15
    origin under early Hasmoneans, 14, 86–88
    political position and role, 4–5, 14, 41–42, 75–81, 96–102, 114–15
    resisted Hasmoneans, 14, 62, 92–93, 96–97
    resisted imperial rule, 15, 18–19
    resisting Herod, 71–73, 103–8
    retainers of temple-state, 76–81, 95–102, 108, 114–15, 117–21
    role in Galilee?, 128–31
    successors of scribes as retainers, 62, 79, 95, 102
    traditions of the ancestors/ elders, 77–80
    under the Hasmoneans, 86–102
    under Herod, 103–9
    under the high priests, 109–13
popular resistance and revolt, 16–17
prophets, supporting temple-state, 11
proprietary theory of the state, 52–53

rabbinic texts, 40–42
    assumed continuity with Pharisees, 40, 63–64
    critical analysis by Neusner, 40
    growing skepticism about continuity with Pharisees, 41–43, 64, 66–68
rabbis
    little authority among the people, 67
    little authority in synagogues, 68
    social-political role of, 41–43
religion as inseparable from political-economy, 2, 116–17
retainers, 3–5, 16–19, 54–57, 75–77
    dissident, 4, 18, 58–60
    Pharisees as, 4, 75–81, 117–23
    ruler-retainer relations, 54–57, 62
Roman governors, 7, 110

Saldarini, Anthony (Tony), 3–5, 6, 116–22, 128–29
Salome Alexandra (Hasmonean queen), 14–15, 31, 35–36, 62, 70, 76, 78, 80–81, 84, 93–98, 100, 102, 109, 114, 119, 129–30, 143
scribes
    adapt customs in support of temple-state, 11
    mediated and resisted imperial rule, 16–18
    resistance against high priestly rulers, 57–60
    retainers of the temple-state, 120
    sense of their own authority from God, 57, 60
    serving (in) the temple-state, 11, 12, 45–47
    training and role of, 12, 48–49
scripture (authoritative written texts) presence/absence, 127–28
sect, concept of, 116
    does not fit the Pharisees, 8
"seekers of smooth things" (code word for Pharisees), 42–43
sociology, historical, 3–5
    of agrarian societies, 45–47, 50–54, 75–77, 118–20
    different structures of, 50–51

sources for the Pharisees, 21–44
  considered in broader literary and historical context, 23–24
  more critical assessment needed, 21–24
synagogues (village assemblies), 121–22

temple
  Herod's temple, 7
  pillar of Judaism, 6
temple-state, 2
  crisis of under Seleucid rule, 12–13, 57–61
  origins under Persian Empire, 9–11
  representative of imperial regimes, 9–15
  revenues, 10–11
  subject to imperial rule, 50
  unstable, 8–9

texts
  text-fragments, 2, 21–23, 37
  whole texts, 2, 37–38
Torah
  not yet stable, 7–8
  pillar of Judaism, 7
Tosefta, 22, 24, 40, 67, 122
(Israelite) tradition(s)
  development of, 125
  "great" (official) tradition, 124–25
  "little" (popular) tradition, 124–25
traditions of the ancestors/elders, 8, 90–91, 96, 148–49
tributary societies, 51–53
tribute to imperial regime, 9–10

village communities, 2, 121–22

Yavneh (Jamnia), rabbinic academy in, 41–42, 128–29
  based on foundational legend, 41–42, 66

www.ingramcontent.com/pod-product-compliance
Lightning Source LLC
Chambersburg PA
CBHW030857170426
43193CB00009BA/643